MW00974830

VCP5-DT
Official Cert Guide

VMware Press is the official publisher of VMware books and training materials, which provide guidance on the critical topics facing today's technology professionals and students. Enterprises, as well as small- and medium-sized organizations, adopt virtualization as a more agile way of scaling IT to meet business needs. VMware Press provides proven, technically accurate information that will help them meet their goals for customizing, building, and maintaining their virtual environment.

With books, certification and study guides, video training, and learning tools produced by world-class architects and IT experts, VMware Press helps IT professionals master a diverse range of topics on virtualization and cloud computing. It is the official source of reference materials for preparing for the VMware Certified Professional Examination.

VMware Press is also pleased to have localization partners that can publish its products into more than 42 languages, including Chinese (Simplified), Chinese (Traditional), French, German, Greek, Hindi, Japanese, Korean, Polish, Russian, and Spanish.

For more information about VMware Press, visit **vmwarepress.com**.

vmware® PRESS

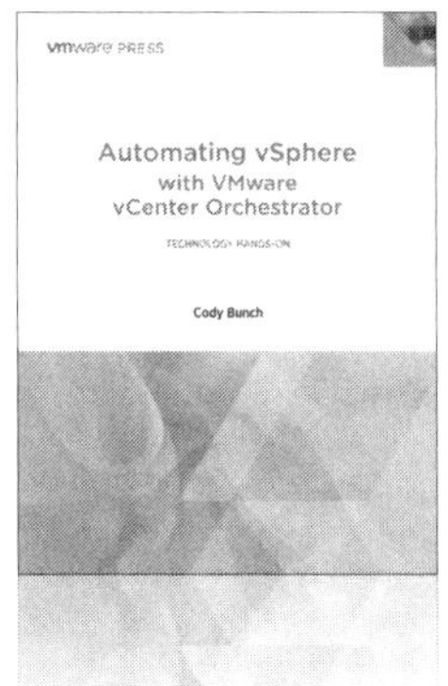

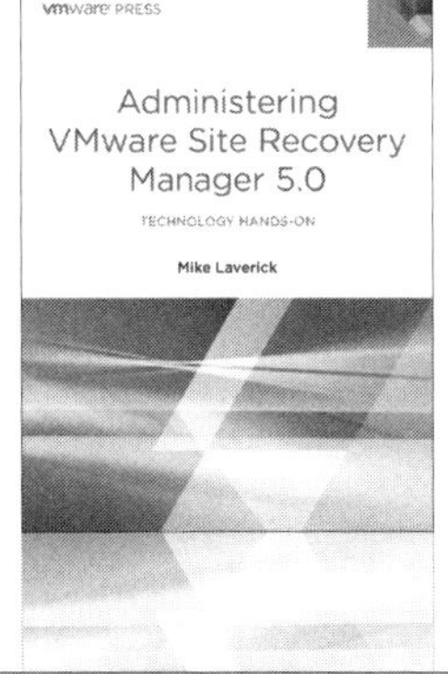

pearsonitcertification.com/vmwarepress

Complete list of products • Podcasts • Articles • Newsletters

VMware® Press is a publishing alliance between Pearson and VMware, and is the official publisher of VMware books and training materials that provide guidance for the critical topics facing today's technology professionals and students.

With books, certification and study guides, video training, and learning tools produced by world-class architects and IT experts, VMware Press helps IT professionals master a diverse range of topics on virtualization and cloud computing, and is the official source of reference materials for completing the VMware certification exams.

Make sure to connect with us!
informit.com/socialconnect

vmware® | PEARSON IT CERTIFICATION | Safari Books Online

VCP5-DT Official Cert Guide

Linus Bourque

vmware® PRESS

Upper Saddle River, NJ • Boston • Indianapolis • San Francisco
New York • Toronto • Montreal • London • Munich • Paris • Madrid
Capetown • Sydney • Tokyo • Singapore • Mexico City

VCP5-DT Official Cert Guide

Published by Pearson plc

Publishing as VMware Press

Library of Congress Control Number: 2013909352

ISBN-13: 978-0-7897-5027-3

ISBN-10: 0-7897-5027-9

Printed in the United States of America

First Printing: August 2013

Text printed in the United States at Courier, Westford, MA.

Warning and Disclaimer

Every effort has been made to make this book as complete and as accurate as possible, but no warranty or fitness is implied. The information provided is on an "as is" basis. The authors, VMware Press, VMware, and the publisher shall have neither liability nor responsibility to any person or entity with respect to any loss or damages arising from the information contained in this book or from the use of the DVD or programs accompanying it.

The opinions expressed in this book belong to the author and are not necessarily those of VMware.

Corporate and Government Sales

VMware Press offers excellent discounts on this book when ordered in quantity for bulk purchases or special sales, which may include electronic versions and/or custom covers and content particular to your business, training goals, marketing focus, and branding interests. For more information, please contact

U.S. Corporate and Government Sales
(800) 382-3419
corpsales@pearsontechgroup.com

For sales outside the United States, please contact:
International Sales
international@pearsoned.com

VMWARE PRESS PROGRAM MANAGERS
Erik Ullanderson
Anand Sundaram

ASSOCIATE PUBLISHER
David Dusthimer

ACQUISITIONS EDITOR
Joan Murray

DEVELOPMENT EDITOR
Ellie Bru

MANAGING EDITOR
Sandra Schroeder

SENIOR PROJECT EDITOR
Tonya Simpson

COPY EDITOR
Keith Cline

INDEXER
Tim Wright

PROOFREADER
Debbie Williams

COORDINATOR
Vanessa Evans

BOOK DESIGNER
Gary Adair

COMPOSITION
Bumpy Design

Contents at a Glance

Table of Contents

About the Author

So, as with any book, there is always this blurb by the author where you learn how great he or she is (or they are). If you have ever attended one of my classes, you know that I am rather personable and love nothing more than sharing everything I can on VMware products. My biggest challenge has always been the "where to start." I suppose it is best to start at the beginning. Let's see. A long, long, long time ago there was this huge big bang.

Oh. Wait. That might be a bit too far back, eh?

So I am Canadian (I bet you can tell by my accent, eh?) and live in the sunny land known as Los Angeles. This year (2013) I will celebrate 8 great years with VMware. I started my career with VMware when a good friend and former Seneca College (Toronto) colleague Scott Laforet said, "Dude! You gotta come and get a job with Andrew and me at this little start-up! It rocks!"

I was skeptical about leaving my life of leisure as a professor at Seneca College. I mean, here I was enjoying a hard week of about 12 to 16 hours, lecturing on the "evils" of "acquiring" access into network systems and how to build PHP games. But it was time for a change and I figured, why not? Couldn't be worse than what I was doing, eh?

So I packed up my two cats and we moved to Burlington, Ontario. I joined the VMware Global Support Services group. At first I was hesitant about doing "telephone support," as I envisioned my day consisting of "Yes, did you turn it on and off again? Did you do it three times?" If anything, it was not that. VMware customers showed me a side of IT support that challenged every little brain cell that eagerly loved puzzles.

But, I missed teaching. There's a joy that comes from seeing people succeed and go beyond what they can imagine when you show them so much more than they expected. So, I decided to get into teaching but for VMware Global Education. Like most instructors, you start with the basics. In this case, it was the Virtual Infrastructure 3.x Install, Configure, Manage class. After doing that for a short bit, I got asked whether I would do the new class: VDM 2.0. For a while, I was the only one teaching it in all of the Americas (for VMware's direct delivery group). VDM evolved into View 3.0 and then 4.0 and then... well, we're up to 5.2 as of now.

During the 4.5 days, I got invited to participate in creating exams for VMware's Certification group. From deciding who the exam targets to even some of the questions (don't ask me for questions; I don't even remember what the answers are to the questions I created, let alone what they are!), I've been part of every one of our desktop certification exams and have been part of the betas for them all.

These days, my life is so much more than just teaching. I still do that, but I also certify who becomes an instructor in the Americas, remain as lead instructor for our End User Computing (EUC) instructor-led classes (as John Dodge says, "I'm the View guy!"), help with creation of classes and labs for the classes, and so much more. I often teach View classes at our education boot camps before PEX (Partner Exchange) and VMworld (USA only). This is my first book, and I already know what I want to do for a second edition (if I get to do it).

When I'm not livin' la vida loca in the virtual world, I stomp around in Warcraft as a Tauren hunter. Or sit out in the warm evening of Los Angeles, a cigar and whiskey in hand, enjoying the night with my girlfriend and our two pugs, Lily and Lawfawda. (If you ever do an online class with me and hear barking or snoring, that's them!) And between all that, I read voraciously all sorts of technical material, philosophy, steampunk, science fiction, and whatever else I find interesting. (So, if you have anything to suggest, send it my way!)

I'll end with a thought from Albert Einstein: "Learn from yesterday, live for today, hope for tomorrow. The important thing is not to stop questioning."

Dedication

I would like to dedicate this to the following: my everything, Kristen Williams, who listens to my ramblings and rants and loves me as I am.

And to my colleagues who are always there when I ask for help, no matter how small or large the task or idea.

Acknowledgments

I never wrote a book until this one. I learned *a lot*! There is so much that goes into producing a book; you'd be amazed! I have to start off by giving huge kudos to Joan Murray and Ellie Bru for keeping at me when I forgot or missed a deadline. I'm sure I drove both of you nuts with missed deadlines and not fully understanding the process.

Thank you to Owen Thomas who helped out with some chapters when the deadline came faster than my brain cells could process. Thanks also to Stephane Asselin, Simon Long, Justin Venezia, and Pranesh Raghavender Rao.

Thanks to my colleagues (Damian Wraa, Brian Watrous, Phil Cohen, John Krueger, Andrew Ellwood) who offered great support and listened to me while I went on about the challenges of writer's block. And a special thanks to Randy Becraft, who suggested this to me in the first place.

Last but not least, thank you to VMware for letting me do this. Very few companies are as supportive of its employees as VMware is. And very few companies make amazing products like we do.

About the Reviewers

Agustín Malanco (VCP 3,4,5, VCAP4/5-DCA, VCAP4/5-DCD, VCP4/5-DT, VCP-Cloud) has been working with VMware's technologies for 6 years, and has worked in various fields, including consulting, support, and training. As a VMware Certified Instructor (VCI4), he taught courses in Latin America. Currently, he works for VMware as a Partner Systems Engineer covering Mexico. Some of his primary responsibilities are enabling partners and distributors from a technical perspective and giving presales support for the whole partner ecosystem. Agustín is a contributor at the official VMware Latam Blog (http://blogs.vmware.com/latam) and he also has his own blog (http://blog.hispavirt.com). He has been recognized as vExpert 2011 and 2012 for his contributions to the community.

Envor Enrico Pillay is currently a part-time consultant and international traveler working as a VMware Certified Instructor (VCI) for a leading IT training provider in Africa, Torque IT. He is certified in many technologies: VMware, Microsoft, and CompTIA, to name a few. He shares his passion for the VMware technology through the VMware authorized classes he delivers, inspiring individuals from all walks of life across Africa. As a virtualization solutions architect, he has provided and assisted in numerous designs and implementations for customers in Africa. He recently received a prestigious award, the EMEA VCI of the Quarter Award for Q1 2013.

Owen Thomas is a senior technical instructor for Global Knowledge, teaching VMware classes and writing white papers for View and vSphere since 2008. Classes include the Install Configure, Manage classes, FastTracks, as well as Design and Troubleshooting. In addition to teaching most of the available VMware classes, his customer-site consulting has included audits, installs, designs, assessments, documenting current environments, and providing road maps for future growth with vSphere and View. Prior to teaching VMware courses, Owen was an analyst in a large enterprise-level network operations center (NOC) in Louisville, Kentucky, where he was first exposed to VMware.

We Want to Hear from You!

As the reader of this book, *you* are our most important critic and commentator. We value your opinion and want to know what we're doing right, what we could do better, what areas you'd like to see us publish in, and any other words of wisdom you're willing to pass our way.

We welcome your comments. You can email or write us directly to let us know what you did or didn't like about this book—as well as what we can do to make our books better.

Please note that we cannot help you with technical problems related to the topic of this book.

When you write, please be sure to include this book's title and author as well as your name, email address, and phone number. We will carefully review your comments and share them with the author and editors who worked on the book.

Email: VMwarePress@vmware.com

Mail: VMware Press
ATTN: Reader Feedback
800 East 96th Street
Indianapolis, IN 46240 USA

Reader Services

Visit our website and register this book at www.informit.com/title/9780789750273 for convenient access to any updates, downloads, or errata that might be available for this book.

Introduction

It's hard to believe how enterprise computing has changed as a whole, but particularly when it comes to virtualization. The idea of taking the four common resources (CPU, memory, disk, and network) and abstracting them into effective processes is not as new as we might think. (The initial starting point can be traced as far back as in 1965, when IBM had memory that was split for the IBM 360/65.) However, it has been advancing at a much more rapid pace in the past decade.

Our traditional datacenters often consisted of lots of physical boxes of varying sizes. Administrators would order new server boxes from a major vendor, install Windows or Linux or some other *Nix on the box, and configure a single application or service to run on it. Once we set these up, we then had to maintain, upgrade, and manage the hardware and software. Updating software was a relatively straightforward aspect of the job, but hardware changes often presented challenges. Even with all the planning and practice, something could still go wrong.

I remember when I first got into IT as a network/system administrator. We were just starting to fit servers into the closet, but we were rapidly discovering that a lack of space, power, cooling, and security was something that we needed to address to ensure a well-running environment. So, we began to assign whole rooms and, sometimes, whole warehouses to be datacenters. They had to have massive cooling infrastructures, complex cabling, and backup power options. And for larger environments, this can be challenging.

If we had to deal with a hardware failure, we had to go to that specific server and get the part from the vendor (hoping for sooner rather than later). We had to plan for some kind of physical failover for each critical server, potentially doubling or tripling cooling costs, power consumption, UPS, and administrative hours to try to minimize our outage risk. Perhaps we would get a new manager who preferred vendor A over vendor B, even though vendor B had been our main vendor for years. Moving over critical systems is not as easy as one might think, and it requires a fair amount of planning, processes, and a lot of luck.

The worst challenge, however, was the orphaned application: that one piece of software that the company needed but whose only source was a vendor that went out of business 10 years earlier. Let's make this even more fun: The original software floppy disks cannot be found, and the application runs only on Windows NT 4 with Service Pack 6 (and not Service Pack 6a). The server it runs on is kept together with glue and duct tape and the occasional wish upon a falling star. All attempts to move it to a new server have failed spectacularly, and the department that depends on it refuses to use a new application that could do the same and more. We've all run into this, even in today's market. These various scenarios have led me to often remark that I will never be out of work in IT (because these challenges ensure a perpetual need for someone to be around to address them). But, the reality of keeping this application running and stable highlights the critical need to migrate it to a more flexible and reliable environment.

And while traditional datacenters were evolving and expanding, a newer technology was emerging in the background: hardware abstraction virtualization (or just virtualization). For me, my first exposure to virtualization occurred more than 15 years ago when I first installed VirtualPC on my Quadra 650. VirtualPC, which was still owned by Connectix, allowed me to run a Windows 95/98 system on my Mac, but to do so, it had to do both the hardware abstraction and the CPU translation. This resulted in some less-than-stellar performance behavior. At this time, virtualization was viewed as something strictly used at the desktop. Over the past 15 or so years, virtualization has dramatically changed both itself and the datacenter.

What Is Virtualization?

Modern virtualization is almost exclusively an abstraction of the four main resource groups: CPU, memory, network, and storage. I sometimes call these the *four food groups of virtualization*. We see this done primarily on the x86 platform in one of two ways: hypervisor (Type 1) or hosted (Type 2). We will start with hosted virtualization (for example, VMware Server, Workstation or Fusion, Parallels). This puts the abstraction layer into an application-like environment. This means that calls to hardware will have to go through the host's operating system (for example, Windows, Linux, OS X) before reaching the hardware and then returning to the virtual machine. For systems like desktops and laptops, this means running operating systems without having to give up the local system. It also means that whatever the local operating system sees as hardware can be presented to the virtual machine. The challenge, in this scenario, is that both the operating system and the virtual machine, the abstracted virtual hardware environment, fight for the limited local resources on the system on which they are installed, usually a laptop or desktop environment for a single user.

This kind of virtualization works great for single users who want to try a different operating system without having to do a new install or multibooting the system, developers who do cross-platform development, and security geeks who want to test or try things that cannot be done on the base operating system. But when we have many more systems to virtualize, this can prove challenging, as mentioned previously.

In comparison, we find that hypervisors, like VMware ESXi (sometimes referred to as bare-metal hypervisors), are better at sharing resources between the virtual machines and the hardware. These hypervisors can ensure that a virtual machine's Guest OS gets access to all the physical resources and then divvy that up between the virtual machines based on their requests, contention, and other factors.

The hypervisor itself is the operating system for the hardware and acts as the go-between for the virtual machine and the hardware, ensuring equitable resource allocation where possible. Normally, an operating system will take full control over a piece of hardware and "own it." This will not work in a virtual environment, where I may have up to 500 virtual machines residing on a single hypervisor host and acting as individual systems. As I often say in class, virtual machines are like 2-year-olds. Everything, for a virtual machine, is "*mine*!" The hypervisor does its best to ensure that the virtual machines share appropriately and do not misbehave.

I will admit it: I'm biased toward ESX/ESXi as hypervisors (and not just because I work for VMware and have been primarily using ESX since it was version 2.5.x). I've always believed in using the tools that best fit and meet the needs of what I need to do. I write this on a MacBook Pro using Office 2011 for Mac (although I could have done it on one of my Fusion Windows 7 virtual machines or my View desktop). There is a reason why the majority of companies use VMware: It works. Over the years, ESX/ESXi has evolved from where the ESX/ESXi server was the most critical piece to recover immediately from an outage (it still is, but it is not as disastrous as it might have once been) to where it does not matter as much as getting the virtual machine running and we do not care where it runs.

vSphere 5

So, this is where vSphere 5 comes in. Introduced in 2011, vSphere 5 was the first version of VMware's hypervisor Type 1 to not offer a service console in it and returned to a single version, this time as just ESXi. (ESX was officially dropped in vSphere 5 as part of the removal of the service console.) Previously, this had been used as a mechanism to manage and bootstrap the hypervisor. Getting rid of this ensured a smaller footprint, fewer security vectors, and a more stable platform. vSphere is the suite name of the VMware enterprise virtualization and cloud computing environment. It includes the two main pieces of ESXi and vCenter as well as Update Manager, Orchestrator, and more. Figure I-1 shows a logical representation of the suite at the time of this writing. New features are added each year, but the core concepts remain the same.

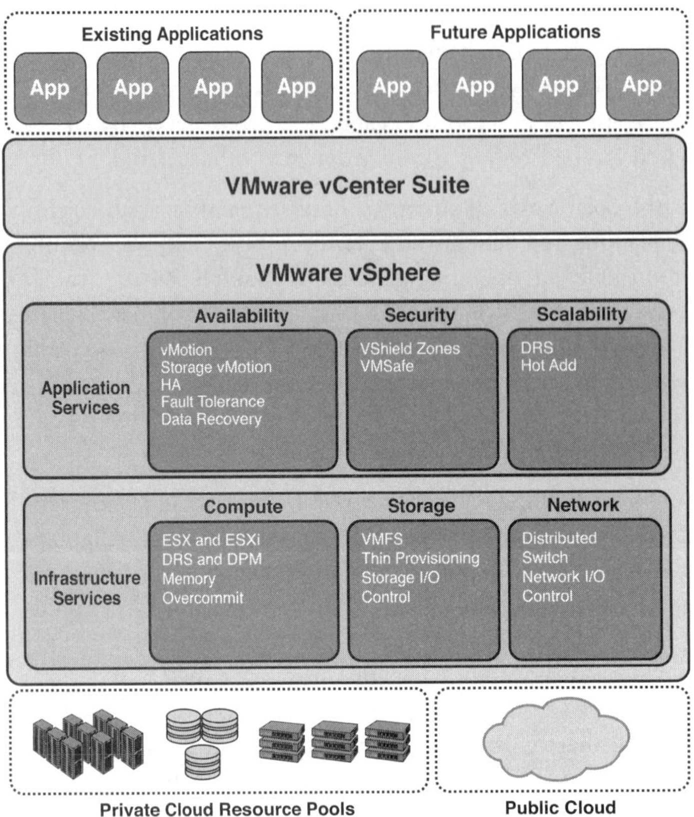

Figure I-1 vSphere 5 virtualization.

More and more, virtualization is more than just the hypervisor. It has instead become how we manage the environment effectively and ensure that the critical virtual machines continue actively running. When you manage multiple ESXi servers, however, individual administration can be too challenging. That is where something like vCenter helps. It brings the management of those servers under the control of a single system. vCenter adds additional features that we would not have available in a single system. As Figure I-1 shows, vSphere is more than just the hypervisor. At the base, we have the actual server hardware, which often represents the CPU and memory resources available to the virtual machines. For vSphere, it is important to ensure that the hardware has been certified on the hardware compatibility list (to avoid common problems that occur when hardware has not been tested to work with vSphere).

In addition to the server, we have storage and network. Storage types come in many flavors, but we tend to see Fibre Channel (also known as FC), iSCSI, NFS, and local storage. On top of FC, iSCSI, and local storage, we can place a VMFS (Virtual Machine File System) and leverage it for many of the features found in vSphere. For the network, we can leverage both standard virtual switches and distributed virtual switches (available only with Enterprise Plus licensing). With these, we can leverage various predictive load balancing, VLANs, basic network security, and bandwidth throttling.

But it really is vCenter that ties everything together. vCenter is the glue that manages a good virtual environment. With it, we can take advantage of features like Distributive Resource Scheduler (DRS), High Availability (HA), Storage DRS (SDRS), vMotion, Template Provisioning, Thin Provisioning, Storage I/O Control (SIOC), Distributive Power Management (DPM), and so on. I could continue with a long list of features, but I think you get the idea. vCenter alleviates some of the tasks that are considered repetitious and does them for us so that we do not have to worry. A feature like DRS helps my environment to balance both CPU and memory utilization better across servers.

And as organizations began to virtualize their servers and to realize significant benefits from doing so, we began to see desktops appear as virtual machines. Administrators and users alike wanted to make it easier to deploy and use desktops. Companies wanted to expand but not deal with new computer costs or the cost of upgrading whole systems (many of which provide many more resources than are truly needed for end users); they also did not want to have to find space for these users (and so on). The reality is that the cost of individuals and providing them with the tools that they need can sometimes outweigh the immediate need to have that person.

We have, as an industry, excelled at server virtualization. When most of IT says *virtualization*, they think of server virtualization (and especially on VMware vSphere). But we now have to look beyond the land of servers.

What Is VDI and View?

So this is where virtualizing the desktop comes in. Virtual desktop infrastructure (VDI) is not a new concept. At the very beginning of server virtualization, administrators began to look for ways to virtualize terminal servers. And when they did, the first virtual desktop environment was started. It was cumbersome, to say the least, but it did alleviate the need for actual desktops in individual cubes. All that was needed was a thin client that could connect, via Remote Desktop Protocol (RDP) or another remote access protocol, back to the terminal server. It was effective enough for small configurations, but what about the environments that wanted to virtualize 300 users? Or 3,000? Or 10,000? This kind of piecemeal setup would, very quickly, become a challenge to manage. And it would require a separate team from those that manage the physical environment.

Many corporations worried *only* about their servers and virtualized those. Meanwhile, employee desktops were changing—or rather, how they accessed those desktops was changing. We are moving from a traditional grey box access from one's cubical to having a variety of devices (such as smartphones or tablets) to access a desktop, which is primarily a Windows flavored desktop (such as Windows XP, Vista, 7 or 8). To make management somewhat easier, we allowed users to look after their system and trusted them to install only what was needed. This meant that organizations allowed some user flexibility, but it also resulted in a kind of a bonding between end users and their desktop. In fact, it became rather a possessive thing.

Back then, if you were to ask a user to give up his desktop, the wrath of some computer deity would come down on your head. A few too many organizations forgot to remind employees that the computer they were using (whether a desktop or laptop) was, in fact, a tool provided to them by the company. Returning that ownership to the organization would mean better control, better security, and a stronger ability to centralize and standardize the desktop image in general. Bringing the desktop into the datacenter would allow this because it would mean that IT would once again control it.

Some organizations started the process of virtualizing their desktops. Often, this form of virtualization, known as VDI or virtual desktop infrastructure, was an ad hoc process. A Windows or Linux system would be created, a remote protocol enabled or installed, and the employee given access. The user would either use an existing full system (laptop or desktop) or a thin client.

But unless organizations were willing to build football field size datacenters just for the desktops (and all the costly support and redundant equipment), the only effective way to achieve this was with virtualization. Back around 2007, VMware purchased a little Swiss company called Dunes. They had a nifty little product called Virtual Desktop Manager. For all intents and purposes, VDM was more of an orchestration kind of tool. It told vCenter what to build, and vCenter went and did. And it was more. It became the central location to manage the desktops. Instead of reinventing how virtual machines were created, we just took what we had and automated the process to make it easier to configure.

And it was easy to set up.

VDM was the first step, but it did need to evolve. A new name and a new protocol did that. From VDM, View emerged as the next generation of VDI. Along with it, we saw the introduction of VMware's linked-clone concept, a mechanism to save on storage space. Further evolutions beyond the initial View 3 introduced a new protocol designed for the end user, regardless of the kind of end user it was. It could have been Georgie, the call center representative who takes your monthly widget order; Sally, the mobile sales representative who pounds the pavement looking for new leads around the Northeast; Angie, the IT administrator who is a Windows-ninja at fixing blue screens; or it could be Kelly, who does the actual CAD design of the widgets and what next year's model will look like. The protocol PC-over-IP (PCoIP) was designed for all these users and those in-between.

The protocol itself was developed by Teradici, who partnered with VMware to make it one of the main features of View. One of the main features of the protocol is that it was designed to be efficient, adaptive, and secure (right out of the box). To have a protocol designed for the modern desktop computing environment is significant because it ensures that we do not need to tack on additional items to achieve a regulatory-compliant environment. As each version of View has come about, we've seen VDI switch from an ad hoc collection of virtual machines that were designated as desktops to complex desktop environments configured with ease and simplicity (and no, that's not contradictory).

Today, you can quickly put up a View environment, usually with little effort. The bigger challenge is the desktop operating system optimization and how the virtual machines play together in memory and storage. But we'll get into that. Understanding where we have come from helps us address some of the challenges that still exist, primarily one of the biggest assumptions that constantly challenges VDI instances: the idea that we can treat desktop virtual machines exactly like we treat server virtual machines.

Virtual desktops behave differently than servers with regard to how resources are used. Although both use the "four food groups," desktops tend to be consistently the same across the board in activities and often do huge bursts (think of Monday morning logins, antivirus updates, and the like). In addition, content changes much more on desktops than it does on servers. The desktop landscape is also being changed by the likes of tablets, smartphones, iPads, zero clients, and more. Figure I-2 provides a logical representation of all the possible features of View. There are other features and pieces not shown, but this figure does highlight how a virtual desktop environment might look for some environments.

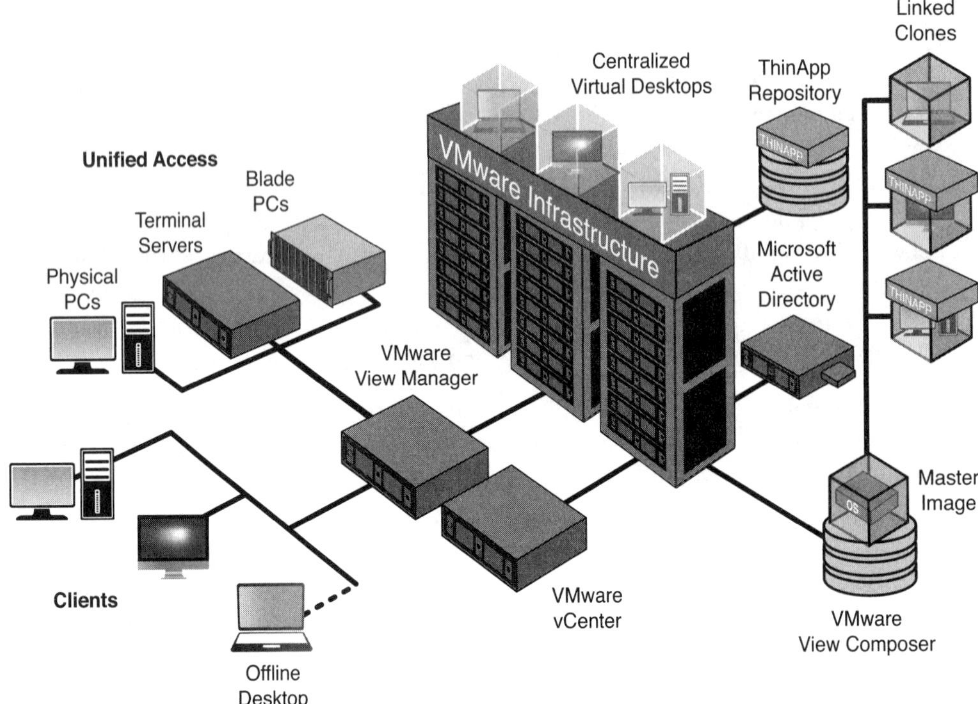

Figure I-2 VMware View components.

So, what makes up View (besides what Figure I-2 shows us)? Well, the central piece of View is the Connection Server. This acts as both the management piece and the point of contact for end users. A single Connection Server, however, cannot manage and handle all the users that would connect to it. Like any system, there are a finite number of resources. Although virtualization does make better use of those resources, there is always a limit to what is there. So, we'll install replica servers to help expand the View instance and allow for a better balance of resource utilization and availability for users. It is through the View Connection Servers that users are able to connect to their desktops that run on vSphere. In addition, the Connection Server allows us to create automated pools, manual pools, or even terminal service pools of desktops if we want. For those pools, we can use the traditional template provisioned virtual machines, but this can eat up a lot of storage space for the environment. So, to help with this, we can leverage the Composer piece that makes linked clones, which can use as little as 90% less space compared to fully provisioned virtual machines. To further help shrink down the size of the virtual desktop, we can leverage a technology like ThinApp to take applications from residing as part of the base image and move them to remote storage for streaming.

When most people think of VDI, they think of the head office or the telecommuter. However, there is a special kind of user whom we need to consider: the remote road warrior user. Normally, our remote users are given a laptop and expected to back up important data once in a while. Because these systems are basically the responsibility of the user, who may or may not make it back into the office occasionally, any number of things can happen to the system over the course of the life of the laptop on the road. Or, worse, it could be stolen or compromised. The desktop support team can monitor systems that are local, but those on the road tend to be a little harder to do.

We often hear in the news about the laptop that got left at the airport or the system that got compromised. These kinds of events result in huge dollar losses. But even when we look beyond that and think of the kinds of people who do business with us (contractors and partners and so on) who might need access to sensitive data or unique applications, we often see that providing a centrally controlled system would be ideal. We do not, however, need to think that broadly. What about the university that has students who do study/work sessions abroad and has research it needs to protect? Maybe the students are part of a special South Pole team that has limited or no network access. Or perhaps they are journalists in the middle of a conflict writing the next Pulitzer Prize-winning article.

In any scenario where you cannot access the environment normally, View provides for a unique kind of desktop: local mode desktop (what used to be referred to as *offline* desktops). If I have a Windows system with the View Client with Local Mode installed on it, I can download a whole virtual machine to my system. Once downloaded and running on the local hardware, any changes I do can be synchronized back to the View environment and the copy that resides, protected, on the ESXi host. If the laptop gets stolen, the virtual machine virtual disk is encrypted. Even if the laptop gets infected with every malware, Trojan, and other nasty thing you can find, the virtual machine remains protected. And, if that local virtual machine shouldn't be used any more, as an administrator I can revoke someone's access easily and when it happens, the virtual machine can delete itself on the remote system once it knows it's not needed any more.

But all that aside, what I find really nice about View is that I do not need to create a separate user environment for this. I can use my existing Active Directory environment and leverage existing Group Policy Objects (GPOs) and add View-specific GPOs to help manage the environment. It is easy to incorporate into the environment. And just as easy to set up. For one customer, I set up a simple proof of concept (POC) in less than 4 hours. The longest piece was tweaking Windows 7 so that it behaved better in a virtual environment.

As you go through this book, you will learn how to configure and set it up based on what the exam blueprint covers. However, I would be remiss if I failed to address a final thought: design. As announced in 2011, we are working on a VCAP5-DT exam. This exam will deal with design issues. No View environment should just be slapped up with the hope that it will work. Unlike other virtual environments, desktops seem particularly sensitive to two specific resources: storage (specifically input/output per second [IOPS] activity) and memory usage.

Before setting up any production environment, ensure that you are aware of what each desktop will actually use for each of these. This does not mean that you ignore the CPU and network; you still need to consider those, too. In my experience, the majority of performance issues with View relate to poor planning, specifically with storage. Although it is easy to create 1,000 linked-clone virtual machines on my storage, that same storage may not be able to handle all of them being created, powered on, refreshed, antivirus scanned, and so on all at the same time on the same storage. What might have been 5 IOPS per virtual machine for behavior may be 100 times greater when doing activities such as power ons, refreshes, rebalances, and so forth.

Because it is so easy to install and configure View, it becomes easy to ignore what needs to be done to ensure optimal performance of the virtual desktops. As the proverb says, "He who fails to plan, plans to fail." This is particularly apt for View. So with that said, let's get un-lulled and install the various parts of View in Chapter 1, "What Makes Up View?"

Who Should Read This Book

The VCP certification was listed on http://www.techrepublic.com/ as one of the top five in-demand certifications to have in 2013. If you are currently working with VMware vSphere virtual datacenters, it could be a valuable certification for you. If you are considering your options in the IT world, you will not go wrong if you learn about virtualization now. In either case, this book will help you obtain the knowledge and the skills necessary to certify as a VCP.

Goals and Methods

My number one goal of this book is simple: to help you pass the VCP5-DT certification exam and obtain the status of VMware Certified Professional 5 – Desktop (VCP5-DT).

To aid you in gaining the knowledge and understanding of key topics, I use the following methods:

- **Opening topics list:** This list defines the topics to be covered in the chapter. Each chapter is a part of the exam blueprint and the chapters and topics are written in blueprint order.
- **"Do I Know This Already?" quizzes:** At the beginning of each chapter is a quiz. The quizzes, and answers/explanations (found in Appendix A), are meant to gauge your knowledge of the subjects. If the answers to the questions do not come readily to you, be sure to read the entire chapter.
- **Key topics:** The key topics indicate important figures, tables, and lists of information that you should know for the exam. They are interspersed throughout the chapter and are listed in table format at the end of the chapter.
- **Review questions:** All chapters conclude with a set of review questions to help you assess whether you have learned the key material in the chapter.
- **Exam-type questions:** Exam questions are included with the printed and digital editions of this book. They are written to be as close to the type of questions that appear on the VCP5-DT exam.

How to Use This Book

Although you could read this book cover to cover, I designed it to be flexible enough to allow you to easily move between chapters and sections of chapters to work on the areas that you feel are the most important for you. If you intend to read all the chapters, the order in the book is an excellent sequence to follow.

The core chapters, Chapters 1 through 9, cover the following topics:

- **Chapter 1, "What Makes Up View?":** This chapter focuses on installing, upgrading, and securing all of the key components in your vSphere. I discuss ESXi hosts, vCenter, datastores, and network components.
- **Chapter 2, "Configuring the View Environment":** This chapter focuses on storage of virtual datacenters and virtual machines. I discuss configuring and managing all forms of storage, including Fibre Channel, iSCSI, and network-attached storage.
- **Chapter 3, "Printing in the View Environment":** This chapter focuses on creating, configuring, and managing virtual machines and vApps. I cover many other topics, including cloning, troubleshooting, and exporting virtual machines and vApps.

- **Chapter 4, "The Protocols":** This chapter focuses on keeping your vSphere running smoothly and recovering quickly from any failure. I cover many topics, including services that improve overall utilization and recoverability.
- **Chapter 5, "Interacting with Active Directory":** This chapter focuses on understanding the key components of your vSphere and how they work together. You learn how to spot a problem and make the necessary corrections. I cover troubleshooting your ESXi hosts, network, storage, and key services.
- **Chapter 6, "Optimizing the Operating System":** This chapter focuses on the "core four" resources in any computer system: CPU, memory, disk, and network. I cover guidelines for monitoring each of the core four. By knowing how to monitor your resources and knowing what you should expect to see, you will be able to spot any metrics that seem to be "out of place" and take the necessary action.
- **Chapter 7, "Kiosk Mode":** This chapter describes the steps required to set up VMware View Clients to behave as kiosk machines.
- **Chapter 8, "Local-Mode":** This chapter illustrates the purposes of local mode and how to configure the VMware View environment to permit this option.
- **Chapter 9, "Troubleshooting":** This chapter discusses the processes involved to assist administrators when problems arise in their View environment.

NOTE I highly recommend that you schedule the test now and then study. Go to Pearson/Virtual University Enterprises (http://vue.com) on the Web and find a testing center close to you. The cost of the exam at the time of this writing is $225. If you put your money down and set the date, you will focus more and study better.

Certification Exam and This Preparation Guide

When I originally started this book, it was more freeflow than I had intended. We then switched to trying to map as many of the chapters to the VCP510-DT Exam Blueprint as we could. Future editions of the book likely will exactly map each chapter to each objective. The idea of mapping the chapters to the objectives makes it easier for you to identify your strengths and weaknesses for understanding the topics. Table I-1 lists the VCP510-DT Exam Blueprint objectives and the chapter of this book that covers them.

Table I-1 VCP5 Exam Topics and Chapter References

Exam Section/Objective	Chapter Where Covered
Section 1: Install View Server Components	
Objective 1.1: Install View Composer	Chapter 1
Objective 1.2: Install View Standard and Replica Connection Server(s)	Chapter 1
Objective 1.3: Install View Transfer Server	Chapter 1
Objective 1.4: Install View Security Server(s)	Chapter 1
Objective 1.5: Prepare Active Directory for Installation	Chapter 1
Section 2: Configure the View environment	
Objective 2.1: Configure View Composer	Chapter 2
Objective 2.2: Configure VMware View Events Database	Chapter 2
Objective 2.3: Configure View Standard and Replica Connection Server(s)	Chapter 2
Objective 2.4: Configure View Security Server(s)	Chapter 2
Objective 2.5: Configure View Transfer Servers	Chapter 2
Objective 2.6: Configure advanced display protocol settings (PCoIP/RDP)	Chapter 4
Objective 2.9: Configure remote and/or location-based printing for View Desktops	Chapter 3
Objective 2.10: Configure the environment for Local Mode	Chapter 8
Objective 2.11: Configure the environment for Kiosk Mode	Chapter 7
Section 3: Create and configure pools	
Objective 3.4: Configure Local Mode use	Chapter 8
Objective 3.5: Build desktop sources	Chapter 6
Section 4: Implementation Troubleshooting	
Objective 4.1: Troubleshoot Composer installation on vCenter Server	Chapter 9
Objective 4.2: Troubleshoot events database	Chapter 9
Objective 4.3: Troubleshoot guest OS customization	Chapter 9
Objective 4.4: Troubleshoot accounts and permissions	Chapter 9
Objective 4.5: Troubleshoot connectivity between View Components	Chapter 9
Objective 4.6: Troubleshoot PCoIP configuration	Chapter 9
Objective 4.7: Troubleshoot View Servers (Connection, Security, Transfer)	Chapter 9
Objective 4.8: Troubleshoot View Persona Management	Chapter 9

Exam Section/Objective	Chapter Where Covered
Section 5: Component features and functions	
Objective 5.1: Describe and differentiate between component functions and feature level (i.e., not only what they do but how they work)	All chapters

Book Content Updates

Because VMware occasionally updates exam topics without notice, VMware Press might post additional preparatory content on the web page associated with this book at http://www.pearsonitcertification.com/title/9780789750273. It is a good idea to check the website a couple of weeks before taking your exam, to review any updated content that might be posted online. We also recommend that you periodically check back to this page on the Pearson IT Certification website to view any errata or supporting book files that may be available.

Pearson IT Certification Practice Test Engine and Questions on the DVD

The DVD in the back of this book includes the Pearson IT Certification Practice Test engine—software that displays and grades a set of exam-realistic multiple-choice questions. Using the Pearson IT Certification Practice Test engine, you can either study by going through the questions in Study Mode or take a simulated exam that mimics real exam conditions.

The installation process requires access to the Internet and two major steps: installing the software, and then activating the exam. The DVD in the back of this book has a recent copy of the Pearson IT Certification Practice Test engine. The practice exam—the database of exam questions—is not on the DVD.

> **NOTE** The cardboard DVD case in the back of this book includes the DVD and a piece of paper. The paper lists the activation code for the practice exam associated with this book. Do not lose the activation code. On the opposite side of the paper from the activation code is a unique one-time-use coupon code for the purchase of the Premium Edition eBook and Practice Test.

Install the Software from the DVD

The Pearson IT Certification Practice Test is a Windows-only desktop application. You can run it on a Mac using a Windows virtual machine, but it was built specifically for the PC platform. The minimum system requirements are as follows:

- Windows XP (SP3), Windows Vista (SP2), Windows 7, or Windows 8
- Microsoft .NET Framework 4.0 Client
- Microsoft SQL Server Compact 4.0
- Pentium class 1GHz processor (or equivalent)
- 512MB RAM
- 650MB disc space plus 50MB for each downloaded practice exam

The software installation process is pretty routine as compared with other software installation processes. If you have already installed the Pearson IT Certification Practice Test software from another Pearson product, there is no need for you to reinstall the software. Just launch the software on your desktop and proceed to activate the practice exam from this book by using the activation code included in the DVD sleeve.

The following steps outline the installation process:

Step 1. Insert the DVD into your PC.

Step 2. The software that automatically runs is the Pearson software to access and use all DVD-based features, including the exam engine and the DVD-only appendixes. From the main menu, click the **Install the Exam Engine** option.

Step 3. Respond to window prompts as with any typical software installation process.

The installation process gives you the option to activate your exam with the activation code supplied on the paper in the DVD sleeve. This process requires that you establish a Pearson website login. You need this login to activate the exam, so please do register when prompted. If you already have a Pearson website login, there is no need to register again. Just use your existing login.

Activate and Download the Practice Exam

After installing the exam engine, you should then activate the exam associated with this book (if you did not do so during the installation process) as follows:

Step 1. Start the Pearson IT Certification Practice Test software from the Windows Start menu or from your desktop shortcut icon.

Step 2. To activate and download the exam associated with this book, from the My Products or Tools tab, click the Activate button.

Step 3. At the next screen, enter the activation key from the paper inside the cardboard DVD holder in the back of the book. Once entered, click the Activate button.

Step 4. The activation process downloads the practice exam. Click **Next**, and then click **Finish**.

When the activation process completes, the My Products tab should list your new exam. If you do not see the exam, make sure you have opened the My Products tab on the menu. At this point, the software and practice exam are ready to use. Simply select the exam and click the **Open Exam** button.

To update a particular exam you have already activated and downloaded, open the Tools tab and click the **Update Products** button. Updating your exams will ensure you have the latest changes and updates to the exam data.

If you want to check for updates to the Pearson Cert Practice Test exam engine software, open the Tools tab and click the **Update Application** button. This will ensure you are running the latest version of the software engine.

Activating Other Exams

The exam software installation process, and the registration process, only has to happen once. Then, for each new exam, only a few steps are required. For instance, if you buy another new Pearson IT Certification Cert Guide or VMware Press Official Cert Guide, extract the activation code from the DVD sleeve in the back of that book; you do not even need the DVD at this point. From there, all you have to do is start the exam engine (if not still up and running), and perform steps 2 through 4 from the previous list.

Premium Edition

In addition to the free practice exam, you can purchase two additional exams with expanded functionality directly from Pearson IT Certification. The Premium Edition eBook and Practice Test for this title contains an additional two full practice exams and an eBook (in both PDF and ePub format). In addition, the Premium Edition title also has remediation for each question to the specific part of the eBook that relates to that question.

If you have purchased the print version of this title, you can purchase the Premium Edition at a deep discount. A coupon code in the DVD sleeve contains a one-time-use code and instructions for where you can purchase the Premium Edition.

To view the Premium Edition product page, go to http://www.pearsonitcertification.com/title/9780133445671.

This chapter covers the following subjects:

- Preparing the Active Directory for a View Installation
- Installing the View Standard and Replica Connection Servers
- Installing the View Transfer Server
- Installing the View Security Server

CHAPTER 1

What Makes Up View?

As with anything, it is worthwhile to start with a plan of what is going to be done in an environment, and most plans start with how to begin. To deploy View in a production environment, you would start with the use cases for that environment. Use cases are defined as how users actually utilize a combination of software and hardware for their daily work activities. Because the use case for our environment is to prepare for the exam, only a small test environment is required.

To create this environment, begin by installing all the pieces that make up a View environment. This will give you a better understanding of how the pieces work and integrate with each other and with Active Directory. This chapter looks at how to install the various components of View and what considerations for Active Directory are required to ensure the various components will work correctly. Getting these parts installed and configured should be enough to allow you to build your own lab environment to practice in preparation for the exam.

"Do I Know This Already?" Quiz

The "Do I Know This Already?" quiz allows you to assess whether you should read this entire chapter or simply jump to the "Exam Preparation Tasks" section for review. If you are in doubt, read the entire chapter. Table 1-1 outlines the major headings in this chapter and the corresponding "Do I Know This Already?" quiz questions. You can find the answers in Appendix A, "Answers to the 'Do I Know This Already?' Quizzes and Review Questions."

Table 1-1 Headings and Questions

Foundation Topics Section	Questions Covered in This Section
Install View Standard and Replica Connection Servers	3–7
Install View Transfer Server	8–9
Install View Security Server	10
Prepare Active Directory for Installation	1–2

1. Which group of Active Directory permissions is required by View Composer?
   a. Create Computer Objects, Delete Computer Objects, Create All Properties, List Contents
   b. Create Computer Objects, Read User Objects, Write All Properties, List Contents
   c. Create Computer Objects, Delete Computer Objects, Create All Properties, Create Contents
   d. Create Computer Objects, Delete Computer Objects, Read All Properties, List Contents

2. Which of the following is not a valid View GPO template?
   a. vdm_client.adm
   b. vdm_composer.adm
   c. vdm_common.adm
   d. vdm_agent.adm

3. Which of the following are ports that must be allowed by the firewall during a View Connection Server installation?
   a. 4000
   b. 8100
   c. 902
   d. 4172

4. What is the maximum number of concurrent connections to a Connection Server?
   a. 2,000
   b. 50
   c. 10,000
   d. 800

5. When installing the View Connection server what cannot be installed on the same server? (Select all that apply.)
   a. Active Directory controller
   b. SQL Server
   c. View Security Server
   d. vSphere Client

6. During the installation of a View Connection Server on Windows 2008, what Windows settings are adjusted to allow for more than 50 connections? (Select all that apply.)
   a. TCB hash table
   b. Remote Desktop protocol
   c. Java virtual machine
   d. IIS service

7. What is the maximum number of Connection Servers that can actively accept connections in a View instance?
   a. 2
   b. 3
   c. 4
   d. 5

8. What does VMware View Local Mode allow an end user to do?
   a. Allows a user to download a virtual machine to a Windows client
   b. Allows a user to download a virtual machine to a Linux client
   c. Allows a user to download a virtual machine to a Mac client
   d. Allows a user to download a virtual machine to an iPad

9. The four SCSI controllers for a View Transfer Server allow for what?
   a. Up to 60 concurrent disk downloads
   b. Up to 60 consecutive disk downloads
   c. Protection against failure
   d. Load balancing

10. The External URL is used for which purpose?
   a. To provide an extra URL to connect to the Security Server
   b. To provide an alternative URL to connect to the Security Server
   c. To provide the client access to the virtual desktop via RDP
   d. To provide the client access to the virtual desktop via PCoIP

Foundation Topics

Installing View

(This section covers Objectives 1.1 through 1.5 of the Blueprint.)

Before reviewing the steps needed to do a full View environment installation, ensure that you have planned the environment out fully so that you know what you will configure, set up, and test. And yes, you should test it. Without testing the environment fully, an administrator runs the risk of having irate end users and a bad user experience. Testing an environment in advance goes a long way toward avoiding future headaches. As I go through each of the steps, you can configure your own environment on which to practice. Although it is not required, familiarizing yourself with the View Manager interface can make a huge difference in how well you do on the exam.

It is best to ensure that Active Directory is configured properly, and this chapter starts with a look at that. You then learn how to install the View Connection Server and any View replica servers needed. After that, this chapter covers the installation of the Transfer and Security Servers. Although not all environments will need these components, it is important to understand their function and place within the View environment.

NOTE As a best practice, the vSphere environment that runs your server virtual machines should be separate from the one that manages your virtual desktops. Also, this book assumes you have the base knowledge necessary to deploy vCenter Server, ESXi, and Active Directory because these components are required for a View deployment. Information on vCenter Server, ESXi, and Active Directory in this book is strictly limited to settings that might need to be adjusted to accommodate a View deployment.

Preparing the Active Directory for a View Installation

(This section covers Objective 1.5 of the Blueprint.)

Although the VMware VCP-DT Blueprint puts this section at the end of Section 1, I believe it is appropriate to place it at the start of the chapter. Before you begin any VMware View installation, it is important to have Active Directory configured properly for VMware View. Currently, VMware View supports Active Directory

2000, 2003, and 2008. View can be easily integrated into an existing domain infrastructure. Although it would be perfect to have a completely new and separate domain just for VMware View, this is not realistic for most companies.

The View Connection Server should be installed on a system that is part of the main domain. From there, you can use any trusts radiating out to allow end users to connect to the environment and connect to a desktop within their domains. Any trusts should be two-way. This can be configured where all domains have two-way trusts with each other or where a central domain has two-way trusts with other domains. For example, Domain A has two-way trusts with Domain B and Domain C, but Domain B and Domain C do not have trusts between each other. This setup can ensure isolation between sensitive domains while utilizing a centralized View environment.

For small Active Domain infrastructures, single-domain environments or environments with a small number of domains (for example, 10 or fewer) can be done as is. If the environment has a large, complex domain structure (for example, more than 75 domains), however, this could result in a challenge for both administrators and end users when trying to select their domain from the list. You can use the `vdadmin` command to filter domains through the use of whitelist or blacklist requirements. This command will be discussed in greater detail in Chapter 9, "Troubleshooting."

A critical best practice is leveraging the use of organizational units (OUs) to isolate or segment VMware View desktops from other systems in the environment. This is particularly important for VMware View desktops like those created by View Composer or those used for kiosk mode. In addition, giving the View Administrator OU administrator privileges avoids the need to give the View administrator full domain administrator privileges. The full list of privileges needed for the View Composer account is as follows:

- Create Computer Objects
- Delete Computer Objects
- Write All Properties
- List Contents
- Read All Properties
- Read Permissions

The Active Directory account must be assigned to the OUs and any child objects within the OUs. These can be used as containers for any linked clones created as part of the deployment, separating them from the physical environment and ensuring proper security within the environment while enabling the VMware View administrator to create desktops as needed.

In addition, you should create a separate group or groups for the end users who will access the desktops. As a best practice, you should entitle groups to the desktop pools rather than individual users. The group name should be something that fits within the environment and yet is understandable. For example, you could have groups such as View Local-Mode Users, View Linked Clone Users, View Kiosk, and so on. This also makes it easier to apply VMware View Group Policy Objects (GPOs) against the View users rather than against individual users. However, if you do need to apply specific GPOs against specific individuals, it's best to put them into another group and apply the GPOs to that group.

Five GPO ADM (administrative) templates, described in Table 1-2, come with the View Connection Server. You can find them in <install_directory>\VMware\VMware View\Server\Extras\GroupPolicyFiles on the View Connection Server itself. You cannot access them until after you have first installed the View Connection Server, but it is a good idea to plan, in advance, what policies you want to apply in your environment.

Key Topic

Table 1-2 VMware View GPO Templates

Template	Description
vdm_agent.adm	This template applies to configuring policy settings related to the View Agent. These will apply to the desktop that the end user will connect to.
vdm_client.adm	This template applies to configuring policy settings related to clients that connect from within the domain. Any clients outside of the domain that the View Connection Server is a member of will not be affected by these policies.
vdm_server.adm	This template applies policies that affect the View Connection Server. This includes any View replica servers that are associated with the initial View Connection Server.
vdm_common.adm	This template allows policies to be applied on all View components (specifically, the View Agent, the View Client, and the View Connection Servers).
pcoip.adm	This policy applies to the PC-over-IP (PCoIP) display protocol. If the remote connection uses RDP, these GPOs will not be applicable.
ViewPM.adm	This applies to policies related to the View Persona Management.

Although each of these is an ADM file, you can use the Microsoft ADMX Migrator to migrate the ADM files over to ADMX for use in Active Directory 2008 environments. You can find it at www.microsoft.com/downloads/en/details.aspx?FamilyId=0F1EEC3D-10C4-4B5F-9625-97C2F731090C&displaylang=en. Each of these templates is discussed in greater detail in later chapters, and you can use Appendix B, "Additional Resources and GPOs," as a quick reference for them.

For kiosk systems, View needs an additional group and accounts created. The group must be named using pre-Windows 2000 naming requirements so that the `vdmadmin` command can configure the kiosk settings. If user account access is used to verify the kiosk to the View Connection Server, the user account must have "custom-" or an alternative prefix (defined in the View ADAM/AD LDS [Active Directory Application Mode/Active Directory Lightweight Directory Services]) for the account. This requirement ensures that View is aware that this is a kiosk-type system.

In addition, if the client allows for generated passwords, there is no need to specify it within the View Client. However, if you explicitly set a password, that will need to be passed to the View Client. This is normally accomplished through the use of a script, and because this means keeping the password in clear text, it could result in a potential security breach. If you have to use this method, you need to adhere to additional local security requirements on the kiosk system. Alternatively, you can use the network card's MAC address to define the account. To do so, you need an account that is named "cm-"<MAC Address>.

Now that the Active Directory is configured, we can look at the actual steps involved to install View in an environment.

Installing the View Standard and Replica Connection Servers

(This section covers Objective 1.2 of the Blueprint.)

One of the things I like about View is that it is really straightforward to install and configure out of the box. Although all environments are unique, many steps are completed in the same way regardless of your environment. One of the first steps in deploying a View environment is to install a View Connection Server. For a new View deployment, you begin by installing the "standard" View Connection Server. If you are going to expand an existing environment or replace an existing server, you install a View Replica Server. As a best practice, you should always have at least two Connection Servers, a standard server and a replica server, regardless of the number of users you have connecting to the servers. This is for failover and redundancy in addition to load balancing of connections to the environment. As an additional best practice, you should also have separate servers to handle connections that are for kiosk systems.

Before you install the View Connection Server onto a Windows server, a few prerequisites need your attention. The first is that the Windows server must be a member of an Active Directory domain. That domain becomes the primary domain for

View. If you have more than one domain in the environment and want users from other domains in the forest to have access to the desktops created by View, ensure that you have a two-way trust in place to allow for those connections. At the time of this writing, VMware View supports Windows 2000, 2003, and 2008 Active Directory domains. As part of the installation, the View Connection Server also installs a version of ADAM or AD LDS, depending on the version of Active Directory that exists at the time of install. This allows View to copy the Active Directory schema down and use it as needed without altering the Active Directory schema.

Second, the Windows server must be a single-purpose server. That is, it should not

- Be an Active Directory controller
- Be a terminal server
- Be a vCenter server
- Be a server that performs other roles (for example, IIS or Apache server, Exchange server)
- Have a View component already installed (for example, Client or Agent, another View server)

This is to ensure that the View Connection Server will not interfere with nor be interrupted by other services and helps eliminate potential conflicts. In the case of Active Directory controllers, View Connection Servers cannot be installed because of the installation of ADAM/AD LDS.

Another factor to consider is the number of concurrent users that will go through the Connection Server. If you use Windows 2008 and configure it correctly, you could have upward of 2,000 concurrent users. A View pod consisting of up to five active Connection Servers and two spare/administrative Connection Servers could handle upward of 10,000 users. For Windows 2003 (supported up to View 5.0), the maximum number of users is 1,500 users. When considering user connections, keep in mind that "concurrent users" is not the same as the total number of users. For example, consider an environment that leverages View for shift work. The environment has 6,000 users total, and each 8-hour shift has 2,000 users. The View installation could be planned for 2,000+ spares (about 500 for this environment). If the environment is large, the View Connection Servers can balance users (with help from third-party load balancers such as F5's BIG-IP, Cisco's ACE, and BalanceNG) across multiple connection servers up to a total of 5 active servers, which means our environment could be upward of 10,000 users. It is also prudent to plan for spare servers in case one of the active servers fails.

You might wonder whether these values are achievable in an actual deployment. VMware has tested these values in the past for View 4.0 and 4.5. In fact, these tests are used to create reference architectures, which can be found and downloaded from VMware's Technical Papers section of the website. So these values definitely are achievable. However, when conducting these tests, VMware assumes that the desktop behavior behaves the same, that the equipment is the same, and so on. In an actual deployment, desktop behavior and equipment is likely to vary, resulting in a variance to what can actually be achieved from deployment to deployment.

To achieve the best possible values for user access to your View Connection Servers, a few settings should be configured before allowing access into the environment. Most settings can be configured at any time, but it is better to have some of them in place on the Windows server before installing the View Connection Server. Ideally, you should have an idea of how many users are going to be using the environment.

Then, you must configure four essential items on the Windows server to ensure that View can handle the maximum user load: ephemeral ports, TCB hash table size, Java virtual machine (JVM) heap size, and the system page file. Just installing View is not sufficient to ensure the environment will be able to handle the number of connections needed. You must adjust these settings for environments that will have more than 50 users connecting to the environment at any one time. Let's start with the ephemeral ports on the Windows server.

Ephemeral ports are used for connections between the Connection Server and the View desktops. Every connection between these two points uses five ports. By default, a View Connection Server installed on Windows 2003 can create a maximum of 4,000 ports. When installed on Windows 2008, a maximum of 16,000 ports can be created. In addition, when installing on Windows 2008, most of the settings that must be manually adjusted are automatically set based on the amount of memory found during the installation of View. If the environment is going to have more than 50 users, it is ideal to confirm that the servers have a minimum of 10GB from the start to ensure that you won't have to adjust this after the fact.

For Windows 2003 in particular, several settings will have to be changed to accommodate the number of connections needed. To determine how many ports are required, use the following formula:

Number of ephemeral ports = ((5 x clients) / servers) + 10

Of particular note in this formula is the *servers* variable. This variable refers to the number of active Connection Servers that clients will access in the environment. That means if you have an environment with 4 active view servers and 2 spares, and 6,500 users (clients) will be connecting in, you will need 8,135 ports on each server (including the spares). Because the spares are not active until one of the four goes down, they do not need to be included in the algorithm. However, the settings should still be adjusted on the spare systems so that when they are added they are ready to handle the load.

After you have determined the number of ephemeral ports, the setting will need to be adjusted on the View Connection Server. To do so, you modify the Windows Registry. As a best practice, use the **rstrui.exe** tool to back up the Registry before adjusting anything. If the required number of ephemeral ports does not exceed the default value, do not adjust the Registry.

Step 1. On the Windows Connection Server, start the Windows Registry Editor by doing the following:

Select **Start > Command Prompt** or select **Start > Run** and type **cmd**.

At the command prompt, type **regedit**.

Step 2. Find the following subkey:

HKEY_LOCAL_MACHINE\SYSTEM\CurrentControlSet\Services\Tcpip\Parameters

Step 3. Click **Parameters**.

Step 4. Choose **Edit > New**, and then add the following:

Value Name: **MaxUserPort**

Value Type: **DWORD**

Value data: **1024** + calculated number of ephemeral ports

Valid Range: **5000-65534**

Step 5. Exit the Windows Registry Editor.

Step 6. Restart the Windows Server.

In addition to the ephemeral ports, connections between the Connection Server and the managed desktops use the Transmission Control Block (TCB) hash table. This table maintains information about the connections. If View Connection Server is installed on Windows 2008, the value for the TCB hash table will be automatically adjusted as needed. For Windows 2003, the value will need to be adjusted to match the number of connections and desktops used. The connection information is kept in memory while connections are active and cleared when a connection is ended. This behavior helps improve network performance and memory utilization. As a result, this is one of the reasons why having connections maintained indefinitely is not supported or encouraged.

The formula for the TCB Hash Table, as shown in Table 1-3, is a little different than the formula used for calculating the required number of ephemeral ports. In addition, the default maximum number of rows in the table will vary depending on the number of CPUs in the server.

Table 1-3 TCB Hash Size on Windows 2003

Number of CPUs	Maximum Number of TCB Hash Table Rows
1	128
2	512
4	2,048
8	8,192

Given these values, the minimum number of CPUs can be determined for a given number of concurrent connections. The formula to use to determine whether more View Connection Servers would be required is as follows:

> Number of TCB hash table rows on each View Connection Server instance =
> ((5 x clients) / servers) + Number of desktops + 5

Using the previous example of 6,500 concurrent connections with 4 active Connection Servers, 2 spare Connection Servers, and 3 Security Servers, and provided that there were 8,000 desktops within the environment, this formula would yield (including the spares) 16,130 rows for the TCB Hash Table. This assumes once again that Windows 2003 is the underlying operating system.

The calculation for View Security Servers has a slightly different formula:

> Number of hash table rows on each Security Server =
> ((5 x clients) / Security Servers) + 10

Using this formula would result in each Security Server requiring 10,843 rows for the TCB Hash Table. Regardless of the number of CPUs on each server, or whether the servers are Connection Servers or Security Servers, you must adjust the Registry setting appropriately.

Step 1. On the Windows Connection Server, start the Windows Registry Editor by doing the following:

Select **Start > Command Prompt** or select **Start > Run** and type **cmd.**

At the command prompt, type **regedit.**

Step 2. Find the following subkey:

HKEY_LOCAL_MACHINE\SYSTEM\CurrentControlSet\Services\Tcpip\Parameters

Step 3. Click **Parameters.**

Step 4. Choose **Edit > New**, and then add the following:

Value Name: **MaxHashTableSize**

Value Type: **DWORD**

Value data: Calculated hash table size

Valid Range: **64-65534**

Step 5. Exit the Windows Registry Editor.

Step 6. Restart the Windows Server.

A final modification to the Registry is required. To help store all connections in active memory, the Windows Java Virtual Machine (JVM) heap is used. By default on Windows 2003, the amount of memory allocated is set to 512MB. This value must be increased to 1GB of memory by changing the following Registry entry:

HKEY_LOCAL_MACHINE\SOFTWARE\VMware, Inc.\VMware VDM\Plugins\wsnm\tunnelService\Params

Specifically, the `-Xmx512m` parameter must be changed to `-Xmx1024m`. Doing so ensures that the JVM heap is set to 1GB and should be able to handle more than 750 concurrent connections.

For Windows 2008 systems, this value is not changed as a Registry entry. In fact, the installer sets the JVM heap based on the amount of memory found during installation. If there is less than 10GB of memory, the JVM heap size will be set to 512MB by default. This value will remain the same even if you later increase the memory on the system to a larger amount. When installing View Connection Server, if 4GB of memory is present at installation, the JVM heap size will be set to 1GB. This is appropriate for environments that might have up to 500 concurrent connections. If more connections are required, the server should have, at a minimum, 10GB present at installation to achieve the maximum of a 2GB Java heap size allocation. Any change of memory, say from 2GB to 10GB, requires a reinstallation of the View Connection Server to take advantage of the new memory and to adjust the JVM heap.

You still need to complete two more steps before beginning the installation of a View Connection Server. First, the server must have a static IP address. If the address is set to DHCP, the View installation stops and prevents any installation until a static IP address is configured. Second, the system page file settings must be configured. The setting should be optimized for the View Connection Server and how it uses the amount of virtual memory within the operating system. This is particularly important if you change the memory assigned to a virtual machine that has the View Connection Server installed on it.

You can change these settings by navigating to the Virtual Memory dialog box. On most Windows system, right-clicking **My Computer** or **Computer** can start this process. You continue with **Properties > Advanced > Performance Settings > Advanced > Virtual Memory > Change**. Deselect **Automatically manage paging file size for all drives** and ensure that **System managed size** is selected. This will ensure that Windows maintains the page file based on current memory usage.

All of these settings are helpful regardless of whether the View Connection Server is a physical or a virtual machine. Although there is no specific requirement to use one or the other, most customer environments use a virtual machine. Using a virtual machine adds many of the benefits realized for virtual machines, including DRS and high availability (HA). Ideally, the virtual machine used for View Connection Server should be on a different ESXi host than the virtual desktops themselves. For this book, all examples will assume the environment is installed using virtual machines.

However, if you want to install using actual physical hardware, Table 1-4 shows the requirements for the View Connection Server (including the replica servers and Security Servers).

Table 1-4 View Connection Server Hardware Requirements

Hardware Component	Required	Recommended
Processor	Pentium IV 2.0GHz processor or higher	Four CPUs
Memory Windows Server 2008 64-bit	4GB RAM or higher	At least 10GB or higher (especially if you are going to have more than 50 desktops)
Memory Windows Server 2003 32-bit R2	2GB RAM or higher	6GB RAM or higher and enable Physical Address Extension (PAE) (especially if you are going to have more than 50 desktops) For the PAE, see this KB from Microsoft: http://support.microsoft.com/kb/283037
Networking	One or more 10/100Mbps network interface cards (NICs)	1Gbps NICs

NOTE As of VMware View 5.1, Windows 2003 is no longer supported as an operating system for View Connection, Transfer, and Security Servers.

One of the choices you have to make is which server operating system you are going to use. The choice you make can have implications with regard to the use of a Security Server and remote PCoIP access. If you choose to use Windows Server 2003 R2 with SP2, only the 32-bit version is supported and you will not be able to use the PCoIP Secure Gateway component for remote access without a virtual private network (VPN). However, using the Windows Server 2008 R2 64-bit, with or without SP1, will ensure that the PCoIP Secure Gateway component is available for use if you want to use it. Remember that all Connection, replica, and Security Servers that are part of a specific View instance should use the same operating system to ensure consistency and proper connectivity.

In addition, if you use Windows 2008, the firewall will be automatically configured by View for the Connection Server. For Windows 2003, the firewall must be manually configured for the appropriate ports to be opened. Table 1-5 details the necessary ports for each protocol that have to be opened and on which component.

Table 1-5 View Connection Server Protocol Port Requirements

Protocol	Ports	View Server Components
JMS	TCP 4001	Standard and replica servers
JMSIR	TCP 4100 in	Standard and replica servers
AJP13	TCP 8009 in	Standard and replica servers
HTTP	TCP 80 in	Standard, replica, and Security Servers
HTTPS	TCP 443 in	Standard, replica, and Security Servers
PCoIP	TCP 4172 in UDP 4172 both directions	Standard, replica, and Security Servers
LDAP/ADAM/AD LDS	TCP/UDP 389	Standard and replica servers
SOAP	TCP 18443	Standard and replica servers
RSA Secure ID	UDP 5500	Standard and replica servers
RPC	TCP 1515	Standard and replica servers

Each protocol listed in Table 1-5 has importance for the View instance and is explained in detail as follows.

The Java Message Service (JMS) API is used for communication between the Connection Servers themselves. You can use the default 512-bit RSA keys, which are used for message validation between the server components, or you can increase the RSA key size to 1,024. This change must be done immediately after the installation of the Standard Server at the start of deploying the View environment and before other components (replica servers, Security Servers, or the View Agent) are installed. To increase the size of the RSA keys, complete the following steps:

Step 1. On the Windows server where the View Connection Server (standard) is installed, start the ADSI Edit (adsiedit.msc) tool. This tool is installed with the View Connection Server.

Step 2. Connect to **DC=vdi, DC=vmware, DC=int**.

Step 3. Select the object **CN=Common**, **OU=Global**, **OU=Properties**, and set the pae-MSGSecOptions attribute to **keysize=1024**.

Step 4. Restart the View Connection Server service.

Java Message Service Inter-Router (JMSIR) is also used for additional traffic between the View Connection Servers.

The Apache JServ Protocol (AJP13) is used for communication between the Security Server and the View Connection Servers. This is to help maintain connections from an external source to the Security Server and into the Connection Servers. Even if you do not plan to use the Security Server, it is worthwhile to ensure that this port is open in case of future changes.

The Hypertext Transfer Protocol (HTTP) and HTTP Secure (HTTPS) protocols are used for client and administrator access for the connection protocol and for client access on the Security Server. HTTPS also is used for tunneled RDP sessions to encrypt the data portion of the connection. Although the PCoIP protocol is not tunneled, the control portion of the protocol still must communicate with the Connection Servers and Security Servers.

The LDAP port is needed to allow for replication between View Connection Servers to ensure that information added to one server is visible to the others. This is the standard port for communication with Active Directory and should already be opened (but if not, definitely open it).

The Simple Object Access Protocol (SOAP) port is used by View Composer to allow for communication between the Connection Server and the Composer service. This allows for commands, such as creation of linked clone pools, recompose operations, and refresh operations to be sent from the View management interface to Composer. In earlier versions, this port was 8443 but was changed to 18443 when vCenter Server started using 8443 for the vCenter Server service.

If RSA authentication is going to be used, it is critical to have that port opened so that the Connection Server can reach the RSA server to verify token authentication as part of the two-factor authentication process.

Prior to the creation of the Microsoft Endpoint Mapper service, a Windows administrator would have to open up a variety of ports for all sorts of services. This was a cumbersome process, and one potentially fraught with error. With Microsoft Endpoint Mapper, services can create ports for their connections as needed. Therefore, it is important to ensure that ports are opened between the Connection Server and the various desktops as well as between the Connection Servers.

Now that the virtual machine is configured and part of the domain, you can begin the installation of the View Connection Server itself. If you haven't done so already, download the installer from the VMware Downloads page. The file should be named something like `VMware-viewconnectionserver-y.y.y-xxxxxx.exe` or `VMware-viewconnectionserver-x86_64-y.y.y-xxxxxx.exe`, where `xxxxxx` is the build number and `y.y.y` is the version number. At the time of this writing, the version is 5.1.1, and the build is 799444. This installer is actually used for four types of servers found within a View environment: the standard server, the replica server, the Transfer Server, and the Security Server. You learn about the Transfer and Security Server installations in the "Install the View Transfer Server" section of this chapter. Start the installation by double-clicking the installer EXE. Remember that the `VMware-viewconnectionserver-x86_64-y.y.y-xxxxxx.exe` should be used for the Windows 2008 server installs, which is what is used for this book. When the installer starts, follow these steps:

Step 1. On the first two screens (the Introduction and the End User Patent Agreement screens), click **Next**.

Step 2. Read the VMware end user license agreement. Then choose **I accept the terms in the end license agreement** and click **Next**.

Step 3. If you want to install the program in a location other than the default, choose **Change**. Otherwise, click **Next**.

Step 4. Choose which of the four server types you are installing. Because this is the start of a View environment, choose **View Standard Server**.

Step 5. Choose whether to configure the Windows Firewall. Because this example uses Windows 2008, View will automatically configure the firewall. Click **Next**.

> **NOTE** If this were Windows 2003, the firewall service would have to be manually configured or disabled altogether. To disable the firewall, ensure that you stop and disable the service itself. Do not right-click the network and try to stop the firewall there; it will not work.

Step 6. Read the summary page to ensure that the install location is correct, and then click **Next**.

View then goes through the installation process, including the installation of ADAM/AD LDS. The amount of time it takes to install depends on how big your current schema is. An environment that has more than 200,000 users and 750,000 computer objects in the domain will take longer than an environment with 30 users and 75 computer objects.

When the installation completes, you can prepare a second server and install the replica server. The operating system should be the same as the initial Connection Server to ensure consistency between versions. Even more important, ensure that memory resources are the same between the initial Connection Server and the replica.

The difference between the standard Connection Server install and the replica server install is minor. All the steps are the same, but because this will be a replica server, the installation will connect to an initial Connection Server to copy the View ADAM/AD LDS, as shown in Figure 1-1. The information copied consists of the domain schema plus View-specific information. As a result, the installation of a replica server will take a little bit longer than the installation of a standard Connection Server. And remember that there are no hierarchies to the servers because all View Connection Servers are peers of each other.

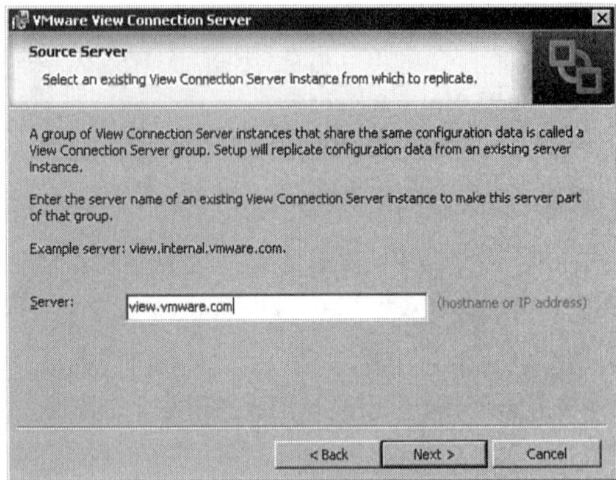

Figure 1-1 Replica installation extra step.

Installing the View Transfer Server

(This section covers Objective 1.3 of the Blueprint.)

One of the more interesting features of View is the local mode option. As companies move more and more toward bring your own PC/employee-owned IT (BYOPC/EOIT) initiatives, the ability to provide a corporate standardized and supported desktop image becomes critical to ensuring IT efficiency while providing users control over the technical tools that they use daily. It can become challenging to meet both goals without increasing the potential for data leakage or sacrificing the corporate image or applications in favor of simplifying employees' lives. Basically, we can have our cake and eat it too in the desktop world by using the local mode option.

Local mode uses a special kind of virtual machine that can have a copy downloaded from an ESXi host to a local physical Windows laptop or desktop. In addition, this option ensures synchronization between the local virtual desktop and the remote one that exists on the ESXi host. This means that if a local physical laptop or desktop fails (say due to a hard drive failure) or gets stolen, a copy of the desktop image is still available on the ESXi host that contains all user data up to when the last save was done. The image on the physical system can be expired and deleted remotely if need be, particularly in the case of a stolen system.

The Transfer Server was introduced in View 4.5. This server alleviates some of the load that is caused by the downloading of virtual machines and the synchronization of changes between local mode desktops and the images stored on the ESXi hosts. The installation of the Transfer Server is just as easy, if not easier, than the View Connection Server. The installation must be done on a virtual machine managed by the vCenter Server where the designated local mode desktops will reside. This allows the Transfer Server to mount the virtual machine virtual disks (VMDKs) as needed.

The requirements for the View Transfer Server are similar to those for the View Connection Server. Again, you want to ensure that the operating system is the same as others in the View environment. This is largely for consistency sake and for ease of installation. One obvious advantage to having virtual machines for the servers is the ease with which you can clone the standard Windows 2008 image and customize with Sysprep afterward (either through the virtual machine cloning process or the template provisioning process). Table 1-6 details the memory requirements for the Transfer Servers.

Table 1-6 Operating Systems and Minimum Memory Supported with View Transfer Server

Operating System	Minimum Memory Requirements
Windows Server 2008 R2, 64-bit Standard or Enterprise (with or without SP1)	4GB
Windows Server 2003 R2, 32-bit Standard or Enterprise (with or without SP2)	2GB

As a best practice, it is recommended to have at least two virtual CPUs to handle the Transfer Server workload. Currently, there is a recommended maximum of 20 concurrent disk transfers per Transfer Server. Also note that initial checkouts will take the longest amount of time and should be planned for. Initial checkouts occur when an end user first connects to the View environment and requests to check out a virtual machine.

This results in the entire virtual machine being downloaded from an ESXi host, through the Transfer Server, to where the View Client with Local Mode is running. As a best practice, users should be attached to the LAN to do this first checkout, to ensure a faster checkout time. For example, if you have upward of 400 users who will participate in a BYOPC program, they should not all check out their desktops at the same time. For that kind of scenario, stagger the checkouts to 15 users each day until all users have downloaded their desktops. You learn more about this process in Chapter 8, "Local Mode."

Part of installing the View Transfer Server is sizing the repository to be able to store the View Composer generated linked-clone base images. These images can be quite large, so size the repository accordingly. The repository can either be a local drive (for example, C:\TransferRepositoryLocal01\ ) or a UNC network drive (for example, \\server.somedomain.com\TransferRepository01\).

NOTE Although it is a best practice to add the View Transfer Server to the View Manager before configuring the View Transfer Server repository, it is not a requirement.

Installation of the Transfer Server requires the virtual machine to be configured with a specific SCSI adapter. This adapter is the LSI Logic Parallel SCSI controller. If the virtual machine is configured with any other controller, the installer will stop. Of particular note is that neither an SAS controller nor the VMware paravirtual controller is supported. This is important because the Transfer Server will transfer any changes done on the local virtual machine to the remote desktop in the datacenter, particularly when using linked clones.

NOTE As of View 5.1, the Transfer Server can use either the LSI Logic SAS or the VMware paravirtual SCSI controller.

Because there is not a page for ports during the installation, it is important to note that the Transfer Server uses a very heavily modified Apache web server. Although it is strongly encouraged to ensure that this is a single-purpose server, if the server is used for other applications that require ports 80 and/or 443, you might experience issues. In this case, the ports for any other processes will need to be changed because the ports for the Transfer Server cannot be modified.

Start the installation by double-clicking the same installer EXE that you used for the Connection Server and replica server installations. In our case, this would be the `VMware-viewconnectionserver-x86_64-y.y.y-xxxxxx.exe` (because I am using Windows 2008). Once the installer starts, follow these steps:

Step 1. On the first two screens (the Introduction and the End User Patent Agreement screens), click **Next**.

Step 2. Read the VMware end user license agreement. Then choose **I accept the terms in the license agreement** and click **Next**.

Step 3. If you want to install the program in a location other than the default, choose **Change**. Otherwise, click **Next**.

Step 4. Choose which of the four server types you are installing. For this section, choose **View Transfer Server**.

Step 5. As shown in Figure 1-2, enter in the appropriate information needed for the Transfer Server configuration. This information must include the domain info, the Transfer Server FQDN, and the View administrator's information. After filling in this information, click **Next**.

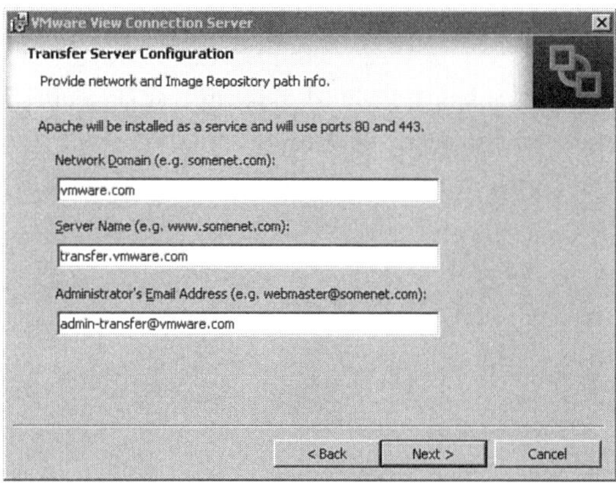

Figure 1-2 View Transfer Server install step 5.

Step 6. Choose whether to configure the Windows Firewall. Because this example uses Windows 2008, View will automatically configure the firewall. Click **Next**.

NOTE If this were Windows 2003, the firewall service would have to be manually configured or disabled altogether. To disable the firewall, ensure that you stop and disable the service itself. Do not right-click the network and try to stop the firewall there; it will not work.

Step 7. Read the summary page to ensure that the install location is correct, and then click **Next**.

Although these steps are all that is required for the installation of the software, additional configuration will be performed when the installation is completed. When the Transfer Server is added to the View environment, View verifies that there are four LSI Logic Parallel SCSI controllers on the virtual machine. If they do not exist, View will do a configuration change to the virtual machine to add them, as discussed in more detail in Chapter 8. These controllers are needed to ensure that the Transfer Server can handle multiple concurrent local disk transfers, up to 60. The value of 60 is a theoretical maximum; at this time, VMware has tested up to 20 concurrent transfers. When performing a large number of concurrent transfers, remember that downloading all those images can saturate bandwidth fairly quickly.

Installing the View Security Server

(This section covers Objective 1.4 of the Blueprint.)

As mentioned previously, one of the things I like the most about View is its installation and configuration simplicity. As you go through this book, you could conceivably build a small proof of concept or even plan a larger one. Either way, the steps are straightforward. My second most favorite part of View is the Security Server. As a security geek who is a huge advocate of transparency and making things secure while making it relatively painless for users to connect, the View Security Server meets my requirements. The installation is similar to that of the View Standard and Replica Connection Servers.

NOTE Although you can install the Security Server on a different Windows version compared to the View Connection Server, it is a recommended best practice to ensure that all View components are using the same operating system and hardware configuration (including the ephemeral ports, the TCB Hash Table, the JVM heap, and the operating system page file).

The View Security Server is a special server that allows users to connect from a not-so-secure environment to the View environment in a more secure location. For example, if users connect from the Internet into a corporate View environment and no VPN exists, the View Security Server provides for a secure mechanism to allow these connections without compromising access. The server will be placed in the DMZ and be configured as a "bastion" host. Bastion hosts expect to be attacked and are fortified against attack, much like the historical meaning behind the word *bastion*. Bastions were specially built fortresses or towers during medieval times that would face catapult attacks. The difference is that this is a computer, and our attackers and the location of their catapults are not as obvious.

NOTE Because it is expected that the View Security Server will face attack from within the DMZ, it should *not* be a member of any domain. The View Connection Servers should *never* be in the DMZ, because they contain the whole domain schema and related information.

What allows for the connection to occur from outside the View environment to a View Connection Server is the creation of a tunnel between the View Connection Server and the View Security Server. Every View Security Server must be paired to a single View Connection Server, but a View Connection Server can have any number of View Security Servers paired with it. Because of the tunnel that is created, VMware neither supports nor allows for load balancers to exist between the View Security Server and the View Connection Server. Breaking this tunnel through the use of a load balancer could compromise a connection between the two servers.

It is a best practice to have a firewall on the external vNIC of the View Security Server and one between the View Security Server and the View Connection Server. This helps enforce a strong DMZ environment, although it is possible to have a single port that behaves as if it is two separate firewalls. To this end, the ports listed in Tables 1-7 and 1-8 will need to be opened on the appropriate firewall.

Table 1-7 External Firewall Ports (In Front of the View Security Server)

Source	Protocol	Ports	Destination	Notes
Any	TCP	443 (or 80)	View Security Server	443 (HTTPS) is the default and should be the port used externally because this will provide basic encryption for connections and requires a Secure Sockets Layer (SSL) certificate. 80 (HTTP) if SSL is disabled.
Any	TCP/UDP	4172	View Security Server	If PCoIP is used externally, this port will need to be used. This feature is available *only* for View environments that use 4.6 and later for both the View Security Servers and the View Connection Server.

Table 1-8 Internal Firewall Ports (Behind the View Security Server and In Front of the View Connection Server)

Source	Protocol	Ports	Destination	Notes
View Security Server	TCP	3389	Any desktop virtual machine	RDP traffic to the virtual desktops
View Security Server	TCP/UDP	4172	Any desktop virtual machine	PCoIP traffic to the virtual desktops
View Security Server	TCP	4001	View Connection Server	JMS traffic for communication between the View Security Server and the View Connection Server
View Security Server	TCP	8009	View Connection Server	AJP13 forwarded web traffic to the View Connection Server
Any desktop virtual machine	TCP	4001	View Connection Server	JMS traffic between the View Agent on the desktops to the View Connection Server

NOTE The firewall rules for ports 4001 and 8009 between the View Security Servers and the View Connection Servers must exist between the paired servers. This means that it can be a specific source-to-specific destination. For example, SecurityServer01 is paired with Replica02, and there should be an explicit firewall rule to allow traffic for those ports with those two servers.

Remember that we will be using `VMware-viewconnectionserver-x86_64-y.y.y-xxxxxx.exe` (because Windows 2008 is being used for the installation example in this book). When the installer starts, follow these steps:

Key Topic

Step 1. On the first two screens (the Introduction and the End User Patent Agreement screens), click **Next**.

Step 2. Read the VMware end user license agreement. Then choose **I accept the terms in the license agreement** and click **Next**.

Step 3. If you want to install the program in a location other than the default, choose **Change**. Otherwise, click **Next**.

Step 4. Choose which of the four server types you are installing. Because this is the start of a View environment, choose **View Security Server** and click **Next**.

Step 5. Enter in the FQDN of the View Connection Server that the View Security Server will be paired with. Click **Next**.

Step 6. Switch to the View Connection Server and log in as a View administrator. Navigate to **View Configuration > Servers > View Connection Servers**. Highlight the View Connection Server you want to pair the View Security Server with.

Step 7. Select **More Commands** and choose **Specify Security Server Pairing Password** from the drop-down. Figure 1-3 shows the pairing password screen.

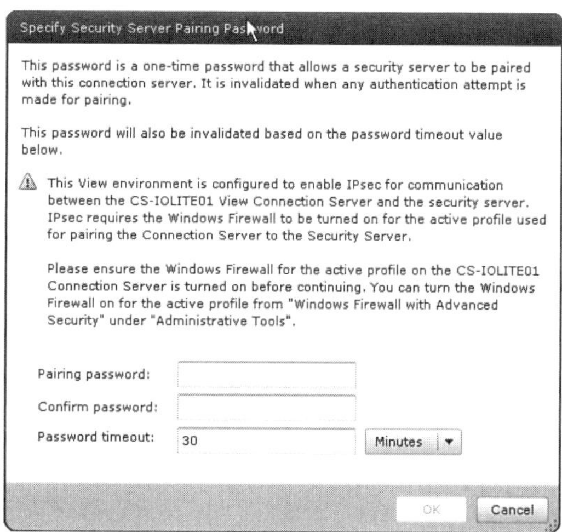

Figure 1-3 View Security Server install step 7.

Step 8. Enter the password to use for the pairing and confirm it. Set the time if you need something greater or less than the 30-minute default. Click **OK**.

Step 9. Return to the View Security Server installer and enter the password. Click **Next**. If the password is correct, the installation continues. If not, reenter the password.

Step 10. Enter the external URL to allow remote RDP access. Enter the external IP address for remote PCoIP if it differs from what View Manager detects as the value. You will not see the external IP address for PCoIP if you use Windows 2003. Adjust ports if you are using ports other than the default. Click **Next**.

Step 11. Choose whether to configure the Windows Firewall. Because this example uses Windows 2008, View will automatically configure the firewall. Click **Next**.

NOTE If this were Windows 2003, the firewall service would have to be manually configured or disabled altogether. To disable the firewall, ensure that you stop and disable the service itself. Do not right-click the network and try to stop the firewall there; it will not work.

Step 12. Read the summary page to ensure that the install location is correct, and then click **Next**.

After the installation is complete, switch to the View Manager and refresh the View Security Servers box on **View Configuration > Servers > View Connection Servers** to verify that the pairing is complete. In step 10, you must configure the External URL. This URL is used as part of the two-part connection process that the View Client performs when connecting to a desktop. The first part is the initial communication with View to verify the user, present entitled desktops, and perform other activities related to the user's initial choices for the desktop. The second connection is the actual connection to the desktop. It is this second connection that the External URL/External IP uses. (The choice between the URL and IP depends on the protocol: URL is for RDP, and IP is for PCoIP.) Essentially, the URL/IP allows the Connection Server or Security Server (depending on which one is used for the initial connection) to act as a proxy on behalf of the desktop to the client. You can change the External URL/External IP later if necessary.

And now you have a simple environment. As previously mentioned, in just a few hours you can create a simple proof of concept (POC) environment to test out View by following these steps. With the installation complete, we can now continue and configure the View environment.

This chapter covered how to prepare Active Directory for a View deployment. You also learned how to install View Composer, the View Connection Server, and associated View replica servers. The chapter finished with a look at the installation process for View Transfer and View Security Servers.

Summary

This chapter covered the various install methods for all the components that could potentially make up a View installation. Properly sizing each component ensures a good foundation and allows the environment to be grown and expanded as the need arises. As a reminder, an environment should always have a minimum of two Connection Servers to allow for failover and load distribution. Planning the environment before starting the installation remains paramount to the success of any virtual desktop infrastructure (VDI) environment.

The next chapter covers how to configure a View environment and what options are available, including one of the more critical pieces, Composer.

Exam Preparation Tasks

Review All Key Topics

Review the most important topics in the chapter, noted with the Key Topic icon in the outer margin of the page. Table 1-9 lists a reference of these key topics and the page numbers on which each is found.

Table 1-9 Key Topics

Key Topic Element	Description	Page
Paragraph	Discusses how to best use OUs for View components like Composer or kiosk mode	8
Table 1-2	VMware View GPO template descriptions	9
Paragraph	Discusses how to migrate files as needed by an environment	9
Paragraph	Discusses best practices to configure AD to be ready for kiosk mode desktops	10

Key Topic Element	Description	Page
List	What not to try to install View Connection Servers with	11
Paragraph	Discussion on settings required for View 5.0 and earlier for larger environments	12
Step list	Steps to modify the Registry for ephemeral ports on Windows 2003	13
Table 1-3	TCB hash size on Windows 2003, depending on number of CPUs on the Windows system	14
Step list	Steps to modify the Registry for a hash table on Windows 2003	14
Paragraph	Parameter needed for Windows 2003 and JVM adjustment	15
Paragraph	Steps to adjust Windows page file	16
Table 1-4	View Connection Server hardware requirements	16
Table 1-5	View Connection Server port requirements	17
Step list	Steps to increase RSA key size on Windows systems	18
Step list	Steps to install the View Connection Server	19
Table 1-6	Operating system and memory requirements for Transfer Server	22
Step list	Steps to install the View Transfer Server	23
Table 1-7	External firewall ports	26
Table 1-8	Internal firewall ports	26
Step list	Steps to install the View Security Server	27

Define Key Terms

Define the following key terms from this chapter, and check your answers in the Glossary:

View Connection Server, Transfer Server, Security Server, Composer, replica, linked clones, ADAM/AD LDS, DMZ

Review Questions

You can find the answers to these review questions in Appendix A.

1. The Active Directory account used for a kiosk system logging in with a MAC address must start with what prefix?
   a. custom-
   b. kiosk-
   c. cm-
   d. mac-

2. Which of the following is not a valid ADM template file?
   a. vdm_client.adm
   b. vdm_common.adm
   c. vdm_pcoip.adm
   d. vdm_agent.adm

3. Which of the following are ports that must be allowed by the external firewall during a View Security Server installation?
   a. 4000
   b. 80
   c. 903
   d. 4173

4. The maximum number of concurrent connections for a View POD could be?
   a. 2,000
   b. 1,500
   c. 10,000
   d. 6,000

5. The LDAP port is used for what purpose in the View environment?
    a. To allow for replication of the ADAM between the replica and standard Connection Servers
    b. To allow for replication of the ADAM between the replica and Security Servers
    c. To allow for replication of the ADAM between Security Servers
    d. To allow for replication of the ADAM between the replica and the desktops

6. Where can you find the ADM?
    a. On the Active Directory server under <install_directory>\VMware\VMware View\Server\Extras\GroupPolicyFiles
    b. On a Connection Server under <install_directory>\VMware\VMware View\Server\Extras\GroupPolicyFiles
    c. On the Active Directory server under <install_directory>\VMware\VMware View\Server\ADM\GroupPolicyFiles
    d. On a Connection Server under <install_directory>\VMware\VMware View\Server\ADM\GroupPolicyFiles

7. Port 4001 needs to be opened between the Security Server and the Connection Servers. What is this used for?
    a. JMS traffic for communication between the servers
    b. SOAP traffic for communication between the servers
    c. SSL traffic for communication between the servers
    d. PCoIP traffic for communication between the servers

8. For a View Connection Server on Windows 2008 for an environment that will have 50 users, how much memory do you need at install?
    a. 1GB
    b. 2GB
    c. 4GB
    d. 10GB

9. What are ephemeral ports used for by the Connection Server?
   a. To connect to Active Directory
   b. To connect to vCenter
   c. To connect to Composer
   d. To connect to desktops

10. The external IP is used for which purpose?
    a. To provide an extra URL to connect to the Security Server
    b. To provide an alternative URL to connect to the Security Server
    c. To provide the client access to the virtual desktop via RDP
    d. To provide the client access to the virtual desktop via PCoIP

This chapter covers the following subjects:

- Configuring the View Events Database
- Installing and Configuring View Composer
- Configuring the Standard and Replica Connection Servers

CHAPTER 2

Configuring the View Environment

Now that the base components for a View implementation have been deployed, let's take a look at how those components are configured. This chapter deals with configuring the components discussed in Chapter 1, "What Makes Up View?", as well as the steps needed to configure the View Events database. We spend considerable time reviewing the installation and configuration of View Composer. Finally, we take a look at roles and permissions and what permissions are needed to conduct specific activities in a View environment.

"Do I Know This Already?" Quiz

The "Do I Know This Already?" quiz allows you to assess whether you should read this entire chapter or simply jump to the "Exam Preparation Tasks" section for review. If you are in doubt, read the entire chapter. Table 2-1 outlines the major headings in this chapter and the corresponding "Do I Know This Already?" quiz questions. You can find the answers in Appendix A, "Answers to the 'Do I Know This Already?' Quizzes and Review Questions."

Table 2-1 Headings and Questions

Foundation Topics Section	Questions Covered in This Section
Configuring the View Events Database	1
Installing and Configuring View Composer	3
Configuring the Standard and Replica Connection Servers	2, 4–10

1. What four tables does the events database maintain?
   a. Event, event_data, event_history, event_data_history
   b. Event, event_data, event_historical_data, event_historical
   c. Event, event_log, event_historical, event_historical_data
   d. Event, event_data, event_historical, event_data_historical

2. Which of the following is not a vCenter permission needed for the View administrator?
   a. Virtual Machine > Configuration > Modify Device Settings
   b. Virtual Machine > Interaction > Create New
   c. Virtual Machine > Configuration > Add or Remove Device
   d. Virtual Machine > Interaction > Power on

3. What additional vCenter permission is needed for the View administrator when using Composer?
   a. Virtual Machine > Provisioning > Clone virtual machine
   b. Virtual Machine > Provisioning > Create linked clones
   c. Virtual Machine > Inventory > Add storage
   d. Virtual Machine > Inventory > Add Thindisk

4. What are the Enable Automatic Status updates used for?
   a. Ensures that desktops have the latest patches
   b. Ensures that the pools have the latest image
   c. Ensures that the desktop sessions do not time out
   d. Ensures that the Administrator interface does not time out

5. When you are using View tag restrictions, which of the following scenarios restrict a user in PoolA to a specific connection server?
   a. Check the Only connect to this connection server check box.
   b. Assign to the Connection Server a tag of EXTERNAL and PoolA INTERNAL.
   c. Assign to the Connection Server a tag of INTERNAL and PoolA INTERNAL.
   d. Assign to the Connection Server with a tag of INTERNAL and PoolA EXTERNAL.

6. The Display warning before forced logoff setting is used in what scenario?
   a. A View administrator logs a user off his desktop.
   b. A View desktop pool is scheduled for a recompose.
   c. A vCenter administrator logs a user off their desktop.
   d. A vCenter administrator schedules a recompose.

7. Which of the following are not predefined roles in View?
   a. Global Configuration and Policy Administrators (Read Only)
   b. Global Configuration and Policy Administrators
   c. Agent Registration Administrator (Read Only)
   d. Agent Registration Administrator

8. Which of the following privileges is specific to a desktop object?
   a. Manage Composer Pool Image
   b. Manage Remote Sessions
   c. Manage Pool
   d. Manage Persistent Disk

9. The maximum number of folders in View is what?
   a. 100
   b. 99
   c. 1,024
   d. 2,048

10. Folders for View can be created in two locations. What are those locations?
    a. View Configuration > Administrators > New Folder
    b. View Configuration > Administrators > Folders
    c. Inventory > Administrators > Folders
    d. Inventory > Pools > New Folder

Foundation Topics

Configuring the View Events Database

(This section covers Objective 2.1 of the Blueprint.)

Troubleshooting environments remains one of my favorite pastimes. I love puzzles of all sorts, and when environments do not work, they can, in fact, present interesting challenges. However, to troubleshoot anything, it helps to understand what the issue actually is, and that is where logs prove priceless. Unfortunately, not all logs provide enough detail to identify the problem at hand. That is where the View Events Database comes in handy. This database records the events of user activities in relation to View. Specifically, it records information in four tables: **event** (keeps the metadata info and optimizes data for searching for recent events only), **event_data** (the actual data for recent events only), **event_data_historical** (all data, both recent and historical), and **event_historical** (includes metadata info and optimizes data for searching).

The View Events Database records when users log in, when a View administrator sends a message to a desktop, when a user logs out, and so on. All information is displayed in plain English. The information can be exported from the database and into a third-party tool like Crystal Reports so that you can see how long individuals connect to their desktops, when they normally log in and out, and other activities. You do not have to have an events database, but it can prove extremely valuable when a problem arises, so setting it up is worthwhile.

Configure VMware View Events Database

(This section covers Objective 2.2 of the Blueprint.)

To configure an events database properly, you first need to create the database itself. For the events database, you create either a SQL database or an Oracle database. The versions that can be used match what View Composer can use (see Table 2-5). However, the View Events Database should be created as a separate database instance. Unlike vCenter Server, View Composer and the View Events Database do not support IMB DB2 as a database option. You do not have to configure an Open Database Connectivity (ODBC) connector, because that is part of the interface in View itself. If you are using a SQL server, you must ensure that you are using SQL Server Authentication (Integrated Windows Authentication is not supported) and that the TCP/IP protocols for the server are enabled. After doing this, you can then configure the events database.

Step 1. Log in to the View Administrator page and navigate to **View Configuration > Event Configuration**.

Step 2. Click **Edit** and enter the necessary information. Figure 2-1 shows an example of this screen filled in. Note that the actual values depend on organizational naming policy and could differ from what is shown. The port number defaults to the port that the database needs (1433 for SQL, 1521 for Oracle).

Step 3. Click **OK**.

Figure 2-1 Events database configuration screen.

After you have configured the database, you can then configure the event settings to determine how long event items are classified as new and how long they will be present in the View Events display (found under **Monitoring > Events**). The data itself remains in the database even when it is past the time to display events.

Configuring View's Connection to vCenter Server

(This section covers Objective 2.3 of the Blueprint.)

One nice thing about View is that you can configure it as a turnkey operation. That is, someone can set it up and then hand it over to someone else to manage the day-to-day operations. Whether View will be used as turnkey or not, an account must be created on vCenter Server to be used by View to connect to vCenter Server and allow View to provision, delete, and otherwise alter virtual machines. To begin, create a custom role on vCenter Server and give it a name like ViewAdministrator. Once created, the account can then be assigned the permissions shown in Table 2-2.

Table 2-2 VMware View Administrator Permissions

Privilege Group	Privileges to Enable
Folder	Create Folder Delete Folder
Virtual Machine	In the **Configuration** section: Add or remove device Advanced Modify device settings In the **Interaction** section: Power off Power on Reset Suspend In the **Inventory** section: Create new Remove In **Provisioning** section: Customize Deploy template Read customization specifications
Resource	Assign virtual machine to resource pool

If View Composer will be used, you must add additional permissions to the role. In addition to the default permissions listed here, the vCenter Server account for View must also have the permissions shown in Table 2-3.

Table 2-3 VMware View Administrator Composer Additional Permissions

Privilege Group	Privileges to Enable
Datastore	Allocate space Browse datastore Low level file operations

Privilege Group	Privileges to Enable
Virtual Machine	Inventory (all permissions)
	Configuration (all permissions)
	State (all permissions)
	In **Provisioning**:
	Clone virtual machine
	Allow disk access
Resource	Assign virtual machine to resource pool
Global	Enable methods
	Disable methods
	System tag
Network	All permissions

Adding local mode into the mix means more permissions must be added. In addition to the default permissions and the ones that Composer requires, you must add the permissions shown in Table 2-4 to the custom role.

Table 2-4 VMware View Administrator Local Mode Additional Permissions

Privilege Group	Privileges to Enable
Global	Set custom attribute
Host	In **Configuration**:
	System management

Determining which permissions are needed for the environment requires some planning in advance. Although these permissions can be added afterward, it is a better practice to plan ahead of time to avoid missing permissions that might be needed to perform certain operations.

Installing and Configuring View Composer

(This section covers Objective 2.1 of the Blueprint.)

Installing and configuring View is easy, but before you start the actual process, you should first determine how many people will be connecting to desktops through View (both at the same time and total), what kind of desktop they will need, and specific configurations for their desktop. In a nutshell, you need a plan. VMware View has many moving parts, and not planning in advance can result in problems later on. Although this book is not about View design, it is important to mention the importance of doing a proper design. The planning and process involved with this is enough for a whole separate book. For our purposes, we'll assume that we have a great design and we will begin configuring the environment with a common user type: the task worker.

When initially deploying or planning an environment, the first goal should be to virtualize the desktops of those users who do not need a dedicated desktop. Generally, these kinds of users are ones who all use the same desktop operating system and the same limited number of applications and tend to have the same tasks to do day in and day out. This type of user is commonly referred to as a *task worker*. Job roles like call center representatives, point-of-sale positions (cashiers), hotel front desk clerks, and other similar roles all fall into this category.

For end users like this, we can leverage linked clones and the Composer technology. We get into the details of what linked clones are in Chapter 6, "Optimizing the Operating System." For now, the best way to describe a linked clone is this: Imagine a virtual machine that has the exact same snapshot, multiple times over, and that all those snapshots are active at the same time. Each active snapshot has unique changes being recorded to it. Normally, I cannot create virtual machines this way, but Composer leverages a special application programming interface (API) that is found in vCenter Server. Composer creates a special read-only version of the base disk and then builds special read/write delta locations that represent the individual virtual machines or desktops.

NOTE As this book was being written, VMware released View 5.1.x. This version introduces the option of doing a standalone installation of View Composer. This can be helpful for larger environments or environments with a large amount of changed data. The installation steps remain essentially the same, except that Composer is not on the vCenter Server. The only visible change is in the user interface and relates to configuring Composer to work with vCenter Server and the Connection Server. This change allows View to be supported for use with the vCenter Server Appliance. This can prove particularly helpful for smaller environments. The current release of the vCenter Server Appliance has an internal PostgreSQL and can support 5 hosts or 50 desktops.

So to leverage linked clone technology you must install View Composer. This can be done before or after the View Connection Server has been installed. (I prefer to install it beforehand so that it is configured and ready for my View environment right away.) VMware vSphere 5 saw the introduction of the vCenter Server Appliance. This is a Linux-based version of vCenter Server that can be used with View 5.1 and later. For View 5.0 Composer, a Windows-based vCenter Server installation must be used because the 5.0 version of Composer is a Windows-only piece and is tied directly to the vCenter Server on which it is installed. Before View Composer can be installed, an account with specific permissions is required on the vCenter Server (see Tables 2-2 and 2-3). This account must be a member of the Local Administrators group.

View Composer should then be installed on each vCenter Server on which you will leverage linked clones. Each Composer installation should have a separate database from both other Composer installations and from vCenter Server itself.

After you have verified that you have the correct Active Directory and vCenter Server permissions, create the database that Composer will use. Although not documented officially anywhere, the database does not need to be large. This database stores information about the connections between Composer and vCenter Server, connections between Active Directory and Composer, and the information about the actual linked clones and the replica that they are anchored to. Field deployments with about 2,000 linked clones show about 22MB of database space used. Now, this does not mean that using SQL Express 2008 is sufficient for busy environments. Although it is possible to use the Express version, SQL Express 2008 was meant for testing and development and for small View environments (50 or fewer desktops). So what are your database options? Table 2-5 details all the database types you can choose from. (Some of the choices depend on whether you use vSphere 4.x or vSphere 5.) As a rule of thumb, always check the latest release notes to see whether there are any changes to the supported database list.

Table 2-5 VMware View Composer Supported Databases

Database	vSphere Version Supported
Microsoft SQL Server 2005 Express	vSphere 4.1 U1 or later vSphere 4.0 U3 or later
Microsoft SQL Server 2005 SP3 and later Standard and Enterprise (32-bit and 64-bit)	vSphere 5.0 or later vSphere 4.1 U1 or later vSphere 4.0 U3 or later
Microsoft SQL Server 2008 Express	vSphere 5.0 or later
Microsoft SQL Server 2008 SP1 and later Standard and Enterprise (32-bit and 64-bit)	vSphere 5.0 or later vSphere 4.1 U1 or later vSphere 4.0 U3 or later

Database	vSphere Version Supported
Oracle 10g Release 2	vSphere 5.0 or later vSphere 4.1 U1 or later vSphere 4.0 U3 or later
Oracle 11g Release 2, with Oracle 11.2.0.1 Patch 5	vSphere 5.0 or later vSphere 4.1 U1 or later vSphere 4.0 U3 or later

Composer is not supported with DB2, even if vCenter Server is. The database should be located on a separate database server or installed as a separate database instance on the database server that vCenter Server is using, provided that the server has enough resources to support the additional database. If you have a database administrator (DBA), he or she can configure this for you. If not, the following steps detail what you need to know to create and configure the database.

You need either SQL Server Management Studio or SQL Server Management Studio Express (which you can download from Microsoft's website):

Step 1. From the vCenter Server system, launch either SQL Server Management Studio or SQL Server Management Studio Express (depending on whether you are using a regular Microsoft SQL Server or one of the SQL Express versions). You can find this under **Start > All Programs > Microsoft SQL Server 2008** or **Microsoft SQL Server 2005**.

Step 2. Connect to the existing SQL Server instance.

Step 3. Right-click the Databases entry on the Object Explorer and select **New Database**. Alternatively, if you are using the SQL Server Management Studio Express, when choosing Connect to Database choose **<New Database...>** from the drop-down on Database file option.

Step 4. Assign a new name to the database in the New Database dialog box. Ideally, this should be something meaningful and memorable later on. For example, you could name the database ComposerDB or ViewComposer. Naming the database Database1 may make it harder later on when troubleshooting or if someone else takes over the View environment. For the Studio Express choice, choose a location and name of the new database.

Step 5. Click **OK**. The new database will be created. Exit SQL Server Management Studio/Studio Express.

The process is similar for Oracle. There are a few options unique to Oracle that must be configured as follows:

- Ensure that you select the **General Purpose or Transaction Processing** template.
- Create a unique Oracle system identifier (SID) prefix. It is best to use the global database name for the SID.
- Set a unique password and ensure that **Use the Same Administrative Password for All Accounts** is selected.

After creating the database, you can then create the ODBC connection. One key item to remember is that all database types that are used by VMware connect with System database source names (DSNs) to allow specific users to manage the database. The ODBC connection can utilize an Active Directory or Local User account, allowing the application to access the database as needed without elevated user rights, thus ensuring better security for the database itself.

Step 1. From the vCenter Server system, navigate to **Start > Administrator Tools > Data Source (ODBC)** and select the **System DSN** tab.

Step 2. Click the **Add** button, and then select the appropriate client. If you are using SQL, select **SQL Native**.

Step 3. Click the **Finish** button.

Step 4. In the Name box on the Create a New Data Source to SQL Server window, enter the name of the ODBC connector. You should use the same name as the database. For example, if the database is called ComposerDB, give the same name to the ODBC connector. Enter in a description if you want (optional). Finally, identify the host that the database resides on. If it is local, simply enter **Localhost**. If it is remote, enter the hostname and database server instance. For example, if your host is called DatabaseServer and the instance is called DatabaseInstances, the info is entered in as **\\DatabaseServer\DatabaseInstances**. Click **Next** after completing all the required fields.

Step 5. Leave the **Connect to SQL Server to obtain default settings for the additional configurations options** selected, and then choose the appropriate authentication method. If the SQL Server is on the local system, select **Windows NT authentication**. If the database is remote to the vCenter host, select **SQL Server authentication**. Then click **Next**. If the information is correct, you continue to the next screen. If not, a configuration problem is preventing access. The most common issue here is a mistyped password or mistyped host/database server name.

Step 6. Check the **Change the default database to** check box and choose the name of the database. If you do not see your database, this might be due to a caching issue. Simply click the **Back** button and then **Next** and attempt again.

Step 7. Click **Finish**.

Now that the database is ready, the next step is to install View Composer. One requirement that you need to meet is to select a supported operating system. Table 2-6 details which operating system platforms are supported as of this writing. (As always, check the latest release notes to see if there have been additions, updates, or changes.)

Table 2-6 VMware View Composer Supported 64-Bit Operating Systems

Operating System	vSphere Version Supported
Windows Server 2008 R2, Standard or Enterprise 64-bit	vSphere 4.1 U1 or later vSphere 4.0 U3 or later

Before doing the actual install, you want to ensure that a few things are configured correctly so that View Composer will run with minimal performance impact. First, ensure that Dynamic Name Service (DNS) is operating correctly for both forward and reverse lookups. To verify this, ping the Active Directory domain controllers and View Connection Servers by both IP address and fully qualified domain name (FQDN). If one or both do not respond, verify that the DNS A record is configured correctly. Second, ensure that the database service is running and that the ODBC connection has been configured with a user account with appropriate permissions. Finally, ensure that the following ports are open: TCP 902 from View Composer to the ESXi hosts, TCP 80/443 from the Connection Server to View Composer, and TCP 18443 (inbound and outbound) for the Composer service to talk to vCenter Server.

After these configuration steps are complete, you can install View Composer. Download View Composer from the VMware Downloads page. The file should be named something like VMware-viewcomposer-*xxxxxx*.exe, where the *xxxxxx* is the build number. This number is actually different from the build number for View itself. It is a good idea to make this available on a network share accessible from the vCenter Server or on the vCenter Server itself. Double-click the installer and do the following:

Step 1. Click **Next** twice (once to start and once for the Patent Agreement page).

Step 2. Choose **I accept the terms in the license agreement** and click **Next**.

Step 3. Choose a new install location for Composer (if you want something different than the default) and click **Next**.

Step 4. Enter the ODBC information, or create a System DSN at this point. Click **Next**. If the information is correct, you should be able to go forward; if not, a configuration problem is preventing access. The most common issue here is a mistyped password or mistyped host/database server name.

Step 5. Choose an alternative port for SOAP if you do not want to use the default, and choose whether you want to create default Secure Sockets Layer (SSL) certificates or use existing ones. If you have created certificates from a previous installation, you can use these when you reinstall.

Step 6. Click **Next** and then **Install**.

After Composer is installed, an account must be associated with the Composer environment. This is shown in Figure 2-2. The account will be used for QuickPrep when creating automated pools. The account must match up with all the domains in which desktops will be created. These domains must have a two-way trust in place. If Sysprep is used, the account information in the Customization Specification will be used.

Figure 2-2 Configure the Composer QuickPrep account.

QuickPrep is only designed to join the desktop to the domain and generate a unique computer name and UUID. The security ID, or SID, remains the same for all desktops within the automated pool.

Configuring the Standard and Replica Connection Servers

(This section covers Objective 2.3 of the Blueprint.)

Chapter 1 reviewed the installation procedures for Standard and Replica Connection Servers. This section reviews the procedure for configuring these servers. We begin by configuring global settings, as shown in Figure 2-3. These settings do not just relate to a specific connection server; they help define the entire View environment. The first setting to adjust is the **Session timeout** value. This is set to a default of 600 minutes (10 hours). This setting controls how long a session can remain open on the Connection Server. As long as there are open sessions, Connection Server resources cannot be released and new connections may be denied. The session timeout is a mechanism to keep idle sessions from remaining open indefinitely, thus tying up valuable Connection Server resources. This value may suffice in most cases, but some environments might require sessions to be never disconnected. Although there is no unlimited setting here, you can set this value as high as 10000000 minutes, or about 19+ years, to accommodate for this use case.

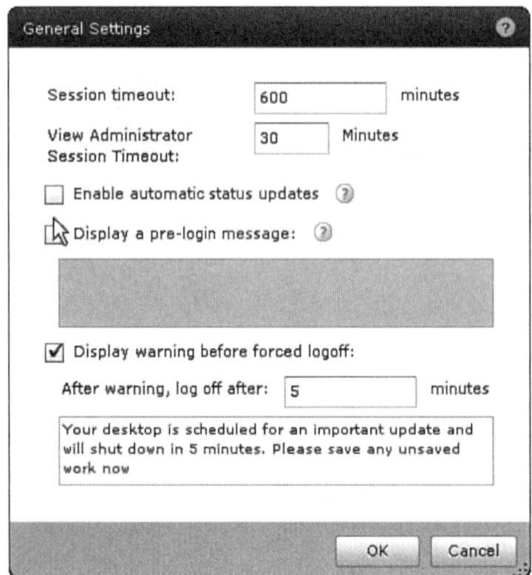

Figure 2-3 View global settings.

The next setting is **Require SSL for client connections and View Administrator**. This setting determines whether access will be granted via HTTP or HTTPS. As a best practice, it is best to use the default value of enabled. This ensures that all communication is done through a secure SSL tunnel. If you have replaced the self-signed certificates with properly signed certificates, this can help ensure that communication is done in a more secure manner and reduces the possibility of man-in-the-middle (MITM) attacks.

To help further mitigate the risk of a MITM attack, the setting for **Reauthenticate secure tunnel connections after network interruption** can be enabled. Although not enabled by default, enabling it can provide an extra security measure. When an unexpected disconnect occurs (that is, one that is not initiated by the user or administrator), end users are asked for their login credentials again to connect to their desktops.

Because we are looking at reducing MITM and other rogue communications between components, an additional global setting should be configured, the **Message security mode**. This setting determines whether View components verify the signed certificate. There are three options for this setting: Disabled, Mixed, and Enabled. By default, this is set to Disabled because the initial configuration of View uses self-signed certificates. If you used signed certificates, changing the setting to Enabled reduces the possibility of a rogue View component being introduced into the environment. However, components earlier than View 3.x do not support this setting. If your environment will contain a mix of product versions, configure this setting to Mixed. Setting Message Security Mode to Enabled with a mixed environment will prevent desktops from being launched in that environment.

Local mode is discussed in Chapter 8, "Local Mode." Local mode uses a special kind of virtual machine that can have a copy downloaded from an ESXi host to a local physical Windows laptop or desktop. If this is something you plan to use in a View deployment, consider how single sign-on (SSO) will be used (and should be configured) for local mode operations. If you check the box for **Disable Single Sign-On for Local Mode**, users are asked again for their credentials when they try to access a local mode virtual machine after providing them to the View Client with Local Mode. Although enabling SSO can be convenient to your users, as a best practice this feature can provide an extra layer of security in case a laptop gets stolen or left out in the open.

Security is very important to a View deployment, up to and including the View Administrator interface. When I teach View to students and do demos, the interface often times out. By default, if the interface remains idle for 5 minutes or more, the administrator is required to log in again. Although it's an effective security measure, this functionality is not ideal when doing demonstrations or when you constantly get calls and are distracted from configuring the environment throughout the day. This can be adjusted using the **Enable automatic status updates** setting, which ensures that the View Administrator interface remains logged in as long as the browser is open or until the administrator explicitly logs off. In a nutshell, this feature refreshes the screen every few minutes to avoid an idle timeout from occurring.

The risk from enabling this setting is that if an administrator walks away from his or her desktop without locking the desktop, someone could access the environment and potentially do damage (for example, delete pools). Data from the desktop pools themselves cannot be accessed from this interface, but if security and role separation is a requirement, this feature should not be enabled. In fact, if you do enable this setting, a warning appears highlighting the potential risk. So if you plan to use this feature, ensure that additional security precautions are in place.

NOTE As this book was being written, VMware released View 5.1.x. and 5.2.x. Version 5.1.x and later introduced an additional option associated with the Enable Automatic Status Updates. **View Administrator Session Timeouts** was added as a fixed timeout option for more security-minded environments. By default, this is set to 30 minutes. You can change this, though, with a maximum value of 720 hours (or a month).

Sometimes, however, even with all the security precautions we put in place we have to remind end users how we expect them to use the environment. This can be done by enabling the **Display a pre-login message** setting. This setting can be used to display a message containing any legalese that is required for your organization. One recommendation that I often make for students is to ensure that the message starts with "By clicking the OK button, you agree...." Quite often, users do not read messages like this, and by having this terminology at the start they cannot claim they did not know what they were allowed or not allowed to do with the desktops. This message will appear for any client accessing the environment before credentials are requested and cannot be configured on a per-desktop, per-pool, or per-Connection Server basis. If you need slightly different verbiage for other desktops beyond the global message, you should include it as part of the desktop image.

The last global setting to be configured is the message to display when a logoff must occur due to a scheduled event like a rebalance, recompose, or refresh. By default, the **Display warning before forced logoff** setting is enabled and set to 5 minutes. Both the message and the time can be changed. Keep in mind that this is a global setting and will be used for all desktops. It is important to set this to a value that is long enough to enable end users to save important data before finally being forced off. Any data not saved is lost, and that is *not* a good thing. Although you could conceivably set this value to 1 minute, it is unlikely that users would be able to save all their data in that time. At the same time, setting this value too high can result in users forgetting the logoff is going to happen. A value between 5 and 15 minutes should provide a sufficient amount of time.

Identifying and Modifying View Global Polices

(This section covers Objective 2.3 of the Blueprint.)

Whereas global settings define the View environment behavior for all Connection Servers, Global Policies define client sessions for all users. Global Policies can be used at a high level and can be modified and/or overridden by setting either pool policies or user-exception policies. To see which global policies are in place and to modify them, go to **Policies > Global Policies**. There are two sets of global policies that you can adjust: View Policies and Local Mode Policies (as discussed in Chapter 8). To edit the settings, click the **Edit Policies** button, as shown in Figure 2-4.

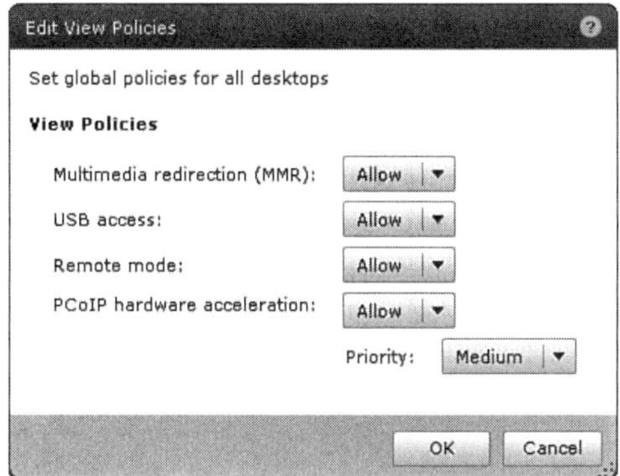

Figure 2-4 View global policies.

The first policy is **Multimedia redirection (MMR)**, which is set to **Allow** by default. This allows the work for video rendering to be performed by the client and allows for an improved video experience. This is helpful for remote desktop protocol (RDP) sessions because RDP does not have a mechanism to separate out multimedia traffic. PC-over-IP (PCoIP) has multimedia redirection (MMR) built in as part of the protocol. Although enabled by default, it is important to recognize that not all operating systems support MMR, particularly Windows 7. Windows XP and Windows Vista both support MMR. To take advantage of MMR redirection, you must have a supported operating system for both the desktop and the client or an MMR-enabled ThinClient. (To determine whether a client supports MMR, search using the compatibility guides found on the VMware website: www.vmware.com/resources/compatibility/search.php?deviceCategory=vdm.) Although Windows 7 does not support MMR, RDP 7 can be used with Windows 7 to enable MMR functionality (see VMware KB1026179: http://kb.vmware.com/kb/1026179).

USB access can be used to control whether users can connect a USB device through the client to the remote desktop, even if the USB virtual hub has been installed with the agent. Currently, VMware does not maintain a list of supported USB devices, but in general View supports USB flash drives and smart card devices. USB access is set to **Allow** by default.

Remote mode determines whether users can connect remotely to their desktops or if they must download them as a local mode desktop. Although set to **Allow** by default, this setting can be disabled if there are limited resources or if View is configured only for local mode.

The last policy is **PCoIP hardware acceleration** and is set to a default value of **Allow – Medium** priority. This setting is observed only if there is a hardware acceleration card on the ESXi host. This policy can be used with single VM-to-card support or with a Teradici offload card like the Teradici APEX 2800, which allows for many VMs-to-single card support. The choice to allow or deny this policy would depend on the environment and use case, and would be required if PCoIP hardware will be used. The policy has three different priority options: Low Priority, Medium Priority (default), or High Priority. The setting should be adjusted based on the level of graphics acceleration provided to desktop sessions. Because this setting is likely to be application specific, you can overwrite this global policy at the pool or user level.

Identifying and Modifying View Connection Server General Settings

(This section covers Objective 2.3 of the Blueprint.)

Global policies and global settings define the overall environment. There are also settings that are done on an individual Connection Server basis. This section reviews how to configure settings specific for end user connections to a specific Connection Server.

Step 1. Log in to the View Administrator page and navigate to **View Configuration > Servers**.

Step 2. Select the Connection Server you want to modify, and then click the **Edit** button. You should see a screen similar to the one shown in Figure 2-5. The restriction tags should be empty unless they have been previously configured.

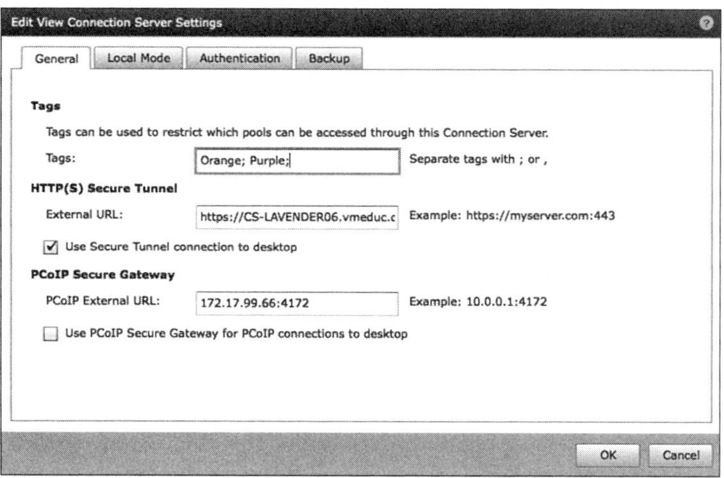

Figure 2-5 View Connection Server settings.

Step 3. Adjust settings that you need on a particular tab or multiple tabs.

Step 4. Click **OK** to save those settings.

Now that you know where to make changes, let's review each setting to determine what changes might be required. The first tab is the General tab. This tab deals with general settings specific to a particular Connection Server. One of the first settings you can configure is *restriction tags*. These tags, when applied, can help restrict which Connection Server an end user connects through. These tags can provide an additional security measure. The example shown in Figure 2-6 has two pools, Orange and Purple. An end user, Purple, is entitled to access the Purple pool. The Connection Servers for the View instances have each been given restriction tags, one tagged Orange and one tagged Purple. When the Purple end user connects to the Connection Server with the Purple tag, the user can access his desktop. However, if the same user tries to connect to his desktop using the Connection Server with the Orange tag, the user would be denied access.

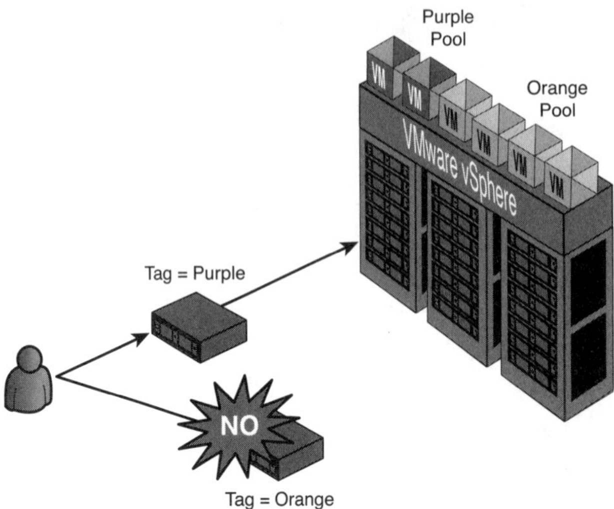

Figure 2-6 View Connection Server tags.

Restriction tags are often used to prevent users from accessing the environment from an external or less-secure source. A tag can be no more than 64 characters and should be limited to letters (no case sensitivity), numbers, and a limited set of special characters (hyphen and underscores). A tag must exist on at least one Connection Server in a View environment to be assigned to a pool. A tag that needs to be removed cannot be assigned to any pools. Table 2-7 explains the effect of tags on end user access.

Table 2-7 VMware View Tag-Restriction Matching

Connection Server	Pool	Able to Get Access?
No tags	No tags	Yes.
No tags	One or more tags	No. At least one server must have a valid tag.
One or more tags	No tags	Yes.
One or more tags	One or more tags	Only if the tags match.

When an end user connects into the environment, the View Client creates two connections. The first is a TCP connection that is used for authentication and to present desktops for selection. The second connection is the actual connection to the desktop. If that address is not resolvable, the end user will not be able to connect to the desktop. To set the values for the second connection, if different from the original installation (for example if the public Internet address differs from the internal address), put the external URL for RDP and the IP address for PCoIP in the appropriate boxes. For RDP, this is the HTTP(S) Secure Tunnel. This value is initially populated with the FQDN for the Connection Server, obtained during installation by the installer, and the port number for HTTPS (port 443). The use of HTTPS is to add additional encryption for RDP connections. By default, the **Use Secure Tunnel connection to desktop** check box is checked to ensure that the RDP session is SSL encrypted through the connection server to the desktop.

For PCoIP, the value is initially populated with the IP address of the Connection Server and the default port for PCoIP (port 4172). However, the PCoIP secure gateway is not enabled by default. This must be explicitly enabled by checking the box for **Use PCoIP Secure Gateway for PCoIP connections to desktops**. This option is available only on Connection Servers that are installed with Windows 2008.

Identifying View Connection Server Backup Settings

(This section covers Objective 2.3 of the Blueprint.)

As part of any best practice, there should always be backups of important data. For the View environment, backups should be made for vCenter Server, the ESXi host configuration, the end user's data, the Active Directory Application Mode/Active Directory (ADAM/AD) Lightweight Directory Services (LDS) (which contains the Connection Server info), and, if installed, the Composer database. For the vSphere components, you must use a separate backup mechanism. For vCenter Server, you use the standard mechanism for backing up the database in question (Oracle, Microsoft SQL, or IBM DB2). For ESXi hosts, you can use `vicfg-cfgbackup` or a third-party backup mechanism. The end-user data backup would be performed with either vSphere Data Protection or a third-party tool. This section focuses on backing up Connection Servers themselves, which in turn backs up not only the ADAM/AD LDS but also the Composer database, if used.

For the Connection Servers, you can adjust backup settings on a per-server basis. Although you cannot change the location of backups or change the time of day of a backup, you can change how often and how many backups are performed. The backup takes a copy of the ADAM/AD LDS schema and the contents of the schema and stores it in a predefined location. Because the location of the backup is static, you might want to add a layer of protection by backing up the contents stored in this location to tape or some other media to ensure a method of recovery.

NOTE Although the GUI does not allow for the location of the backup to be changed, it is possible to do so. KB1010285 details how to do this, but VMware strongly advises against doing so.

To perform a manual backup, follow these steps:

Step 1. Log in to the View Administrator page and navigate to **View Configuration > Servers**.

Step 2. Select the Connection Server you want to back up and select **Backup Now**.

Step 3. (Optional) If you want to adjust the backup settings, select the Connection Server and then click the **Edit** button.

Step 4. Choose the **Backup** tab and adjust the frequency and maximum number of backups, as shown in Figure 2-7.

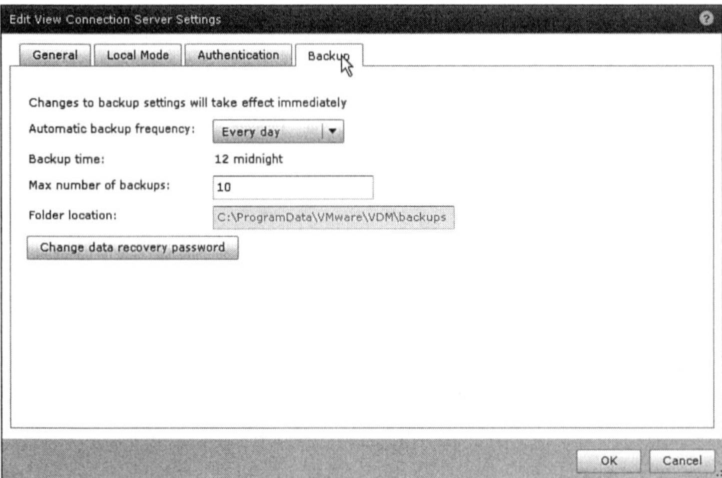

Figure 2-7 View Connection Server Backup tab.

Step 5. (Optional) Change the backup recovery password.

Step 6. Click **OK**.

The backup will include the Composer database if Composer is associated with this Connection Server. The Composer backup is not vendor specific but rather a generic SQL backup. This allows for restoring into either database option (Microsoft or Oracle) if need be. When performing a restore, it is critical to note that if either the ADAM/AD LDS backup fails or gets corrupted, or if the Composer backup fails, you should not restore from that backup. As a rule of thumb, you should restore both ADAM/AD LDS and Composer from the same time period. However, even when restoring both you might need to do a manual adjustment for newly created or deleted virtual machines (whether linked clone or fully provisioned).

When doing backups, however, things can always go wrong. If an error appears during a backup, as one did in Figure 2-8, click the ellipses to help determine where the issue is.

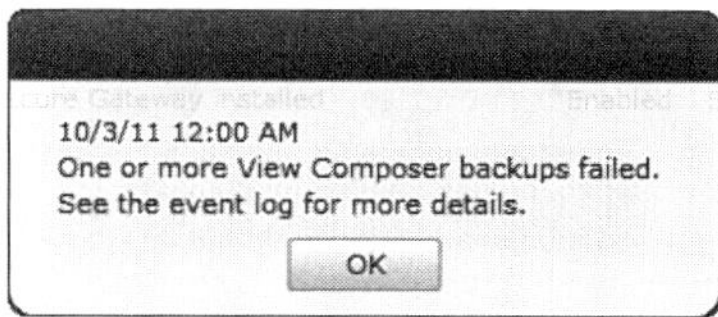
10/3/11 12:00 AM
One or more View Composer backups failed.
See the event log for more details.
OK

Figure 2-8 View backup error.

In this example, it appears that the Composer service was not running when the backup ran. In this scenario, the fix is relatively simple: Determine why the Composer service did not start, correct the issue, and then restart the service.

Identifying Default Roles, Custom Roles, and What Permissions Are Available

Key
Topic

(This section covers Objective 2.3 of the Blueprint.)

One of the nicer features of View is that a turnkey installation can be performed. A consultant or architect can initially configure and set up the environment and then hand it off to a day-to-day administrator while Tier 2 support looks after pool creation and Tier 1 support deals with simple support questions. Many support questions center around access. This section deals with roles and permissions and defining access to View resources. If you have worked with vCenter Server permissions, the implementation of View permissions should look familiar.

A number of privileges exist in View. Each privilege allows an action to be performed. These privileges are grouped into roles according to what actions need to be performed by that role. The role is then assigned to one or more users on one or more View objects. This comprises a user's permission set. There are some predefined roles, as defined in Table 2-8. If a predefined role does not quite fit what you need, you can create custom roles based on the privileges found in Tables 2-9 and 2-10. Read-only roles are good roles to give to auditors who need to evaluate an environment without accidentally modifying something that could be detrimental to production.

Table 2-8 VMware View Predefined Roles

Role	Privileges	Can Be Applied to a View Folder?
Administrator	Has all privileges. If a View administrator needs to do any of the following, they *must* use the predefined Administrator role: ■ Add/delete folders ■ Manage ThinApp through View ■ View and modify Transfer Servers and the repository ■ Use the `vdmadmin` and `vdmimport` commands	Yes
Administrator (Read only)	Has full access to everything but cannot modify any settings. If this is applied against a specific folder, then the administrator can only see objects in that folder.	Yes
Agent Registration Administrators	Can register unmanaged desktops, such as physical systems, virtual machines not managed by vCenter Server, or terminal servers.	No
Global Configuration and Policy Administrators	This role is specifically for modifying global policies and configuration settings for servers except for administrator roles and permissions, anything related to ThinApp applications and settings, and the Transfer Servers and their repository.	No
Global Configuration and Policy Administrators (Read only)	Much like the Administrators (Read only) role, this role does the same as its predecessor but cannot modify anything.	No
Inventory Administrators	Manages the pools, desktops, sessions, persistent disks, and Composer operations against a linked-clone pool. When applied against a specific folder, Inventory Administrators can only make changes against any pools found within those folders	Yes

For many environments, the predefined roles will suffice. Because the Administrator role allows for all tasks to be carried out, it is often used in new deployments by multiple administrators. This is not a good practice. Even if an individual is the View administrator, this role should not be the day-to-day role used for administration. This role should be assigned to a user or group and used only when troubleshooting or when needing to perform specific steps, such as creating folders.

Day-to-day activities should be performed using either the Inventory Administrator or the Global Configuration and Policies Administrator roles, depending on need. Starting with View 5.1, during the installation the Administrator role can be either assigned to the Local Administrators group (which also includes the Domain Administrators) or to a specific group or user. This can prevent, for larger environments, domain administrators from being able to modify or adjust View settings.

As previously mentioned, roles are made up of privileges. These privileges are broken down into three groups: global privileges, as shown in Table, 2-9, object-specific privileges, and internal privileges.

Table 2-9 VMware View Global Privileges

Privilege	Actions	Predefined Roles
Console Interaction	Ability to log in to and use the View Administrator web interface.	Administrators Administrators (Read only) Inventory Administrators Inventory Administrators (Read only) Global Configuration and Policy Administrators Global Configuration and Policy Administrators (Read only)
Direct Interaction	Allows user to run all PowerShell commands except for `vdmadmin` and `vdmimport`. To run those commands, the full Administrator role is required.	Administrators Administrators (Read only)
Manage Global Configuration and Policies	Allows a user to be able to view and modify all global policies and configurations except for Administrator roles and permissions.	Administrators Global Configuration and Policy Administrators
Manage Roles and Permissions	Allows a user to create, delete, and modify Administrator roles and permissions.	Administrators
Register Agent	Allows a user to install the View Agent and register a system with View. This is required for non-vCenter Server managed virtual machines, terminal servers, and physical desktops	Administrators Agent Registration Administrators

Global privileges are used to adjust the View environment (the Connection Server, Transfer Server, or security server settings). These are never applied against folders because those are specific objects within the View environment. For the inventory or for specific objects like desktops, pools, and so on, we use object-specific privileges, as detailed in Table 2-10. All of these privileges are found in the Administrators and Inventory Administrators predefined roles.

Table 2-10 VMware View Object Specific Privileges

Privilege	Actions	Object
Enable Pool	Allows the ability to enable or disable a desktop pool.	Desktop pool
Entitle Pool	Allows the ability to assign a user/group to a desktop pool.	Desktop pool
Manage Composer Pool Image	Allows the ability to apply the three *R*'s (refresh, rebalance, and recompose) to a linked-clone pool. Also can change the default pool parent image.	Desktop pool
Manage Desktop	Allows the ability to perform desktop and session activities (for example, reboot a desktop, log out a user).	Desktop
Manage Local Sessions	Allows the ability to roll back a local mode desktop as well as initiate replication between the local desktop and the one that resides on the ESXi host.	Desktop
Manage Persistent Disk	Allows the ability to do all persistent disk operations such as attaching a persistent disk to a desktop, detaching a disk, or importing a disk.	Persistent disk
Manage Pool	Allows the ability to create, modify, and delete desktop pools as well as add or remove desktops from the pool.	Desktop pool
Manage Remote Sessions	Allows the ability to disconnect and log off users from their remote sessions. Can also send messages to desktop users through the View Administrator interface.	Desktop
Manage Reboot Operation	Allows the ability to reboot a View desktop.	Desktop

The last privilege in Table 2-10 is often used for a custom role. This is often used for Tier 1 support roles (that initial level of support that gets calls from end users) to help users with their desktops. When a simple reboot of a Windows desktop fails to resolve these issues, create a custom role following these steps:

Step 1. Log in to the View Administrator page and navigate to **View Configuration > Administrators**.

Step 2. You have three tabs to choose from. Choose the **Administrators and Groups** tab.

Step 3. Click the **Add User or Group** button.

Step 4. In the Add Administrator or Permissions window, click the **Add** button.

Step 5. In the Find User or Group window, leave both Users and Groups checked, or uncheck the one you are not looking for.

Step 6. Select the domain or leave it set to **Entire Directory**. Keep in mind this could be quite large in a forest with multiple domain trusts.

Step 7. For the Name/User name option, select either **Contains**, **Starts with**, or **Is Exactly** and in the box put at least one character.

Step 8. For Description, if necessary, select either **Contains**, **Starts with**, or **Is Exactly** and in the box put at least one character.

Step 9. Click the **Find** button. From the results click each name of the user/group you want.

After creating the role, you can assign it to users or groups, and then add the users or groups to the folders as needed. The following steps detail how to add a user or multiple users and/or a group or multiple groups to a role:

Step 1. Log in to the View Administrator page and navigate to **View Configuration > Administrators**.

Step 2. You have three tabs to choose from. Choose the **Administrators and Groups** tab.

Step 3. Click the **Add User or Group** button.

Step 4. In the Add Administrator or Permissions window, click the **Add** button.

Step 5. In the Find User or Group window, leave both **Users** and **Groups** checked or uncheck the one you are not looking for.

Step 6. Select the domain or leave it set to **Entire Directory**. Keep in mind this could be quite large in a forest with multiple domain trusts.

Step 7. For the Name/User name option, select either **Contains**, **Starts with**, or **Is Exactly** and in the box put at least one character.

Step 8. For Description, if necessary, select either **Contains**, **Starts with**, or **Is Exactly** and in the box put at least one character.

Step 9. Click the **Find** button. From the results, click each name of user/group you want and click the **OK** button.

Step 10. After you have all the users/groups you want, click the **Next** button.

Step 11. In the Select a Role window, select the role you want to apply. Only one role can be chosen. Click the **Next** button.

Step 12. If the role has object-specific permissions, you are asked to select a folder if more than the root folder exists. Select the folders you want to apply the role against and click the **Finish** button

A View environment can have up to 100 folders, including the default root folder, which appears as Root (/) in View Administrator. You cannot delete or modify the root folder, and folders cannot be nested into other folders. You can create folders in two ways. The first is in the Global Administrators view, as follows:

Step 1. Log in to the View Administrator page and navigate to **View Configuration > Administrators**.

Step 2. You have three tabs to choose from. Choose the **Folders** tab.

Step 3. Click the **Add Folder** button.

Step 4. In the Add Folder window, enter a name for the folder and a description if necessary. Folder names cannot be the same as role names.

Step 5. Click the **OK** button.

Alternatively, you can create folders in the Pools section under Inventory. Click the **Folder** drop-down in the Pools section and choose **New Folder**. Then enter a name and a description, if needed.

Summary

This chapter dealt with configuring the View infrastructure components discussed in Chapter 1, as well as the steps needed to configure the View Events database. You reviewed the steps to install and configure View Composer and reviewed roles, permissions, and permission assignments.

As Chinese philosopher Lao-tzu said, “A journey of a thousand miles begins with a single step.” This chapter completes the first step in building the overall virtual desktop infrastructure.

In the next chapter, you learn how to establish printing capabilities in a View environment, even for the user who has that old printer that does not have any modern drivers for Windows 7.

Exam Preparation Tasks

Review All Key Topics

Review the most important topics in the chapter, noted with the Key Topic icon in the outer margin of the page. Table 2-11 lists a reference of these key topics and the page numbers on which each is found.

Table 2-11 Key Topics

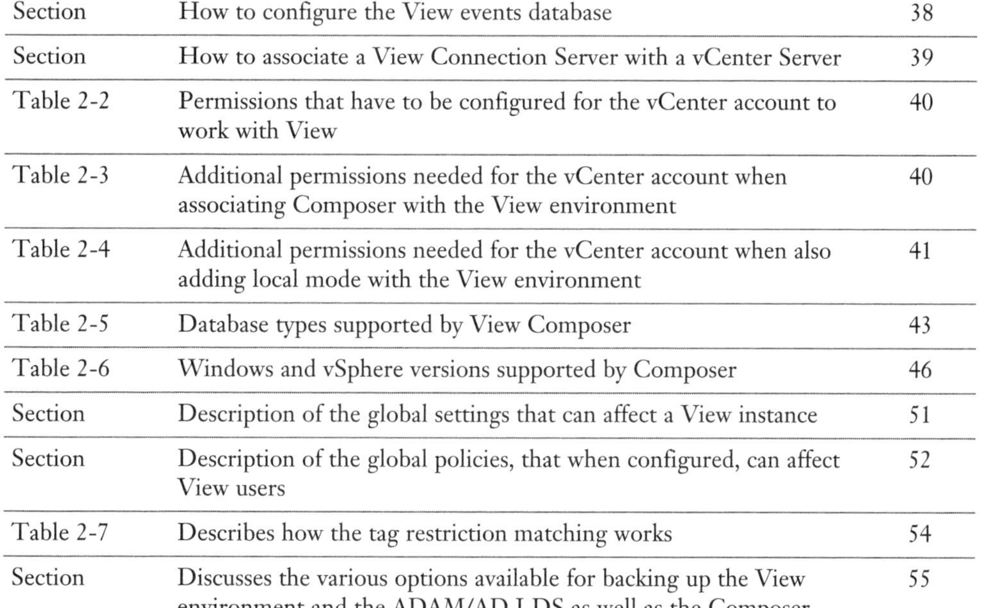

Key Topic Element	Description	Page
Section	How to configure the View events database	38
Section	How to associate a View Connection Server with a vCenter Server	39
Table 2-2	Permissions that have to be configured for the vCenter account to work with View	40
Table 2-3	Additional permissions needed for the vCenter account when associating Composer with the View environment	40
Table 2-4	Additional permissions needed for the vCenter account when also adding local mode with the View environment	41
Table 2-5	Database types supported by View Composer	43
Table 2-6	Windows and vSphere versions supported by Composer	46
Section	Description of the global settings that can affect a View instance	51
Section	Description of the global policies, that when configured, can affect View users	52
Table 2-7	Describes how the tag restriction matching works	54
Section	Discusses the various options available for backing up the View environment and the ADAM/AD LDS as well as the Composer database	55
Section	Discusses the default roles, how to create custom roles, and what each of the permissions are that are available to administrators to configure	57
Table 2-8	List of default predefined roles in View	58

Key Topic Element	Description	Page
Table 2-9	List of View global privileges that can be used for custom settings	59
Table 2-10	List of View object-specific privileges that can be used for custom settings	60

Define Key Terms

Define the following key terms from this chapter and check your answers in the Glossary:

View events, View Composer, View global policies, View global settings, Connection Server restriction tags, ADAM/AD LDS, automatic pools, manual pools, persistent disk

Review Questions

You can find the answers to these review questions in Appendix A.

1. Which of the following is not a vCenter Server permission needed for a View administrator?
   - a. Virtual Machine > Inventory > Create New
   - b. Virtual Machine > Interaction > Reset
   - c. Virtual Machine > Inventory > Power Settings
   - d. Virtual Machine > Interaction > Power Off

2. What additional vCenter Server permission is needed for a View administrator when using local mode?
   - a. Global > Set custom attribute
   - b. Global > Set local desktop
   - c. Global > Create new
   - d. Global > Add or delete virtual machine

3. Which of the following is not a supported database for View Composer 5.x?
   - a. Microsoft SQL 2008 Express
   - b. Microsoft SQL 2008 SP1
   - c. Oracle 9g Release 2
   - d. Oracle 10g Release 2

4. What is the message security mode used for?
   a. To ensure messages sent to desktops are secure
   b. To ensure that communications between View components are verified as authentic
   c. To ensure that messages sent from desktops are secure
   d. To ensure that communications between View components are encrypted

5. MMR is not supported by which of the following?
   a. RDP
   b. Windows 7
   c. PCoIP
   d. Windows XP

6. A user is about to access his desktop. The desktop is part of a pool that has the tag External, and the Connection Server has no tags. Will the user be able to access the desktop?
   a. Yes, because a Connection Server with no tags acts as a wildcard, allowing access to all pools.
   b. No, because a Connection Server with no tags automatically denies access to all pools.
   c. Yes, because the pool has been configured with the External tag.
   d. No, because the Connection Server has not been configured with the External tag.

7. The View Connection Server backup feature backs up which components?
   a. The event database
   b. The Active Directory Lightweight Directory Service
   c. The vCenter Server database
   d. The Composer database

8. An administrator using a custom role cannot log in. What privilege is likely missing?
   a. View Direct Interactions
   b. Direct Interaction
   c. Console Interaction
   d. View Console Interaction

9. Which of the following roles cannot be applied to a View folder?
   a. Administrators
   b. Global Configuration and Policy Administrators
   c. Inventory Administrators
   d. Administrators (Read only)
10. Besides the Root(/) folder, how many folders in the View interface can be created?
   a. 100
   b. 99
   c. 1,024
   d. 2,048

This chapter covers the following subjects:

- ThinPrint
- Location-Based Printing

(This chapter covers Objective 2.9 of the Blueprint.)

CHAPTER 3

Printing in the View Environment

One of the bigger challenges for remote desktops, whether physical or virtual, is printing. Printing to a printer on the same network as a physical desktop is a trivial task. Even when printing from a virtual desktop, the task is fairly simple if the virtual desktop and the printer are both on the same corporate network infrastructure. However, when an end user is accessing a virtual desktop, and both the user and the printer are in a remote location (say, a student or a telecommuter employee), things become a bit more challenging. Print jobs are the proverbial "hot potato" of remote virtual desktops because of the processing power often required to produce them. Furthermore, when the virtual desktop is a stateless desktop, with different users accessing the same desktop at different times, user rights can become an issue. This is because installing print drivers typically requires having local administrator rights. In this section, we cover the various printing options for virtual desktops, including the ThinPrint driver, location-based printing, and various Group Policy Object (GPO) settings.

Before getting into the print options, let's start by looking at how Windows handles document processing. First, a user creates a document of some kind and chooses **Print** from the application that created it. The application then sends the print job to the Microsoft Windows graphics device interface (GDI). Next, the GDI takes the print job and turns it into an Enhanced MetaFile (EMF). EMF is the spool format used by Windows when preparing a print job, particularly when dealing with multiple print jobs. Think of EMF as a universal language format. After the EMF is generated, the application sits back while the Windows print spooler takes over. The print spooler takes the EMF and translates it into a format that the printer can understand (for example, Adobe PostScript or PCL 6). The resulting file is now a printer spool file (extension .spl), which is then sent to the printer through the printer port (either a Line Print Terminal [LPT] port or a TCP/IP print port). Simple enough, right? Even if it were that simple, the abundance of printers and drivers in the marketplace increases the difficulty exponentially. When you consider the increasing complexity of user applications and the increasing size of resulting print jobs, it is easy to see that the simple print job has evolved into something new and challenging.

In environments where print jobs can spool for a significant period of time, having a print server to manage those jobs can be extremely beneficial. The sooner the print job is off to the printer, the better the overall performance to the desktop. In environments where users are sending print jobs to local printers, sufficient bandwidth must exist to support both the desktop and the print job. A number of optimizations can be performed, but in the end if the amount of bandwidth is not sufficient, user performance will suffer. In extreme cases, this bandwidth issue can even cause the network itself to be impacted.

"Do I Know This Already?" Quiz

The "Do I Know This Already?" quiz allows you to assess whether you should read this entire chapter or simply jump to the "Exam Preparation Tasks" section for review. If you are in doubt, read the entire chapter. Table 3-1 outlines the major headings in this chapter and the corresponding "Do I Know This Already?" quiz questions. You can find the answers in Appendix A, "Answers to the 'Do I Know This Already?' Quizzes and Review Questions."

Table 3-1 Headings and Questions

Foundation Topics Section	Questions Covered in This Section
ThinPrint	1–5
Location-Based Printing	6–7

1. Windows first sends the print job to which interface?
   a. EMF
   b. GDI
   c. PCL
   d. AIO

2. If the View Client for local mode is used, what port is used to send the print job using ThinPrint?
   a. USB port
   b. TCP/IP port
   c. UDP/IP port
   d. COM port

3. The .print service appears to be unresponsive. What service must be restarted to return the .print service to operational readiness?
   a. TP Print Service
   b. TP AutoConnect Service
   c. TP PrintConnect Service
   d. TP VC Gateway Service

4. Instead of turning the print job into an EMF, what format does .print turn the job into?
   a. RAW
   b. RDP
   c. PCL
   d. COM

5. What is the next step to troubleshooting a ThinPrint issue after stopping the connection service?
   a. Reinstall the View Agent and tools
   b. Restart `TPAutoConnect -d`
   c. Remove VMware Tools and the View Agent
   d. Restart `TPPrintConnect -d`

6. Which DLL should you use for location-based printing?
   a. Location.dll
   b. TPlocalmap.dll
   c. TPVMGPoACmap.dll
   d. Print.dll

7. Which of the following is not a value that can be filled in for location-based printing?
   a. IP range
   b. Client name
   c. Computer name
   d. MAC address

Foundation Topics

ThinPrint

When remote access to a desktop was in its earliest days, the only way you could use the printer at your desktop was with printer redirection. This required installing printer drivers on the remote desktop for it to be able to print. Although this can be acceptable in some environments, many desktop administrators do not want users to have the ability to install anything. In addition, some users still have old printers that do not have drivers for Windows 7 but are determined to use them until they completely fall apart. As I often joke in class, it is the user who still has a dot-matrix printer and a garage full of perforated paper who wants and needs to print locally. And drivers for older printers don't typically work on more modern operating systems like Windows 7.

Printer redirection is possible by enabling this capability on Remote Desktop Protocol (RDP), which then enables the remote system to redirect its print job to a client's locally connected default printer. However, to utilize this capability, the necessary printer drivers must be installed on the remote desktop, and to do so a user must have local administrator rights. Both of these concerns are the main reasons why printer redirection is avoided, because it requires lots of desktop micromanagement, providing excessive rights to users, or both.

However, if the environment is meant to support telecommuters, having centralized printing might not suffice. Providing a better mechanism for localized printing is critical. So to make this possible, VMware has partnered with Cortado (formerly ThinPrint) and included a universal print driver in both the View Client and the View Agent. This driver, known as the ThinPrint.print universal print driver, is located on the client. It detects the printers it can see and presents those to the remote desktop. When a print job is created, the ThinPrint server turns the print job into a universal language and encrypts it for transport. An end user can then print to a nearby printer rather than to a network printer attached to the remote desktop.

For me, this proved handy when I was in New York City and wanted to print material from my View desktop (located in our California datacenter) to the classroom in which I was located. I was able to print the material I needed without installing any drivers for the printer in the classroom other than those that were already on my local desktop. In this case, the physical desktop in the classroom was a Windows XP desktop with a Samsung printer driver installed. I installed the View Client and connected to my View Windows 7 desktop. When I went into the Printer and Fax section, I could see the local Samsung printer even though I did not install a driver for it into my View desktop. When I logged out and later logged in again, I got a new desktop from the floating pool, and the Samsung printer still appeared.

How a print job goes from one end to another depends on how you are connecting into the environment itself. If a print job is going over a network, either PC-over-IP (PCoIP) or RDP channels are used to transport the job. If local mode is used, a COM port or a named pipe is used. Either way, the print job is sent from the virtual desktop to the client in the form of a compressed, encrypted universal formatted file. Upon receipt at the client, it is decompressed, decrypted, and sent to the print driver on the client system to be translated into the language of the printer (usually something like Adobe PostScript or Printer Control Language [PCL]). Figure 3-1 depicts this process.

When installing the View Client, the default setting always installs the virtual printing driver. If you deselect the USB redirection option when installing, the virtual print components are not installed.

This feature works for both remote desktops and for local mode desktops. It alleviates the need to install drivers and leverages any printers found on the client system, whether they are local or network-attached. This eases supportability.

To enable this support, first install the View Agent with virtual printing into the virtual desktop, and then install the View Client. That's it. The necessary drivers for ThinPrint are included, and you need do nothing more but have end users connect, wait about 30 to 60 seconds for the printer to appear, and then print. The agent installs a couple of services, one that is used for printing and to create the .print objects (the TP AutoConnect Service), and one that communicates with any .print servers, if they exist in the environment, over RDP/ICA connections (the TP VC Gateway Service). If you stop the TP AutoConnect Service, you cannot print using the virtual printing piece. Furthermore, this service checks every 30 seconds to see whether there are any new printers to add to the virtual desktop environment. For these two reasons, it is critical to ensure that this service is continually running.

Now, let's compare the process for typical Windows printing to the process using the ThinPrint .print driver. A user still creates a document and prints it. The application still sends the print job to the Microsoft Windows graphics device interface (GDI), but the print job is now turned into a simple RAW format. The file is encrypted and compressed then sent to the printer through the ThinPrint .print port, which in the View environment is either a COM port or a named pipe (for local mode desktops), or via PCoIP or RDP, to the client. The client then hands it off to the local printer much like was done before: It turns it from the RAW format to the language of the printer (PostScript or PCL) and hands it off to the proper port (either an LPT port or a TCP/IP print port) to send to the physical printer.

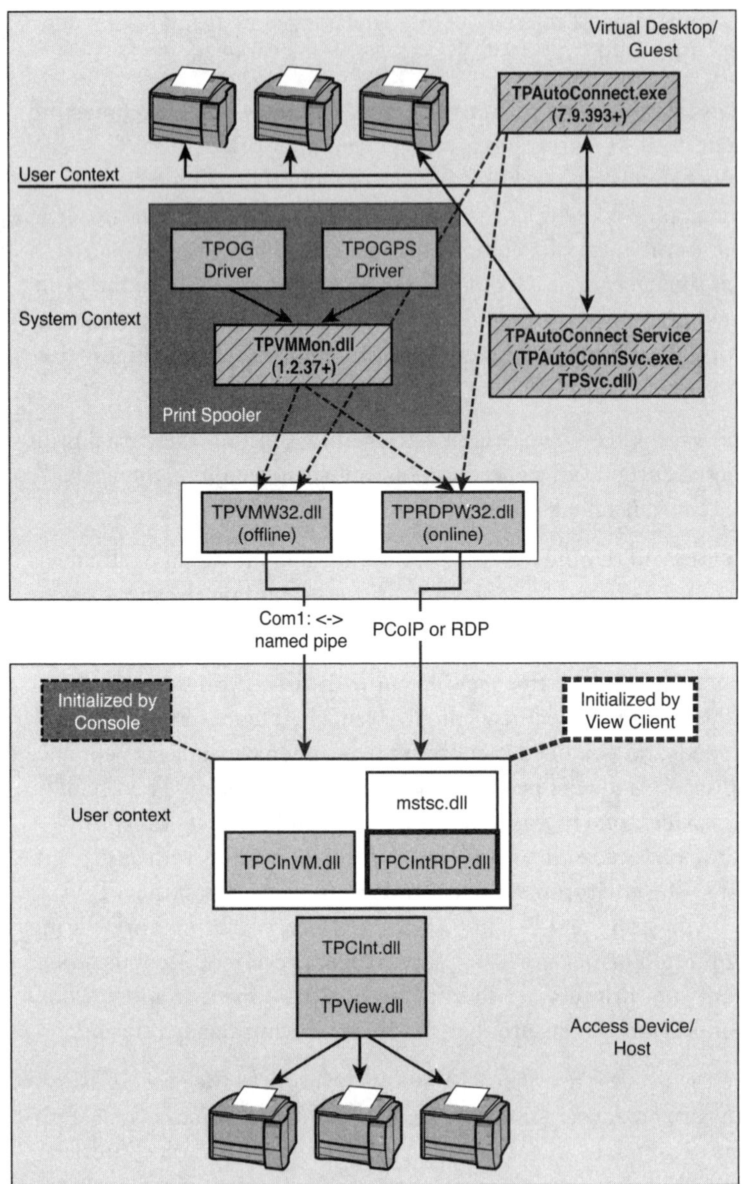

Figure 3-1 ThinPrint driver.

An advantage to this process is that users do not have to install any drivers, so users do not need local administrator rights. This enables View administrators to have better control over the environment.

Although printing through the use of Cortado should work as is without issue, life in IT is never complete without a visit from Murphy's Law. And printers seem to be one particular area of specialty for Murphy. When an issue arises, the following methodology can be used to attempt to resolve ThinPrint issues:

1. Remove all printers. To remove printers, click **Start > Run >** and enter the following command: **C:\Program Files\VMware\VMware Tools\TPAutoConnect –d**.
2. Stop the ThinPrint connection service by running the following command from the command line:

   ```
   net stop TPAutoConnSvc
   ```
3. Go to **Control Panel > Add or Remove Programs** and remove VMware Tools and the View Agent.
4. Install VMware Tools.
5. Install the View Agent.
6. The print driver will attempt to rescan all printers found. This might take a while, so be patient.

Location-Based Printing

So, ThinPrint addresses use cases for telecommuters and remote users, but we still face the challenge of finding an answer for location-based use cases. Imagine a hospital where a doctor starts her day in the E.R., printing patient reports at the nurses' station there. By mid-afternoon, the doctor must do rounds up in I.C.U., all the way on the 10th floor of the hospital. If the doctor is using a tablet device (for example, an iPad or an Android tablet) and the hospital wireless network, the desktop can be configured to pick up the IP address where the doctor is and print to the closest available printer.

For example, suppose the E.R. uses a subnet range of 192.168.14.xx, while the I.C.U. uses a subnet range of 192.168.56.xx. Under normal circumstances to print, a list of every printer on every floor would be required, even when using the same driver would otherwise be possible. So for 10 floors the desktop would need to have at least 10 different instances of the printer on the desktop.

With View, however, we can enable location-based printing, and the Group Policy Object changes the settings for the print driver based on the options configured for the GPO. This enables a single print driver to accommodate the change in location and associated printer configuration changes. In environments like the one portrayed in this example, where a user is in a single location but may be mobile within that location, this can prove handy. To enable this functionality, you must import the location-based printing dynamic link library (DLL) into either Active Directory in the appropriate organizational unit (OU), or into the desktop itself to make it part of the base image.

The steps are basically the same regardless of which option you choose. The one difference, however, is where the changes are made. For Active Directory, changes are made on an Active Directory controller. This means that each user who will use this feature must have the GPO applied to him or her. To limit the number of GPOs loaded at login, you can load DLL on the desktop itself instead of loading it as part of the end user's profile.

If the goal is to have location-based printing follow the user across devices, it is better to load the DLL into the Active Directory OU to which that user's group belongs. In this case, the DLL is loaded onto the AD controller. You can find the DLL at the following location on the View Connection Server: <install drive>:\Program Files\VMware\VMware View\Server\extras\GroupPolicyFiles\ThinPrint\x64\TPVMGPoACmap.dll. (You can find the 32-bit version of the file in the ia32 directory.) After locating the file, you can then load it onto the desktop as follows:

Step 1. Log in to the desktop with local administrator rights.

Step 2. Ensure that all printer drivers are installed on the master image or template.

Step 3. Go to **Start > Run** and type **regsvr2 <drive letter/path>/TPVMGPoACmap.dll**. Choose the **x64** folder if the desktop is a 64-bit OS, or choose the **ia32** folder for a 32-bit OS.

Step 4. Once installed, again go to **Start > Run** and type **mmc**.

Step 5. Once the console launches, choose **File > Add/Remove Snap-in**.

Step 6. Click the **Add** button.

Step 7. From the Add Standalone Snap-in list, select **Group Policy Object Editor** and click **Add**.

Step 8. Leave the default GPO set to **Local Computer** and click **Finish**.

Step 9. Click **Close** and **OK**.

Step 10. Click the plus (+) beside Local Computer Policy to open it. Then open the **Computer Configuration Software Settings** and select **AutoConnect Map Additional Printers for VMware View**.

Step 11. In the right column, select **Configure AutoConnect Map Additional Printers** to open the tab.

Step 12. On the top right of the table, select **Enable**.

Step 13. Either click the first button on the top left of the table (see Figure 3-2) or press **Ctrl+A** to add an empty row.

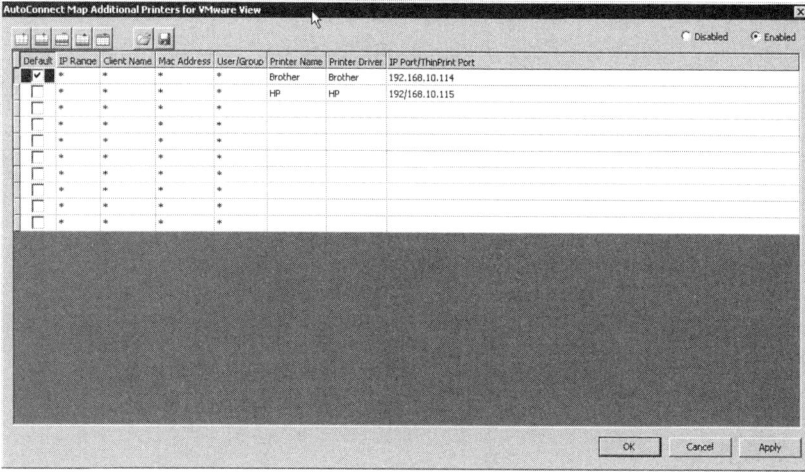

Figure 3-2 Location-based printing table.

You now can choose how you want printers to be presented to the end user. Using the asterisk (*) option will enable any printer. Use the check box under Default to identify whether a printer will be the default. Other values that can be configured include the following:

- **IP Range:** IP range or subnet address that an end user could be identified with (for example, 192.168.42.1-192.168.42.3 or 192.168.42.0/24)
- **Client Name:** Computer name of the client connecting to the desktop (for example, Linus Laptop)
- **Mac Address:** MAC address of the client (for example, 01-02-03-04-05-06 for Windows clients or 01:02:03:04:05:06 for Linux clients; note the difference in formatting depending on client type)
- **User/Group:** The username or a group name (for example, lbourque or Instructors)

- **Printer Name:** The printer's network name (for example, CTRL-HP-COLOR-FLR6)
- **Printer Driver:** Name of the print driver (for example, HP Color LaserJet 5700 PS)
- **IP Port/ThinPrint Port:** IP address (for example, IP_192.168.14.104)

Summary

This chapter discussed the challenges involved with printing in a View environment and the various ways to meet those challenges. The concept of printer redirection was discussed, and configuration options were detailed. These included the use of ThinPrint and the configuration of location-based printing. These print configuration choices can make printing a simple process for almost any remote printing use case.

In the next chapter, you learn what protocols can be used with virtual desktops and the benefits each protocol option can provide.

Exam Preparation Tasks

Review All Key Topics

Review the most important topics in the chapter, noted with the Key Topic icon in the outer margin of the page. Table 3-2 lists a reference of these key topics and the page numbers on which each is found.

Table 3-2 Key Topics

Key Topic Element	Description	Page
Paragraph	Discussion about how the .print process works in View	73
Paragraph	How to install the printer driver	73
Step list	How to troubleshoot printer issues	75
Paragraph	How to install location-based printing	76
List	Discussion about options to use for location-based printing	77

Define Key Terms

Define the following key terms from this chapter and check your answers in the Glossary:

ThinPrint, .print, location-based printing, EMF, GDI

Review Questions

You can find the answers to these review questions in Appendix A.

1. EMF represents what in the print process?
   a. The spool format
   b. The application
   c. The printer port
   d. The graphics interface

2. If the View Client is used, what type of port is used to send the print job using ThinPrint?
   a. USB port
   b. TCP/IP port
   c. UDP/IP port
   d. COM port

3. How often does the TP AutoConnect Service check for new printers?
   a. Every 10 seconds
   b. Every 30 seconds
   c. Every 60 seconds
   d. Every 90 seconds

4. The View Agent is responsible for what two activities when processing a print job?
   a. Compressing the print job
   b. Decompressing the print job
   c. Encrypting the print job
   d. De-encrypting the print job

5. What command enables you to delete all the printers on a remote desktop when troubleshooting printer detection?

   a. `TPPrint -d`

   b. `TPAutoConnect -d`

   c. `TPVCGateway -d`

   d. `TPPrintConnect -d`

6. What is the path to find the DLL that should be used for location-based printing?

   a. c:\Program Files\VMware\VMware View\Server\extras\GroupPolicyFiles\ThinPrint\x64\

   b. c:\Program Files\VMware\VMware View\Server\extras\GroupFiles\ThinPrint\x64\

   c. c:\Program Files\VMware\VMware View\extras\GroupPolicyFiles\ThinPrint\x64\

   d. c:\Program Files\VMware\VMware VDM\Server\extras\GroupPolicyFiles\ThinPrint\x64\

7. Which of the following is a value that can be configured for location-based printing?

   a. Connection Server name

   b. Virtual desktop name

   c. Client computer name

   d. Printer vendor

This chapter covers the following subjects:

- RDP: The Historical Protocol
- PCoIP: The Modern Protocol

(This chapter covers Objective 2.6 of the Blueprint.)

CHAPTER 4

The Protocols

Although the exam does not explicitly cover the protocols in a single given objective or section, knowledge of both Remote Desktop Protocol (RDP) and PC-over-IP (PCoIP) is expected. These are the two protocols that View can use to communicate between the end user and the View Connection Server. Understanding how they work, and how to leverage the Group Policy Objects (GPOs) associated with them, is critical, especially the PCoIP GPOs, because PCoIP is the default protocol. This chapter looks at how each protocol works and how to optimize them for the best possible end-user experience.

"Do I Know This Already?" Quiz

The "Do I Know This Already?" quiz allows you to assess whether you should read this entire chapter or simply jump to the "Exam Preparation Tasks" section for review. If you are in doubt, read the entire chapter. Table 4-1 outlines the major headings in this chapter and the corresponding "Do I Know This Already?" quiz questions. You can find the answers in Appendix A, "Answers to the 'Do I Know This Already?' Quizzes and Review Questions."

Table 4-1 Headings and Questions

Foundation Topics Section	Questions Covered in This Section
RDP: The Historical Protocol	1–2
PCoIP: The Modern Protocol	3–10

1. The version of RDP included with Windows Vista provided a new feature that would verify the computer as well as the user. What is the name of that feature?
   a. Network Link Authentication
   b. Network Layer Authentication
   c. Network Link Aggregation
   d. Network Layer Aggregation

2. What feature was added to RDP 7.1 to help with 3D graphic rendering and game playing?
   a. MMR
   b. NLA
   c. Remote3D
   d. RemoteFX

3. PCoIP is what kind of protocol?
   a. UDP
   b. TCP
   c. IP
   d. FC

4. PCoIP uses what kind of image rendering?
   a. Build-to-lossy
   b. Build-to-lossless
   c. Perceptually lossless
   d. Perceptually lossy

5. What is the default value to configure the clipboard in PCoIP?
   a. Enable both directions
   b. Enable server to client only
   c. Enable client to server only
   d. Disabled

6. The default maximum frame rate for PCoIP is what value?
   a. 12 FPS
   b. 24 FPS
   c. 30 FPS
   d. 120 FPS

7. For PCoIP, if FIPS 140-2 approved mode is enabled, what option will not be available?
   a. Disable AES-128-GCM encryption
   b. Disable AES-192-GCM encryption
   c. Enable AES-128-GCM encryption
   d. Enable AES-192-GCM encryption

8. A vCenter Server administrator goes to look at the console of an end user's session. The screen is blacked out. What is the cause of this?
   a. The PCoIP port is not opened for 4172.
   b. The RDP port is not opened for 3389.
   c. This is default behavior of the View Agent for privacy.
   d. This is default behavior of the vSphere Client for privacy.

9. What is the default value for the maximum PCoIP session bandwidth (in Kbps)?
   a. 1
   b. 10
   c. 11.25
   d. 90000

10. The default audio bandwidth level is what value?
    a. 50Kbps
    b. 250Kbps
    c. 500Kbps
    d. 1600Kbps

Foundation Topics

RDP: The Historical Protocol

Remote Desktop Protocol, or RDP, has been around for a while, first making an appearance with Windows XP. At the time of its creation, the Internet was in relative infancy compared to what it is today. The goal for many of the protocols of the day was merely to connect and allow end users to reach whatever service was on the other end. For RDP, this was a full desktop. At the time, there was no need to consider security or speed because the use cases at the time did not require high levels of security or bandwidth.

RDP is part of a family of protocols based on the ITU T.128 Standard. The historical background tracing RDP's evolution from Citrix's WinFrame to where it is today is interesting. RDP's humble beginnings originate from within Windows NT 3.5. There, a precursor to what we know to be Terminal Services was first introduced. At the time, Windows needed some kind of remote management mechanism as networks became more and more prevalent and network services had to be regularly maintained (such as email and file sharing services). So Microsoft partnered with Citrix to implement MetaFrame on top of Windows NT 4.0, replacing the earlier WinFrame that was found on 3.5, and RDP was born. You could almost refer to this first version of RDP as RDP 4.0.

With the advent of Windows 2000 Server, additional channels were introduced to provide local printer access and improved network access, resulting in RDP 5.0. Windows XP ushered in additional features like 24-bit color and sound redirection, resulting in RDP 5.1. In fact, the release of Windows XP and the increased use of the Internet is what really started to drive development of the RDP protocol. By the time Windows 2003 Server was released, RDP was updated to version 5.2. This version introduced console mode connections (the infamous `mstsc -console` mode), the ability to map to local resources (for example, local drives), and other features. It was at this point that we saw the separation of Remote Desktop Connection (RDC, often just referred to as RDP) from the Terminal Services Client (often just Terminal Services). RDC would be used for single-user remote access while Terminal Services would provide for access to a system by multiple users. The version of RDP released with Windows 2003 Server was also the first version to offer encryption (even if it was only TLS 1.0 and was for server authentication only). This was critical because use of the protocol was growing and the lack of encryption was creating a growing security concern. The 64-bit version of Windows XP and the 32 and 64-bit versions of Windows 2003 Server contained this updated version of RDC.

The release of Windows Vista introduced RDP 6.0, which included more changes, particularly one of my favorites: Network Layer Authentication (NLA). NLA gave RDP the ability to verify that the user was who he claimed to be while ensuring that the user was connecting from an expected computer. This capability was aimed at reducing man-in-the-middle (MiTM) attacks against RDP that were becoming increasingly prevalent. RDP 6.0 also added limited support for multimonitor (initially all monitors had to be the same resolution and orientation). Support was also added for Windows Presentation Foundation (WPF) to leverage additional graphics options for 2D, 3D, and user interface options. Finally, support was added for larger desktop environments and full TLS 1.0 support was added (not just for the server portion).

RDP 6.1 was released with Windows 2008 Server and Windows Vista SP1. Support was added for Windows XP with the release of SP3. The addition of this support was critical because many corporations were still running XP rather than migrating to Vista. RDP 6.1 provided an avenue by which to run individual applications, a new print driver (the TS Easy Print driver), client-side printer redirection, and overall improvements. Windows 7, not surprisingly, introduced RDP 7.0. This release added Windows Media Player Redirection (which differs from MMR or Multi-Media Redirection extensions provided by companies like Wyse), bidirectional audio support, Aero Glass remote support, full multimonitor support, and more. As of this writing, the current version of RDP is RDP 7.1. This version was released with Windows 7 SP1 and Windows 2008 R2 SP1 and added RemoteFX to help provide additional support for graphics such as 3D rendering and game playing.

The idea behind the RDP protocol was simple: Split the desktop into various channels. For every change made to the desktop, the protocol sends the necessary packets for that channel. The channels used depend on the version of RDC (Remote Desktop Connection) that both sides used: the local client (client) versus the remote desktop (server). The two sides establish communications and agree, as part of their initial handshake, upon the lowest common denominator level of RDP to utilize. With each release of RDP, new features and new channels have been added. Today, the following features are supported overall for RDP:

- 8-bit to 32-bit color (higher color options are available with newer versions of RDP)
- RC4 encryption with version 6.0 and later
- Audio redirection (from remote desktop to client system)
- Printer redirection
- Port redirection (allowing access to local serial and parallel ports)
- Clipboard shared between the local and remote system

- Remote application execution (available with version 5.0 and later)
- RemoteFX allowing for virtualized GPU (with version 7.1 and later)
- Support for Windows Management Instrumentation (WMI)

There remain, however, two large issues with RDP. The first is the lack of security protocols. As mentioned earlier, it's important to recognize why the protocol was first created and who was the expected audience: internal LAN administrators looking after users on different floors of a building. Although this use case might still be appropriate for some environments, it's not valid for all, and the landscape has changed dramatically from when the protocol was first introduced. At that time, it was uncommon for security breaches to happen internally. Today, about 40% of all attacks and breaches of data come from internal sources. In today's environments, data needs to be protected internally as much as it does from external threats. To help address this, the use of the TLS 1.0 protocol and RC4 encryption should be required at a minimum. An additional option would be to include virtual private networks (VPNs) to provide external encryption of the protocol while communication occurs between the client and the remote desktop.

The second issue is more of an end-user satisfaction issue. One way to ensure buy-in to a virtual desktop infrastructure (VDI) is by ensuring that the end users' experience is the same, if not better, than when they were in front of their physical desktop. Within a LAN, RDP performs well. But in today's day and age of telecommuting, many connections are made external to the LAN. In this case, RDP might not be a viable option due to performance considerations. As an example, I have had to connect sometimes when I'm on a plane 39,000 feet in the air. I've done it a few times, but only by using PCoIP as my protocol option. RDP would not be able to handle that kind of connection well without help from a WAN accelerator. One of the reasons behind this is that RDP uses channels. A single change means resending all the data for a given channel. This means that a simple icon movement results in the screen being redrawn. The more objects or the more complex a desktop, the greater the refresh rate and the slower the connection because of all the redrawing that must be performed.

Certainly RDP/RDC can be used, but design considerations must be strongly taken into account before considering this for 10,000+ remote users connecting into the environment. Assuming that a variety of devices and platforms exist in that environment, even more design considerations must be addressed. When you add in the need for security, particularly for companies where users are telecommuting, it becomes evident that although RDP might be adequate for some scenarios, it is not for all scenarios. In particular, the example I gave on the plane would have been frustrating, to say the least, if I had used RDP. Because we cannot solely design VDI environments for LAN users, and we cannot expect environments to have the funds to add large WAN accelerators at the drop of a hat, we need a protocol that is light, fast, has built-in security, and can have tolerance for latency. That's where PCoIP comes in.

PCoIP: The Modern Protocol

PCoIP (PC-over-Internet Protocol) was first introduced in 2005, when Teradici, a small and unknown Canadian company from the wilds of British Columbia, first introduced it to the world. The idea was that a remote user's experience when connecting to a desktop should be neither limiting nor wide open. Teradici had previously introduced hardware adapters called TERA cards that were designed to allow for intense graphic design with the aid of NVIDIA chipsets. These cards were focused on remote access use cases where latency and bandwidth utilization often had a performance impact. For most environments, the cost of the cards was enough to live with the current remote access model. For those environments where intensive computing puts a strain on an environment regardless of how many WAN accelerators are in place, an alternative was needed. For this use case, PCoIP provides an excellent alternative. A largely User Datagram-based Protocol (UDP), PCoIP also has the benefit of built-in encryption. The hardware version that comes with the TERA cards uses AES-128 and can be configured to support AES-256. The software version, which is co-developed with VMware, utilizes AES-128 (up to AES-192) and Salsa20-256round12 for its encryption method (by default). Whether a hardware version or a software version of PCoIP is utilized, it is secure out of the box. This removes the need for a VPN because encryption is part of the protocol itself. However, for some environments, you might still need a VPN for remote authentication. It's important to know that Transmission Control Protocol (TCP)-based Secure Sockets Layer (SSL)-type VPNs will actually cause worse performance for the protocol.

PCoIP is the default protocol of View, and that's not surprising. The flexibility of this protocol allows for virtually any user from nearly any location to connect to his or her desktop, even when the network is subpar and bandwidth is limited. The protocol uses codecs to represent changes done on the desktop remotely. These are installed as part of the PCoIP server, or in the case of View, from the View Agent. These codecs allow for changes to the desktop to be handled in a more dynamic fashion. For example, if a user moves an icon on the desktop, just the pixels associated with the move are transmitted, rather than the whole desktop image. Because the protocol only needs to burst the pixels that represent the changes, the protocol behaves better in poor-latency and low-bandwidth scenarios than some other protocols normally would.

One of the biggest features of this protocol is the way it builds images and text for the remote session. PCoIP uses a concept known as *build-to-lossless*. For those unfamiliar with this concept, there are two important terms to understand before continuing: *lossless* and *lossy*. Lossless means the desktop image displayed to the end user is perfect, with every pixel or bit in its place. Lossy means the desktop image is an approximation or rough outline of the actual image. If you've ever had your eyes checked, you might remember a test by the optometrist where he compares lenses to see which one causes the letters on the wall to appear perfect. The fuzzy state where you are trying to strain and guess the letters is what is referred to as lossy; we experience lossless when the lenses match and result in 20/20 vision.

What PCoIP does is initially download images from the remote desktop. The starting point is a default of 50% quality. For most images, this results in a fuzzy appearance to the naked eye (lossy). Text, however, is completely lossless. As more bits come in over the wire, graphic images continue to build to a lossless state. Depending on the bandwidth available, this can be within a blink of an eye or a few seconds. What is ideal about this process is that the end user does not have to wait for images to fully download before using the desktop. And when the user scrolls, rather than redownloading everything all over again, only the changed data is required. The result is a faster and more consistent experience for the end user, reduction in bandwidth, and better performance. And this is just one benefit of using PCoIP. Another great feature of PCoIP is that it can adapt its bandwidth utilization. If bandwidth in an environment is less than optimal (or becomes less than optimal at any point), PCoIP will attempt to adjust itself to work within the confines of the bandwidth that is available. It does so through a variety of mechanisms, such as audio compression, reduced frames per second, and increased display compression.

For many protocols, specifically TCP-based ones, a WAN accelerator is often used to address issues such as latency. For a protocol like PCoIP, this will not work. Optimizing the protocol through the use of GPOs discussed in this chapter will achieve the best results because optimization can be done on a use-case basis, either based on the user or the desktop itself. That said, one thing *must* be done as part of the network configuration itself: PCoIP should be the second-highest prioritized protocol for either quality of service (QoS) or class of service (CoS). Generally speaking, most UDP-based protocols fall under the category of "garbage" protocols because they are associated with peer-to-peer networking. This prioritization can result in dropped packets, which would be a bad thing for an important protocol like PCoIP. Changing the priority by moving it up to just under a protocol like Voice over IP (VoIP) will help ensure that PCoIP performs as expected.

As mentioned, a lot of PCoIP features (for example, frames per second for video and audio rate) can be controlled through GPOs. This allows the protocol to be flexible and responsive to changing situations within the environment. One thing to be aware of is that some of the GPOs apply to only the "soft" version of PCoIP. This means that if an offload card like an APEX2800 is used, changes you have made to the GPOs might not be applied because the changes do not apply to the "hardware" version of PCoIP. Any references in the GPOs to "soft host only" refer to the View Agent on a virtual machine. These GPOs are meant as a computer policy, which means they must be applied to the template virtual machine or master virtual machine image.

To install the GPOs (whether locally on a desktop or into the domain), follow these steps:

Step 1. On the system where you want to implement the GPOs, launch a Microsoft Management Console (MMC) by typing **mmc** in the Run box.

Step 2. When the MMC opens, press **Ctrl+M** to choose **Add/Remove Snap-in** from the File menu.

Step 3. From the Add or Remove Snap-ins window, scroll down on the left side until you locate Group Policy Object Editor. Click the **Add** button.

Step 4. Once it loads, open **Administrative Templates** under Computer Configuration.

Step 5. Right-click **Administrative Templates** and choose **Add/Remove Templates**.

Step 6. Click **Add** and browse for the PCoIP GPO by navigating to the following location on the Connection Server: <drive letter>/Program Files/VMware/VMware View/Server/extras/GroupPolicyFiles.

Step 7. Select **pcoip.adm** and click the **Open** button.

Step 8. Click the **Close** button if you've selected all the GPOs you need. You should see the PCoIP Sessions Variables folders under Classic Administrative Templates.

The PCoIP GPOs are categorized into the following topics: View PCoIP General Session Variables, View PCoIP Session Bandwidth Variables, and View PCoIP Session Variables for the Keyboard. Before making any changes, it is good practice to make a backup of the Registry for the system where the changes will be made. You also should evaluate the reason for the change and, for future reference, record why the change was made. For example, if you disable audio because you determine that end users will not use it, only to find out that one group does require it, you can easily locate which GPO you altered (as this can be disabled in a couple of places). Let's start by reviewing the General Session Variables, shown in Table 4-2 and Figure 4-1.

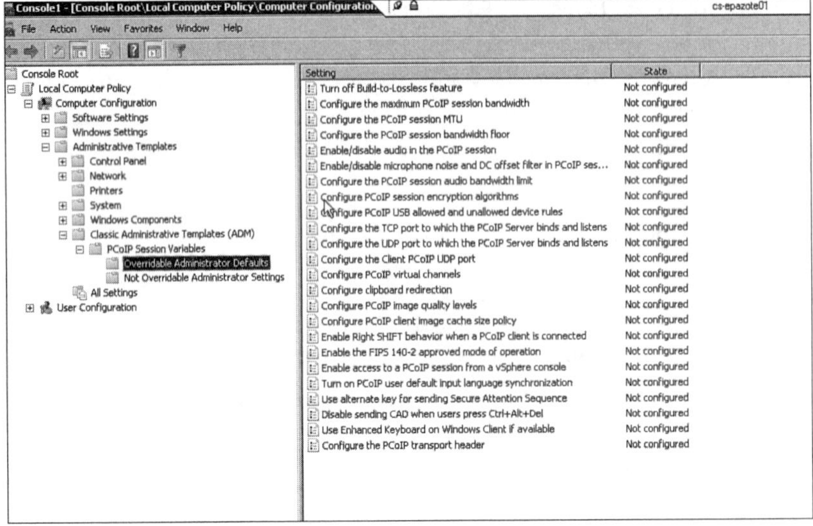

Figure 4-1 Group Policy Objects for PCoIP configuration screen.

Table 4-2 View PCoIP General Session Variables

GPO	Description
Configure Clipboard Redirection	Defines whether to allow clipboard copy from the client to the View desktop only, from the View desktop to client only, in both directions, or if the setting should be disabled. The default value is to Enable client to server only (from View client system to View desktop).
Configure PCoIP Client Image Cache Size Policy	Sets the size of the PCoIP client image cache. This cache ensures that frequently used images are not transmitted over and over again (for example, desktop icons). The default value is 250MB and can be adjusted to a size ranging from 50MB to 300MB. This GPO affects only Windows and Linux clients. At the time of this writing, Mac and other VMware View clients do not support a PCoIP client image cache.

GPO	Description
Configure PCoIP Image Quality Levels	Defines how PCoIP will display images when the network is congested. Three settings can be adjusted. The first is Minimum Image Quality, which defines how the image will initially appear. This setting defaults to a value of 50 and can be changed to anything from 30 to 100. The lower the value, the faster an image is displayed, but at the cost of quality. Images appear fuzzier at lower values. This value cannot be set higher than Maximum Initial Image Quality. Maximum Initial Image Quality helps to reduce the peaks that could be created by additional pixels (for changed areas) being sent during the initial stage. This value cannot be less than Minimum Image Quality. It defaults to 90 and can be set to any value from 30 to 100. It's important to consider what kind of images you are viewing. It's possible to make this value (and other graphic values) lower, but if image quality is required to be high (for example, for medical imaging or CAD/CAM applications), lowering these values could be detrimental. Maximum Frame Rate helps to control how much bandwidth is consumed by limiting how often the screen is updated per second. The default value is 30 frames per second (FPS). To provide some context, film uses 24FPS, whereas U.S. television often uses 30FPS. The value for this setting can be anything from 1 to 120. Setting this value too low may result in stuttering of motion video. This GPO applies only to the soft host. If the GPO is disabled or not configured, it uses the default values.
Configure PCoIP Session Encryption Algorithms	Determines which algorithm will be used for session negotiation. At least one algorithm must be selected. By default, both AES-128-GCM and Salsa20-256round12 are enabled. If FIPS140-2 approved mode is selected, the Disable AES-128-GCM encryption option will not be available because AES-128-GCM is required for FIPS140-2.

GPO	Description
Configure PCoIP USB Allowed and Unallowed Device Rules	Determines which USB devices are allowed or not allowed to be used with zero clients. (These are clients that use the Teradici firmware to connect to a View desktop.) The default setting is to allow all devices to connect. For both the authorization and unauthorization tables, a maximum of 10 rules can be defined. The rules can be either a combination of a Vendor ID (VID) and a Product ID (PID), or it can define a class of USB devices. Class rules can allow or disallow a whole device class, a subclass, or a protocol within a class. The rule format for VID/PID usage is `Rule#VIDPID` and is formatted as `1aaaazzzz`, where `1` is the rule number, `aaaa` is the VID hexadecimal, and `zzzz` is the PID hexadecimal. For example, if I want to block all 8GB Apple Nano devices (fourth generation), I create a rule for the VID of 0x05ac and a PID of 0x1263, so it would be `105ac1263`. If I want to specifically allow webcams, I can use the rule of `22030eXXXX`. This means regardless of the vendor, webcams will be allowed. If a device is listed in the USB unauthorization table, it will not be allowed. If the device is listed in the USB authorization table, it will be allowed.
Configure PCoIP Virtual Channels	Defines the virtual channels that are allowed or disallowed during PCoIP sessions.
Configure the Client PCoIP UDP Port	Defines the UDP port to be used by the software PCoIP clients. It identifies the base port to use and possible port range. (This allows for other ports to be used if the base port is unavailable.) The default values are a base port of 50002 and a port range of 64. (This means that the range starts at 50002 and could possibly be 50066 at its highest value.)
Configure the TCP Port to Which the PCoIP Host Binds and Listens	Defines what TCP port the View Agent (on software PCoIP desktops) will attempt to bind to and what port range might be used (a value between 0 and 10). The base port depends on which version of the View Agent is being used. The default value for View Agents that are version 4.0.x or earlier is 50002, and the default value for View Agents that are version 4.5 and later is 4172.

GPO	Description
Configure the UDP Port to Which the PCoIP Host Binds and Listens	Defines what UDP port the View Agent (on software PCoIP desktops) will attempt to bind to and what port range might be used (a value between 0 and 10). The base port depends on which version of the View Agent is being used. The default value for View Agents that are version 4.0.x or earlier is 50002, and the default value for View Agents that are version 4.5 and later is 4172.
Enable Access to a PCoIP Session from a vSphere Console	By default, when a PCoIP session is active, the vSphere Client console screen is blacked out to ensure privacy of the desktop (often required to comply with policies like the Health Insurance Portability and Accountability Act [HIPAA] and the Sarbanes-Oxley Act [SOX]). In environments where this is not a requirement, you can enable access (both to see and interact with it) through the vSphere Client console. To enable access to the desktop through the vSphere Client console on Windows 7 desktops, the virtual hardware must be version 8 or later. (Hardware version 8 is found only on ESXi 5.x and later.) To allow for vSphere Client input on Windows 7, any hardware version is allowed. For Windows XP or Vista systems, any hardware version is allowed.
Enable the FIPS 140-2 Approved Mode of Operation	Ensures that only FIPS 140-2-approved cryptographic algorithms and protocols are used for PCoIP sessions. When this is enabled, it prevents AES128-GCM from being disabled, because this is a required cryptographic algorithm for FIPS 140-2. Note that this GPO is available only for View 4.5 and later. If View 4.0 and earlier is being used, this GPO is ignored. This setting can be applied to the agent, the client or both. Ideally, it should be applied to both to ensure that all algorithms can be used.
Enable/Disable Audio in the PCoIP Session	Allows audio to be enabled or disabled in the PCoIP session. Audio tends to be a large bandwidth waster, and this particular GPO provides an easy way to disable audio to alleviate excess bandwidth usage. Most employees don't require audio. The default setting is enabled.
Enable/Disable Microphone Noise and DC Offset Filter in PCoIP	Either allows or prevents the use of microphone noise and DC offset filters for microphone input while in a PCoIP session. This can be applied against the View Agent and Teradici audio driver only. (At the time of this writing, this can be found only in the Windows View Client.) By default, the use of microphone noise and DC offset filters is enabled.

GPO	Description
Turn on PCoIP User Default Input Language synchronization	Allows the View Agent to determine what language the client is inputting via the keyboard (for example, French, English, Korean). By default, the View Agent will not attempt any synchronization. Note that this setting can be applied only against the View Agent.

When evaluating bandwidth usage, you might find it necessary to adjust some settings, depending on the situation, to improve performance. These changes should not be made without first investigating the reason to do so. For example, if everyone can get to his or her desktop with good performance and bandwidth usage is only at 20%, there really is no need to change anything. However, if you are in a LAN environment, bandwidth is saturated to 90%, and users are complaining about poor performance or dropped connections, it might be worthwhile to investigate some of the GPOs listed in Table 4-3.

Table 4-3 View PCoIP Session Bandwidth Variables

GPO	Description
Configure the Maximum PCoIP Session Bandwidth	Defines in kilobits per second the maximum bandwidth a specific session may use. This setting includes all graphics, audio, USB, control traffic, and the virtual channels. The PCoIP server (View Agent) will adhere to the value set, which could prevent poor performance or packet loss. You should set this value to the maximum capacity you want the session to have. It should be equal to or less than the value of what the endpoint can handle. For example, if the endpoint has a 10MB network interface card (NIC) and connects to the Internet through a 4Mb connection, the value should be equal to or less than the 4Mb. (If you need a quick conversion of kilobits to megabytes to megabits, you can visit www.easycalculation.com/bandwidth-calculator.php.) If the client and the View Agent have different values, the lower of the two values is used when transmitting data. This value can be applied to both the View Client and the View Agent. The default value is 90000Kbps.

GPO	Description
Configure the PCoIP Session Bandwidth Floor	Defines in kilobits per second what the lower bandwidth limit of a session can be set to. This can prove helpful for networks that are particularly congested by reserving bandwidth for sessions, thus ensuring that the end user does not have to wait for the congestion to clear. If this setting is used, it is important to plan appropriately and ensure that the sum total of all the "floors" does not exceed the bandwidth itself. By default, a minimum bandwidth value is not defined. (The value of 0 is used.) Although this setting can apply to both the View Agent and the View Client, it will affect only the endpoint for which it is configured.
Configure the PCoIP Session MTU	Defines the maximum transmission unit (MTU) size for the UDP packets of a PCoIP session. The default size of the packets is 1300 bytes, but the value could be set to anything between 500 and 1500 bytes. It is rare to change this value. However, in cases where the network has a unique configuration, you might need to adjust the MTU to avoid packet fragmentation. Both the View Agent and View Client can have this attribute applied to them, but if the values differ, the lower of the two sizes is used.
Configure the PCoIP Session Audio Bandwidth Limit	Defines the maximum amount of bandwidth that can be used for audio (sound replay) for PCoIP sessions. The default value is 500Kbps (which allows for high-quality stereo audio but compressed). The minimum value can be set to 50Kbps (which could mean no audio or audio being disabled). A value greater than 1600Kbps means uncompressed high-quality stereo audio. Values between 50Kbps and 450Kbps can result in qualities similar to that of FM radio or phone calls. This value applies only to View 4.6 and later. If the View environment is 4.0 or earlier, this GPO is ignored.
Turn Off Build-to-Lossless Feature	Defines whether to build images to a lossless state. By default, Build-to-Lossless is enabled. To disable this feature you must agree to do so by checking **I accept to turn off the Build-to-Lossless feature**. This will enable the GPO setting. For environments that do not require pristine "every pixel" images, enabling this GPO can result in performance improvements.

The last PCoIP GPO, shown in Table 4-4, is for values that affect how the keyboard behaves when the client connects to the remote desktop.

Table 4-4 View PCoIP Session Variables for the Keyboard

GPO	Description
Disable sending CAD when Users Press Ctrl+Alt+Del	Controls what occurs when a user presses Ctrl+Alt+Del. By default, when users press Ctrl+Alt+Del, both the local Windows client and the remote desktop screens may lock. To help avoid confusion for end users, this setting can be enabled, which results in users pressing Ctrl+Alt+Ins to lock/unlock the remote desktop session when using PCoIP. By default, this GPO is not enabled.
Enable Right Shift Behavior When a PCoIP Client Is Connected	Controls functionality of the right Shift key. If you use View Agent 4.5 or earlier and access an RDP session from within the PCoIP session, the right Shift key does not work as intended. Enabling this GPO substitutes the right Shift key with the left Shift key. This applies *only* to the View Agent. For View Agents 4.6 and later, this GPO has no impact.
Use Alternate Key for Sending Secure Attention Sequence (SAS)	Enables you to define an alternative key other than the Insert key for sending the Secure Attention Sequence (SAS) to lock/unlock a remote desktop session using PCoIP. This GPO is particularly helpful in environments where the vSphere Client is used to access the console of a virtual machine. By defining an alternative key with this setting, you avoid confusion between the SAS for the remote desktop and the one to use for the vSphere Client console. If this value is enabled, you *must* select a value for the third key in the SAS sequence from the drop-down list.
Use Enhanced Keyboard on Windows Client If Available	Allows for the use of special keys found on extended or enhanced keyboards (for example, Win+L) to be recognized by the PCoIP remote desktop. This can also be used for international keyboards. Before you enable this GPO, the Windows client *must* have the keyboard filter driver (vmkbd.sys) installed and configured. If VMware Workstation, Player, or the View Client with local mode is installed, this driver is already installed and configured.

Summary

This chapter took us through the two protocols that View uses, specifically highlighting the default protocol of PCoIP. We also looked at how we can optimize the bandwidth and performance of PCoIP when needed. Before we continue to look at more GPOs in Chapter 5, "Interacting with Active Directory," it's important to reiterate that changes to GPO settings should be made only after evaluating the need for the change and not just *because*. As I often say in class, just because you can change something doesn't mean you should!

Exam Preparation Tasks

Review All Key Topics

Review the most important topics in the chapter, noted with the Key Topic icon in the outer margin of the page. Table 4-5 lists a reference of these key topics and the page numbers on which each is found.

Table 4-5 Key Topics

Key Topic Element	Description	Page
Section heading	Reviews the RDP protocol and the features it provides for Windows desktops	86
Section heading	Takes a look at the features of PCoIP and how it works	89
Table 4-2 and Figure 4-1	Identifies which GPOs can be used to help optimize PCoIP	92
Table 4-3	Identifies which GPOs can be used to help optimize PCoIP bandwidth	96
Table 4-4	Identifies which GPOs can be used to help modify PCoIP behavior for keyboard interaction	98

Define Key Terms

Define the following key terms from this chapter and check your answers in the Glossary:

RDP, NLA, PCoIP, build-to-lossless

Review Questions

You can find the answers to these review questions in Appendix A.

1. An end user connects with the 6.1 RDC client to a Windows 7 virtual machine using RDP 7.0. What's the effective level of RDP being used?
   a. 6.x
   b. 6.1
   c. 7.x
   d. 7.0

2. To help improve the overall performance of an RDP connection, what network tool can be used?
   a. RDP Accelerator
   b. WAN Accelerator
   c. LAN Accelerator
   d. RDC Accelerator

3. One of the default encryption algorithms for the software version of PCoIP is what?
   a. AES-256
   b. AES-192
   c. Salsa20-256round12
   d. Salsa12-256round20

4. What is the minimum value that can be configured for the PCoIP client-side image cache?
   a. 50MB
   b. 100MB
   c. 250MB
   d. 300MB

5. Which GPO can be configured to ensure the screen is updated at a specific rate?
   a. PCoIP refresh quality levels
   b. PCoIP image quality levels
   c. PCoIP FPS quality levels
   d. PCoIP maximum frame rate levels

6. In the unauthorization table, a system administrator has placed a VID of `22030eXXXX`. What is the result of this setting?
   a. All fourth-generation 8GB Apple Nanos are not allowed.
   b. All fourth-generation 8GB Apple Nanos are allowed.
   c. All webcams are allowed.
   d. All webcams are not allowed.

7. What port is used for PCoIP in View 5.0?
   a. 4271
   b. 50066
   c. 50002
   d. 4172

8. A View use case does not require audio. What GPO would be used to disable audio?
   a. Enable/Disable Audio in the DC Offset Session
   b. Enable/Disable Audio in the PCoIP Session
   c. Enable/Disable Audio in the View Client Session
   d. Enable/Disable Audio in the RDP Session

9. What is the default value for the maximum PCoIP session bandwidth (in MB)?
   a. 1
   b. 10
   c. 11.25
   d. 90000

10. Setting the audio bandwidth limit to the lowest value of 50Kbps will set it to what audio level?
    a. Compressed stereo audio
    b. Uncompressed stereo audio
    c. FM audio
    d. No audio

This chapter covers the following subjects:

- Preparing the Active Directory for a View Installation
- Describing the GPO Template Files
- OUs for Machine Accounts and Kiosk Mode Client Accounts
- Verifying Trust Relationships

(This chapter covers Objective 1.5 of the Blueprint.)

CHAPTER 5

Interacting with Active Directory

One of the nice features of View is that it ties in with the most commonly used directory service in enterprise environments today: Windows Active Directory. Designing and configuring Active Directory so that it works well with View, and ensuring that your virtual desktop environment adheres to organizational policies, is a critical part of any successful View deployment.

To be clear, this chapter is *not* a chapter about how to implement Active Directory. There are lots of great books out there on how to work with Active Directory. Instead, this chapter examines what you need to consider when it comes to using Active Directory and the various Group Policy Objects (GPOs) specific to various components of View, including the View Agent, the View Client, and View Server components.

"Do I Know This Already?" Quiz

The "Do I Know This Already?" quiz allows you to assess whether you should read this entire chapter or simply jump to the "Exam Preparation Tasks" section for review. If you are in doubt, read the entire chapter. Table 5-1 outlines the major headings in this chapter and the corresponding "Do I Know This Already?" quiz questions. You can find the answers in Appendix A, "Answers to the 'Do I Know This Already?' Quizzes and Review Questions."

Table 5-1 Headings and Questions

Foundation Topics Section	Questions Covered in This Section
Preparing the Active Directory for a View Installation	8
Describing the GPO Template Files	1–7
OUs for Machine Accounts and Kiosk Mode Client Accounts	9
Verifying Trust Relationships	10

1. A large organization wants to ensure that when users log in to their desktops they sign in again. Which of the following GPOs would need to be configured?
   a. AllowSingleSignon
   b. DisallowSingleSignon
   c. AllowDesktopSignon
   d. DisallowDesktopSignon

2. What is the GPO ConnectionTicketTimeout setting used for?
   a. Sets the timeout for the Active Directory token
   b. Sets the timeout for the administrator session connection
   c. Sets the timeout for View Client SSO authentication
   d. Sets the timeout for the View desktop uptime

3. In which ADM template would you find the Logon Password GPO?
   a. View Agent Configuration
   b. View Common Configuration
   c. View Client Configuration
   d. View Server Configuration

4. In a small environment, an administrator cannot create a signed certificate for a connection server and doesn't want users to be prompted to approve one. Which GPO and which setting need to be set?
   a. Certificate Verification Mode, No security
   b. Certificate Verification Mode, Unsigned Verified
   c. Signed Certificate Mode, No Security
   d. Signed Certificate Mode, Unsigned Verified

5. A large manufacturing environment has a shared desktop used by multiple users connecting to different connection servers. The security team wants to make sure that the current user does not see a previous user's connection server information. What GPO needs to be disabled to meet the security team's requirement?
   a. Enable Client Connection Servers
   b. Enable Client Connection Server List
   c. Enable Jump List on Client
   d. Enable Jump List Integration

6. The Desktop Composition GPO is used to enable what feature in Windows?
   a. Themes
   b. Aero
   c. WordPress
   d. AutoCorrect

7. When using the override (o) modifier for USB splitting on the View Agent, what is the final policy?
   a. A unification of the policies of the View Agent and View Client
   b. Just the policies of the View Agent
   c. Just the policies of the View Client
   d. Just the policies of the USB device

8. Which of the following View components must be a member of Active Directory? (Select all that apply.)
   a. Connection Server
   b. Virtual desktop
   c. View client
   d. Transfer Server

9. What command enables you to configure a kiosk system?
   a. vdmadmin
   b. viewadmin
   c. sviconfig
   d. vdmkiosk

10. What kind of trust is supported by the View Connection Server?
   a. Two-way
   b. One-way
   c. Workgroup
   d. None

Foundation Topics

Preparing Active Directory for a View Installation

In a perfect world, Active Directory would be deployed at the same time the View infrastructure is deployed. But in most cases, View is deployed into an existing environment containing Active Directory. I had one customer who inherited his Active Directory with no instructions, guides, or anything. Myriad GPOs were in place. When deploying into an environment with an existing Active Directory structure, a separate child domain for View is the best option. If this cannot be done, a separate organizational unit (OU) should be used to separate the virtual environment from the physical environment. Whatever the choice, have a plan as to how you want to implement View into an existing Active Directory structure, and investigate any concerns and existing GPOs to try to identify where potential conflicts might arise in relation to View and the View GPOs.

One of the most important concepts to understand is where Active Directory *must* be used versus where it *could* be used. For example, for most labs performed in a VMware classroom environment, the vCenter Server does not require domain access. Certainly, if we were going to create separate roles for vCenter Server access it would make sense to utilize the domain, but it really is not needed or required for that scenario. Even in the case where I'm a sole "Jack of all trades" kind of administrator who looks after everything (for example, network, storage, different server types), a workgroup would suffice for vCenter Server.

A View Connection Server, however, *must* be a member of Active Directory. It is a best practice to have the server on which you are deploying View be a member of the domain before installation. This domain will become the primary domain for the Connection Server. DHCP is also required for the View desktops, particularly those created through the automated mechanisms of either template-provisioned desktops or linked-clone-provisioned desktops. The various View server components require static IP addresses, and the entire View environment requires solid DNS resolution for both forward and reverse lookup. Because Active Directory is a core component of the environment, configuring DNS and DHCP services as part of Active Directory can make it easier to configure and administer.

In addition to the Connection Server, the desktops themselves must be members of the domain, either at creation (particularly for linked-clone parent virtual machines) or added during customization as part of using Sysprep or QuickPrep. You can leverage additional GPOs in the domain or on the local desktop to optimize or customize the desktop specifically for View. Leveraging central profile management ensures a better experience for the end user. A successful View deployment strives to provide an optimal user experience while adhering to organizational policies.

Other components like the Transfer Server can be part of the domain or not. However, it is highly recommended that the Security Server *not* be a part of the domain, given where it will reside (in the DMZ) and the risks that come from being in that location.

Describing the GPO Template Files

View has a total of six Group Policy Object (GPO) ADM templates available to help customize the virtual desktop environment. In Chapter 4, "The Protocols," we looked at how the PCoIP ADM template works. Here we focus on the other four templates that cover GPOs for View components: the Agent template, the Server template, the Client template, and the Common template (which covers common GPOs that can be applied to the Agent, Server, or Client). These templates are located in install_directory\VMware\VMwareView\Server\extras\GroupPolicyFiles and can be imported either into AD itself or into, in the case of the Agent GPO, the local desktop. You can either import the ADM files as is or, if need be, use the Microsoft ADM Converter (http://www.microsoft.com/en-us/download/details.aspx?id=15058) to convert the files to ADMX. Not all of the ADM templates are required for every View deployment. It's fairly common to use the Client and Agent GPOs. Regardless of which GPOs are configured for use, the GPOs will be applied only if downloaded as part of a profile or if already installed into the base desktop.

Although AD GPOs offer a variety of features and settings that can be adjusted, they should be changed only when a specific use case requires it.

The first ADM template that we look at relates to View Agent configuration settings. This template incorporates all settings other than those related to USB. Table 5-2 describes how settings specific for the agent will be enforced by the agent.

Table 5-2 View Agent Configuration ADM Template

GPO	Computer	User	Description
AllowDirectRDP	X		Enabled by default, this setting allows non-View clients to connect directly to View desktops using Remote Desktop Protocol (RDP). By disabling this, you can force clients to connect through the Connection Server to reach the desktop. If an environment uses the Mac client, this GPO should not be disabled because it would prevent the users from connecting to the environment.

GPO	Computer	User	Description
AllowSingleSignon	X		Enabled by default, this setting allows for the use of single sign-on (SSO). For an end-user experience, this can be helpful. However, for environments that require extra security, it may be beneficial to disable this GPO.
CommandsToRunOnConnect	X		Lists any commands or lists of commands that are needed to run when the user connects, for the first time, to the desktop.
CommandsToRunOnReconnect	X		Lists any commands or lists of commands that are needed to run again after first connect.
Connect Using DNS Name	X		Disabled by default, this setting can be helpful for environments that have a Network Address Translation (NAT) in place when the View Client or View Connection Server cannot connect directly via IP address.
ConnectionTicketTimeout	X		Determines how long the View Clients use the connection ticket for verification and SSO requirements. If authentication does not occur within that time, the session times out. By default, the connection ticket timeout is set to 900 seconds (30 minutes). You can change this as needed depending on security requirements.
CredentialFilterExceptions	X		Specifies the files for which you do not want to load the agent CredentialFilter. In some cases, the credentials passed through the agent are not needed or wanted for specific files. No path or suffix should be used. If more than one filename exists, use a semicolon (;) to delineate between various filenames.

GPO	Computer	User	Description
Disable Time Zone Synchronization	X	X	Enables the desktop to keep the time zone in which it was created rather than the time zone in which the client resides. Disabled by default, in some situations it will be necessary to enable this setting. Note that if this setting is enabled, the Disable Time Zone Forwarding GPO setting for the client is not enabled.
Enable Multi-Media Acceleration	X		Ensures that multimedia redirection (MMR) sends multimedia content to the client to decode instead of having the virtual desktop do it. Enabled by default, this can result in a better end-user experience, but only if the client has sufficient resources to do so. To take advantage of this setting, the View Client must have overlay support. This setting does not apply to local mode desktops.
Force MMR to Use Software Overlay	X		Ensures that MMR will utilize a software overlay to allow multiple monitor support. MMR uses hardware overlay where possible. However, if the client has multiple monitors, MMR is only applied to the primary monitor, and moving multimedia content to any secondary monitors will result in it not being displayed. This particular setting is disabled by default.
ShowDiskActivityIcon	X		This setting is no longer supported.
Toggle Display Settings Control	X		Ensures that when using the PC-over-IP (PCoIP) display protocol the Settings tab is available in the Control Panel. This setting is enabled by default. Kiosk-type desktops may benefit from having this setting disabled.

The Client ADM template is specific to the Windows versions of the View Client because it must be part of the domain or has to be installed locally on the client system. The first part of the client ADM template, as identified in Table 5-3, consists of GPOs specific to the use of scripts that would populate a View Client or have choices related to noninteractive View Client usage (as in the case of kiosk-type systems).

Table 5-3 View Client Configuration ADM Template: Scripting Definitions

GPO	Description
Connect All USB Devices to the Desktop on Launch	Defines a scripting option to ensure all devices are connected at launch. (Devices such as smart cards, USB printers, barcode scanners, and other dependent devices would benefit, as would kiosk systems.)
Connect All USB Devices to the Desktop When They Are Plugged In	Autoconnects devices when attached. Kiosk systems, barcode scanners, and other optional devices can be autoconnected when the client detects them after login to the desktop.
DesktopLayout	Specifies the layout options that users can have upon login, including the following: ■ Full Screen ■ Multimonitor ■ Window - Large ■ Window - Small The GPO DesktopName to Select setting must be configured for this setting to apply.
DesktopName to Select	Identifies which desktop to use.
Disable 3rd-Party Terminal Services Plugins	Disables the ability for the View Client to check for third-party Terminal Services plug-ins, if enabled. (These are often installed as normal RDP plug-ins.) This will not affect any View-specific plug-ins like USB redirection.
Logon DomainName	Specifies the NetBIOS domain name (derivative of the AD domain name) to be used by the View Client.
Logon UserName	Allows the script to insert the username that the View Client will use for authentication.
Logon Password	Specifies the password to be used. This will be stored in clear text in the AD.
Server URL	Identifies the URL for the Connection Server to be used by the View Client (for example, http://view.company.com). The URL can be either the address of the Connection Server or the load balancer that will lead to the Connection Server.

GPO	Description
Suppress Error Messages (When Fully Scripted Only)	Hides error messages when the View Client logs in (when enabled). This setting applies only when the login is fully scripted.

As a reminder, Table 5-3 is specific for a scripted connection to a View Connection Server from a Windows View Client. The rest of the View Client Configuration can be applied regardless of whether a script is used to log in or the end user interactively logs in.

The next section of the View Client Configuration ADM template file is for security settings. Settings are applied to either the computer configuration or user configuration. In cases where the GPO can apply to both the user and computer, the user configuration setting takes priority over the computer configuration setting. Table 5-4 details the various security settings for the View Client.

Table 5-4 View Client Configuration ADM Template: Security Settings

GPO	Computer	User	Description
Allow Command Line Credentials	X		Allows for user credentials to be passed through command line. Enabled by default, this option cannot be used with SmartCardPIN and password options.
Servers Trusted for Delegation	X		Specifies which Connection Servers will recognize Log In as Current User. This is useful for mixed environments where some users connect from a non-domain location and some connect from within the domain (for example, internal employees and external partners). By default, all Connection Servers recognize Log In as Current User. When restricting this capability to one or more specific servers, you can specify the server(s) by entering the server information in one of three formats: ■ domain\system$ ■ system$@domain.com ■ The SPN (service principal name)

GPO	Computer	User	Description
Certificate Verification Mode	X		Establishes the default verification mode for the View Client and prevents users from changing this option, although they can see the current setting. The setting can be configured to one of the following three options: ■ **No Security:** The View Client doesn't check or verify the certificate. ■ **Warn but Allow:** The View Client checks the certificate, and if it is not signed, is expired, or is not valid, it gives a warning. ■ **Full Security:** Forces the View Client to use a signed and valid certificate. If the certificate is not valid, is expired, or is unsigned, the user will not be able to connect. If this GPO is not enabled, the default behavior of the View Client is to Warn but Allow, and end users can change this setting on the client. Alternatively, CertCheckMode can be enabled on the client system. For 32-bit Windows systems: HKLM\Software\VMware, Inc.\VMware VDM\Client\Security For 64-bit Windows systems: HKLM\Software\Wow6432Node\VMware, Inc.\VMware VDM\Client\Security For this Registry key, changing the value sets the client system to use one of the earlier described options: 0 = No Security 1 = Warn but Allow 2 = Full Security If both the GPO and Registry key are used, the GPO overrides the Registry key.

GPO	Computer	User	Description
Default Value of the 'Log in as Current User' check box	X	X	Ensures SSO (single sign-on) behavior for an environment. By default, this GPO is not enabled. If all end users are going to connect from within the domain, this can help reduce the number of times users must enter their login information. If a user logs in to the View Client via the command line with the command `logInAsCurrentUser`, those values override this setting.
Display option to Log in as Current User	X	X	Provides end users with the option to select or deselect the Log in as Current User. Enabled by default, this setting can be helpful for users who access the View environment from both within the domain and outside the domain.
Enable Jump List Integration	X		When disabled, ensures that users will only see the Connection Servers that they are entitled to connect through. By default, the View Client keeps a list of recently accessed View Connection Servers.
Enable Single Sign-On for Smart Card Authentication	X		Allows the View Client to temporarily cache the smart card PIN in memory when logging in to the end user's desktop. If this option is disabled, the View Client will not display the smart card PIN dialog for login.
Ignore Bad SSL Certificate Date Received from the Server	X		Suppresses any errors that relate to the date on the certificate, usually after the date has passed for the certificate. Only applies to View 4.6 and earlier releases.
Ignore Certificate Revocation Problems	X		Suppresses any errors that relate to a certificate being revoked. Only applies to View 4.6 and earlier releases.
Ignore Incorrect SSL Certificate Common Name (Host Name Field)	X		Suppresses any errors that relate to a certificate hostname that does not match the hostname of the server that sent the certificate. Only applies to View 4.6 and earlier releases.

GPO	Computer	User	Description
Ignore Incorrect Usage Problems	X		Suppresses any errors that relate to a certificate that was intended to be used for something other than verifying the sender and ensuring that the connection is encrypted. Only applies to View 4.6 and earlier releases.
Ignore Unknown Certificate Authority Problems			Suppresses any errors where the server certificate is associated to an unknown certificate authority (CA), usually the result of a certificate signed by an untrusted third-party CA. Only applies to View 4.6 and earlier releases.

As discussed earlier, View has a variety of GPOs that were specifically designed for PCoIP. Similarly, there are GPOs specific to RDP. Most of these GPOs apply to behavior in relation to the View Client and the View Agent. Table 5-5 shows how RDP settings can be adjusted in relation to the View Client.

Table 5-5 View Client Configuration ADM Template: RDP Settings

GPO	Description
Audio Redirection	Redirects audio to the client by default. However, you can explicitly set the audio behavior to one of the following: ■ **Disable Audio:** This setting disables audio from being played. This can help reduce bandwidth requirements. ■ **Play VM (this is needed for VoIP USB support):** Audio will be played on the View desktop and requires that a USB audio device exists on the client system. ■ **Redirect to client:** Audio will be redirected to the client system. This setting is for RDP only. If audio is redirected as part of MMR, it will be played on the client system and not the View desktop.
Audio Capture Redirection	Redirects audio input from an audio device connected to the client to the remote View desktop. By default, this setting is disabled.

GPO	Description
Bitmap Cache File Size in XX for YY bpp Bitmaps	Establishes the size of the cache (in kilobytes or megabytes) for bitmap color settings, or color depth, (specified in a bits per pixel or bpp sizing). The options for this setting are as follows: KB/8bpp MB/8bpp MB/16bpp MB/24bpp MB/32bpp
Bitmap Caching/Cache Persistence Active	Enables a persistent bitmap cache to improve performance. This increases disk space usage by the client.
Color Depth	Specifies the color depth of the View desktop as 8bit, 15bit, 16bit, 24bit, or 32bit. For Windows XP systems, you need to enable the Limit Maximum Color Depth policy in **Computer Configuration > Administrative Templates > Windows Components > Terminal Services** and ensure that it is set to 24 bits, the maximum for that operating system.
Cursor Shadow	Enables or disables the cursor shadow. By disabling this, you can improve performance.
Desktop Background	Enables or disables the desktop background when a View client connects to a View desktop. By disabling the background, you can improve performance.
Desktop Composition	Enables Windows Aero. This setting requires Windows Vista or later. Although enabling this setting can improve the end-user experience, performance can be degraded if limited bandwidth is available.
Enable Compression	Utilizes compression to reduce bandwidth utilization. This setting is enabled by default.
Enable Credential Security Service Provider	Supports the use of Network Layer Authentication (NLA) for operating systems that support this feature. This setting is disabled by default. If you are using Windows Vista or Windows 7 desktops that have NLA enabled, this setting must be enabled. In addition, both the client and the View desktop must support the use of NLA. This setting can only be used in a direct connect mode and is not supported with tunneled connections.

GPO	Description
Enable RDP Auto-Reconnect.	Ensures that the RDP client tries to connect again when the RDP connection fails. This setting is disabled by default and, when enabled, only works with View Agent 4.5 and later on the remote desktop.
Font Smoothing	Enables font anti-aliasing where needed. This setting applies only to Windows Vista or later.
Menu and Window Animation	Enables animation for menu and windows. Enabling this could adversely affect performance.
Redirect Clipboard	Allows for local clipboard information to be copied to the View desktop when enabled.
Redirect Drives	Allows for local drives on the client system to be redirected to the View desktop. By default, this setting is enabled. If data security is of concern, this option should be disabled. Other methods of enforcing this type of security include setting the GPO policies for folder redirection for remote sessions and for drive redirection.
Redirect Printers	Allows for local printers to be redirected to the View desktop.
Redirect Serial Ports	Allows for local COM ports to be redirected to the View desktop.
Redirect Smart Cards	Allows for local smart cards to be redirected to the View desktop. This particular setting applies to both RDP and PCoIP sessions.
Redirect Support Plug-And-Play Devices	When enabled, allows local plug-and-play devices and point-of-sale (POS) devices to connect to the View desktop. This is not the same as the USB redirection piece of the View Agent.
Shadow Bitmaps	Enables bitmap shadows except in full screen mode. Enabling this could adversely affect performance.
Show Contents of Window While Dragging	When enabled, displays the contents of a folder when dragging that folder to a new location. Enabling this could adversely affect performance.
Themes	When enabled, allows themes to be used by end users on their remote desktop. Enabling this could adversely affect performance.
Windows Key Combination Redirection	Allows key combinations (for example, Shift+F2) to be redirected the remote View desktop. When this is not set, all key combinations apply locally only.

Some general settings can also be applied to the client and its behavior on a Windows system. Some of the General Setting GPOs can be applied against the user only or the computer only. User settings override any equivalent computer settings. Table 5-6 goes over the various general settings that can be applied against the View Client.

Table 5-6 View Client Configuration ADM Template: General Settings

GPO	Computer	User	Description
Always on Top		X	Ensures that the View Client will be the topmost window on the client system. Enabled by default, this prevents the Windows taskbar from covering the View desktop.
Default Exit Behavior for Local Mode Desktops		X	Changes the exit behavior to a simple logoff (the virtual machine will remain powered on). By default, when a user connects to a local mode desktop, it shuts down.
Delay the Start of Replications When Starting the View Client with Local Mode	X		Delays the start of replication until after starting the View Client with local mode. This helps to ensure that the local client system has been given enough time to ensure that it has network connectivity. This setting applies to the first replication only. Remaining replications would be performed using the interval setting value in the View Administrator local mode policies. The value has a default value of 900 seconds, or 15 minutes. Setting the value too low might not provide enough time to ensure that the network is active.
Determines If the VMware View Client Should Use proxy.pac File	X		Allows the View Client to use a Proxy Auto Configured (PAC) file. A PAC file is a JavaScript file that identifies a specific proxy for a specific URL. Note that if this setting is enabled on a multicore system, the WinINet application (part of the View Client that looks for the PAC file) may crash. This setting affects only direct connections and is not used with tunneled connections. Only applies to View 4.6 and earlier releases.
Disable Time Zone Forwarding	X		Ensures that the View Client will not synchronize its time with the local client system.

GPO	Computer	User	Description
Disable Toast Notification			Disables toast notifications. These are those little pop-up messages that you get when you receive an email or when a new instant message comes in. The messages normally appear at the corner of the screen; actual location varies depending on the application. Note that if this setting is enabled it will prevent the 5-minute warning for session timeout from appearing.
Don't Check Monitor Alignment on Spanning		X	Prevents the View Client from spanning multiple monitors if multiple monitors are connected. By default, this setting is disabled.
Enable Multi-Media Acceleration		X	Allows multimedia redirection (MMR) on the client if the client operating system allows it and if the client hardware supports it. The underlying hardware must have overlay support to use this setting.
Enable the Shade		X	Allows the shade bar at the top of the remote desktop session if available. By default, this setting is enabled for standard desktops and disabled for kiosk mode desktops.
Redirect Smart Card Readers in Local Mode	X		Allows the View Client to redirect card readers to the local mode virtual machine. Enabled by default, this should be disabled if a smart card reader is not used with the local mode desktop.
Tunnel Proxy Bypass Address List	X		Provides a list of specific addresses that the proxy would not be used with. The separator for each address is a semicolon (;).
URL for View Client Online Help	X		Provides an alternative URL that can be used if the end user is unable to access remote help (for example, local mode desktops that are not connected to a network).
Pin the Shade		X	Shows the pin option for the shade. If the shade is disabled (as with kiosk mode connections), this setting has no impact on the shade. This setting is enabled by default.

One of the trickier functions for View to provide is support for USB. Because there are so many vendors, devices, and products there is no way to validate every device type on the planet and whether it will work with View 5.x. With each release, the USB framework gets better and better, but it is still hard to know what will and will not work within a View environment. In addition, there might be some devices that an organization will not want to be used in their View environment. USB policies can be defined for both the View Client and the View Agent. Understanding where a USB policy must be defined depends on being aware of what the vendor and product IDs are. If you are unsure of the vendor and product IDs, you can find them at http://www.usb.org/kcompliance/view.

To add complexity, quite a few devices are "composite USB" devices, which perform a dual role. Some examples are a USB mouse that also provides storage, a barcode reader that also provides storage, or a tablet device that allows audio input. In some cases, you might want to allow only one function of these USB devices but not both. The most common use case for this is when a device performs a function but also provides storage. In this case, you might want to allow the device functionality but disable storage functionality for protection against data leakage. This is called *splitting*. These settings are made using policies at the View Agent level. Table 5-7 indicates which settings could be used to enable splitting.

> **NOTE** Not all VMware View Clients support USB redirection, and it is important to check for any updates. For example, USB support was added to the Mac client just before publication of this book. To keep up to date on new features, visit http://blogs.vmware.com/euc/.

Table 5-7 View Agent Configuration ADM Template: Device-Splitting Settings

GPO	Description
Allow Auto Device Splitting	Allow for automatic splitting of composite USB devices. This setting is not defined by default.
Exclude Vid/Pid Device from Split	Excludes one or more devices from being split. The syntax for this comes in the form of `{m|o:vid-AAA1_pid-BBB2 [;vid-AAA2_pid-BBB2]`. The value must be specified in hexadecimal, and an asterisk (*) can be used as a wildcard to replace specific digits within the ID.

GPO	Description
Split Vid/Pid Device	Allows splitting of one or more specified devices. The syntax format for this comes in the form of `{m|o}:vid-xxxx_pid-yyyy(exinfo:zz[;exintf:ww])`. The `exintf` value allows you to exclude components by their interface number. This value must be specified in hexadecimal, and an asterisk (*) can be used as a wildcard to replace specific digits within the ID. View does not automatically include a component that is not excluded. A filter policy such as Include Vid/Pid Device is required to include those components.

Because the View Agent overrides what the View Client settings are, especially if merge is not used, the agent-enforced settings add specificity to the device-splitting settings (as identified in Table 5-7). Table 5-8 details the agent-enforced settings.

Table 5-8 View Agent Configuration ADM Template: Agent-Enforced Settings

GPO	Description
Exclude All Devices	If set to true, the Include settings to allow specific devices or family of devices will be passed through the USB framework. Set to false by default. If this value is set to true, it overrides the settings that the View Client may have set.

Exclude Device Family	Allows the exclusion of devices by family (for example, smartphones and flash drives). The syntax for this is as follows:
	
	`{m|o}: family_name1;family_name2...`
	
	For example, to exclude Bluetooth, you use the following syntax:
	
	`o:Bluetooth`
	
	When automatic device splitting is enabled, View looks at the device family of the parent composite device.

Exclude Vid/Pid Device	Excludes a specific device or devices. The syntax is as follows: `{m|o}: family_name1;family_name2..` The device ID numbers must be input in hexadecimal, and an asterisk (*) can be used to replace individual digits for the device.

GPO	Description
Include Device Family	Allows the option to identify which device family or families would be included in the forwarding of USB devices. The syntax is as follows: `{m|o}: family_name1;family_name2..` The device ID numbers must be input in hexadecimal, and an asterisk (*) can be used to replace individual digits for the device.
Include Vid/Pid Device	Allows the option to include the forwarding of specific USB devices. The syntax is as follows: `{m|o}: family_name1;family_name2..` The device ID numbers must be input in hexadecimal, and an asterisk (*) can be used to replace individual digits for the device.

While the View Agent tells the View Client a lot of what it can or cannot do with regard to USB, the client-interpreted settings (as shown in Table 5-9) act like suggestions from the agent to the client (but are not enforced by the agent). The client handles interpretation and enforcement of the settings if a USB device that is affected by the settings is available and ready for forwarding. The following settings are not defined by default.

Table 5-9 View Agent Configuration ADM Template: Client-Interpreted Settings

GPO	Description
Allow Audio Input Devices	Allows for audio input (USB specific) to be used.
Allow Audio Output Devices	Allows for audio output (USB specific) to be used.
Allow HIDBootable	Allows for human interface devices (USB specific), or HIDs, that are neither keyboards nor mice to be used if they are discovered at boot.
Allow Other Input Devices	Allows for non-HID boot devices or keyboards with integrated pointing devices (USB specific) to be used.
Allow Keyboard and Mouse Devices	Allows for keyboards with integrated pointers (USB specific) to be used. Integrated pointers include device types like mouse, trackball, or touchpad.
Allow Smart Cards	Allows for smart card devices (USB specific) to be used.
Allow Video Devices	Allows for video devices (USB specific) to be used. Video devices could include webcams and other similar devices.

By default, the View Client does not allow composite devices to connect, because automatic splitting is initially disabled. View will apply any device's splitting policies before applying any other policy to ensure that it can identify each side of the device. The policy applied will be a combination of the policy settings for both the View Agent and the View Client. Table 5-10 lists the final result of the combined policies depending on which settings are altered, most of which would be done on the View Client.

Although automatic splitting can be enabled to handle the splitting of some devices, the individual USB splitting settings allow for more granular control over splitting behavior beyond the final result of the policies of the agent and the client combinations.

Table 5-10 Results of Combined Disable Splitting Policies of View Agent and View Client

Policy for View Agent: Allow Auto Device Splitting	Policy for View Client: Allow Auto Device Splitting	Effected Result of Combined Policies
Set to default of Allow	False (disable autosplit feature)	Splitting will be disabled.
Set to default of Allow	True (enable autosplit feature)	Splitting will be enabled.
Set to default of Allow	Not defined	Splitting will be enabled.
Override client-side Allow	Any or not defined	Splitting will be enabled.
Not defined	Not defined	Splitting will be disabled.

For the View Client, the GPOs listed in Table 5-9 can be leveraged at the computer level. If no GPO is set, View looks for Registry entries at HKLM\Software\Policies\VMware, Inc.\VMware VDM\Client\USB.

When using the Split Vid/Pid Device option, View will not automatically include devices not found on the exclude list. These devices must be explicitly listed on the include list. Table 5-11 shows modifiers that you can add to determine how the View Client will handle View Agent device-splitting policies.

Table 5-11 View Client Configuration ADM Template: USB Splitting Modifiers for View Agent

Modifier	Result
merge (m)	Ensures that the View Client will apply the device-splitting policy set by the View Agent in addition to the View Client.
override (o)	Ensures that the View Client will use the View Agent's device-splitting policy in place of the View Client setting.

For example, if I set `m:vid-AAAA_pid-BBBB` on the View Agent to be excluded and the View Client has `vid-CCCC_pid-DDDD` on its exclude list, the result will be `vid-AAAA_pid-BBBB; vid-CCCC_pid-DDDD`. Basically, the View Agent's devices are excluded first, followed by the View Client. If we changed the `m` to an `o`, only `vid-AAAA_pid-BBBB` would be excluded. The View Agent will not apply the policy; this is done by the View Client. The client will apply the splitting policy in the following order:

Exclude Vid/Pid Device from Split

Split Vid/Pid Device

A policy that excludes a device from splitting always takes precedence over a policy that sets splitting of a device. You can, to help avoid confusion, change the policy on the View Agent from Allow Auto Device Splitting to Allow - Override Client Setting. This will ensure clarity on what devices are split versus those that are not by centralizing control to the View Agent.

As has been shown, there are a variety of options to allow custom configuration of the View Client independently, the View Agent independently, and both together.

One of our last ADM templates is the Common Configuration Template. This template allows the configuration of settings that are applied across the board for all component types within a View environment. This template applies only to computer configuration settings. Table 5-12 identifies the first group of settings, which are related to log configurations.

Table 5-12 View Common Configuration ADM Template: Log Configuration

Setting	Description
Number of Days to Keep Production Logs	Allows the number of days to keep production logs to be adjusted. By default this value is set to 7 days of logs. In some environments, either because of organizational policy or legal requirements, this might not be a sufficient period of time.
Maximum Number of Debug Logs	Allows the number of debug logs generated to be adjusted. By default, this value is set to 10 logs. Again, in some environments this might not be sufficient due to organizational policy or legal requirements. When the maximum number of logs is reached, the policy will automatically delete the oldest log as newer logs are generated.

Setting	Description
Maximum Debug Log Size in Megabytes	Refers to the maximum log file size before it closes the file and creates a new one. The default value is set to 50MB. Exercise caution when increasing this value and the number of debug logs. If a particular log starts *spewing* (writing nonstop), space on a particular View component could be completely used up and render that particular component unavailable.
Log Directory	Allows a directory to be chosen to place log files. When not specified, the View component writes logs to its regular location. It is important to ensure that the new location has write permissions. The View Client, when changing the log directory location, will create an additional folder with the client name to identify it compared to other clients (which proves helpful when multiple clients share the directory).

Logging within View is important not just because of the reporting of errors; logging also reports CPU and memory usage for various View components. This can allow a View administrator to monitor the overall health of a component or even specific processes within a component. Table 5-13 looks at how to adjust the performance alarm settings for this purpose and specifically applies only to the View Connection Server and View Agent systems. Adjusting these values can result in more information being recorded in the logs and the increased log turnover rate.

Table 5-13 View Common Configuration ADM Template: Performance Alarm Settings

Setting	Description
CPU and Memory Sampling Interval in Seconds	Determines how often, in seconds, CPU and memory is polled for information.
Overall CPU Usage Percentage to Issue Log Info	Sets the threshold at which CPU information, in the form of a percentage, is recorded to the log. In components that have multiple CPUs, this value represents the total percentage of all CPUs.
Overall Memory Usage Percentage to Issue Log Info	Sets the threshold at which committed system memory, in the form of a percentage, is recorded to the log. Basically, this is the percentage of memory that is utilized by a process, whether actual physical memory or whether using the guest operating system's page file.
Process CPU Usage Percentage to Issue Log Info	Sets the threshold at which CPU information for individual processes, in the form of a percentage, is logged. This can prove useful in determining whether a particular process is causing disruption on a component.

Setting	Description
Process Memory Usage to Issue Log Info	Sets the threshold at which memory usage for individual processes, in the form of a percentage, is logged. This can prove useful in determining whether a particular process is causing disruption on a component.
Process to Check, Comma Separated Name List Allowing Wild Cards and Exclusion	Identifies and lists individual processes, delineated by commas, for the purpose of being logged for CPU and memory sampling. In addition, specific characters translate into wildcards or exclusion options: An asterisk (*) means a match of 0 or more characters in the process (for example, `vdm*`). A question mark (?) refers to a single character difference in a process (for example, `wsnm????.exe`). An exclamation mark (!), sometimes referred to as a bang, means exclude this process (for example, `!vmware-svi-ga.exe`).

The last GPO settings are the common general settings. Table 5-14 looks at these settings, and it is important to remember that, much like the previous settings, arbitrarily changing these settings could result in detrimental behavior.

Table 5-14 View Common Configuration ADM Template: General Settings

Setting	Description
Disk Threshold for Log and Events in Megabytes	Refers to the minimum remaining space on a disk for logs and events. The default value is 200MB.
Enable Extended Logging	This setting, when enabled, adds both trace and debug events to logs. This value should be set only at the suggestion of either VMware support or Teradici support. While this setting is enabled, logging behavior is significantly increased.

OUs for Machine Accounts and Kiosk Mode Client Accounts

For design purposes, it is recommended that within the domain there is a separation of the View environment from other resources. As mentioned earlier, creating a separate OU for View is a best practice. Ensure that there are separate OUs for

View users, View administrators, and View computer accounts. The VCP-DT exam does not cover design topics, but it does cover the configuration and administration of View-related OUs implemented as the result of a design.

Kiosk mode is a unique option that allows for a device to log in and connect to a desktop. It is important to configure the Active Directory requirements to ensure that kiosk devices connect properly. The main step is to ensure that Active Directory (AD) has a separate organizational unit (OU) for kiosk clients, named something nifty like kiosk-ou, for example. In addition, a pre-Windows 2000 name for the group must be specified, which is used by the `vdmadmin` command for configuration. Setting up and configuring kiosk mode is covered in more detail in Chapter 7, "Kiosk Mode."

Verifying Trust Relationships

View deployments can be more challenging when Active Directory contains multiple domains within a larger forest. For View, the domain that the Connection Server joins effectively becomes its primary domain. For any other domains that need to be involved in the View environment, there must be two-way trust between the primary domain and the secondary domains, but trust is not required between the secondary domains themselves. If you imagine an old Western wagon wheel with the Connection Server at the center of the wheel, the domains to which it connects would be at the end of each spoke. This ensures that various child domains are kept separate from each other and from the Connection Server but still allows for connectivity to the desktops.

This brings us to the smallest GPO template that is part of VMware View: server.adm. It consists solely of a single GPO:

Recursive Enumeration of Trusted Domains

A common question is this: What kind of two-way domain trusts does View support? The answer is easy: All of them. These trusts include External, Realm, Forest, and Shortcut. They can be nontransitive or transitive. All of these are supported as long as the trust is two way (between the primary and secondary domains). Because the primary domain is the domain that the connection servers are a part of, recursive enumeration allows the View server to find every domain that is trusted to the primary domain. This is enabled by default.

In some cases, you might find it more prudent to disable this setting, either because of the size of the forest or to avoid additional domains being added to the environment. If this is left enabled, recursive enumeration in larger domain forests may take a bit more time to get information from all the domains.

Summary

This chapter might have felt like a laundry list of GPOs, but they are very important for the customization of View, particularly when View is deployed into an existing environment. Many environments often overlook these GPOs based solely on the idea that all that is needed is to install the software and walk away. No two organizations are the same, and neither should two properly deployed View environments be.

Now that the View environment is properly deployed, it is time to begin looking at desktop deployment. The next chapter delves into how to best optimize the operating systems of these virtual desktops.

Exam Preparation Tasks

Review All Key Topics

Review the most important topics in the chapter, noted with the Key Topic icon in the outer margin of the page. Table 5-15 lists a reference of these key topics and the page numbers on which each is found.

Table 5-15 Key Topics

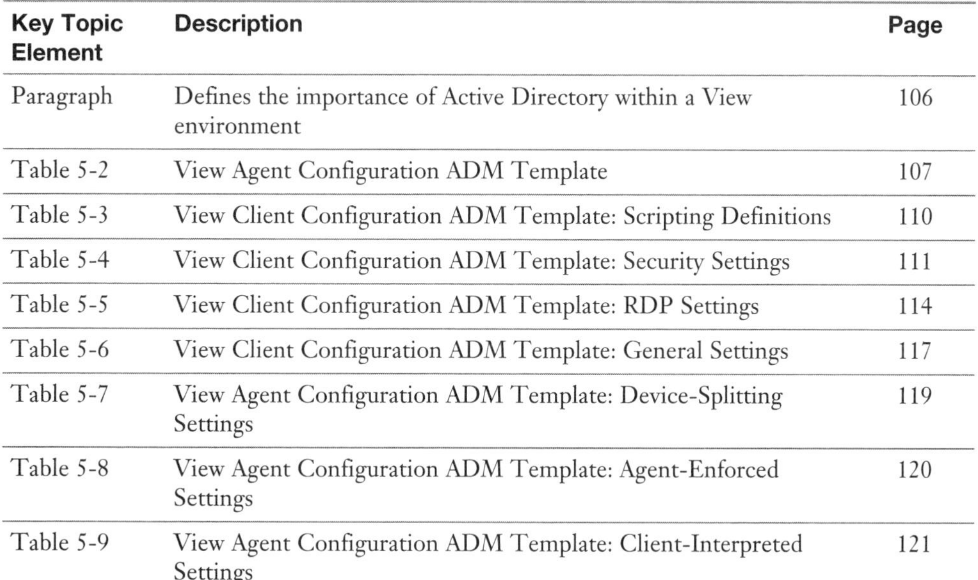

Key Topic Element	Description	Page
Paragraph	Defines the importance of Active Directory within a View environment	106
Table 5-2	View Agent Configuration ADM Template	107
Table 5-3	View Client Configuration ADM Template: Scripting Definitions	110
Table 5-4	View Client Configuration ADM Template: Security Settings	111
Table 5-5	View Client Configuration ADM Template: RDP Settings	114
Table 5-6	View Client Configuration ADM Template: General Settings	117
Table 5-7	View Agent Configuration ADM Template: Device-Splitting Settings	119
Table 5-8	View Agent Configuration ADM Template: Agent-Enforced Settings	120
Table 5-9	View Agent Configuration ADM Template: Client-Interpreted Settings	121

Key Topic Element	Description	Page
Table 5-10	Results of Combined Disable Splitting Policies of View Agent and View Client	122
Table 5-11	View Client Configuration ADM Template: USB Splitting Modifiers for View Agent	122
Table 5-12	View Common Configuration ADM Template: Log Configuration	123
Table 5-13	View Common Configuration ADM Template: Performance Alarm Settings	124
Table 5-14	View Common Configuration ADM Template: General Settings	125
Section	Discusses the importance of understanding how trust works with View	126

Define Key Terms

Define the following key terms from this chapter and check your answers in the Glossary:

ADM, GPO, OU

Review Questions

You can find the answers to these review questions in Appendix A.

1. An administrator wants to prevent non-View clients from connecting to View desktops. What GPO needs to be set for this to happen?
   a. Set AllowNonViewClient to Enabled
   b. Set AllowViewClient to Disabled
   c. Set AllowDirectRDP to Disabled
   d. Set AllowDirectPCoIP to Enabled

2. What is the GPO CredentialFilterException used for?
   a. Allows for credentials to not be passed to certain files
   b. Allows for credentials to be passed to certain files
   c. Allows for credentials to be used for SSO
   d. Allows for credentials to not be passed for SSO

3. What kind of desktop would benefit from having the Toggle Display Settings Control?
   a. Terminal server
   b. Physical desktop
   c. Kiosk desktop
   d. Local mode desktop

4. In which ADM template would you find Disable Time Zone Forwarding?
   a. View Agent Configuration
   b. View Common Configuration
   c. View Client Configuration
   d. View Server Configuration

5. In a large environment, an administrator wants to prevent users from logging in to Connection Servers that do not have signed certificates. Which GPO and which setting in that GPO need to be set?
   a. Certificate Verification Mode, Signed Only
   b. Certificate Verification Mode, Full Security
   c. Signed Certificate Mode, Signed Only
   d. Signed Certificate Mode, Full Security

6. What GPO disables the little pop-up notifications that applications do when things happen like receiving new email or an instant message arrives?
   a. Disable Popup Notification
   b. Disable Notifications
   c. Disable Toast Notification
   d. Disable Notification Popups

7. When using the merge (m) modifier for USB splitting on the View Agent, what is the final policy?
   a. A unification of the policies of the View Agent and View Client
   b. Just the policies of the View Agent
   c. Just the policies of the View Client
   d. Just the policies of the USB device

8. Which of the following parts of a View installation can be a member of a workgroup? (Select all that apply.)
   a. Connection Server
   b. Virtual desktop
   c. View Client
   d. Transfer Server

9. What is the command to be used to configure a kiosk system?
   a. vdmadmin
   b. viewadmin
   c. sviconfig
   d. vdmkiosk

10. What GPO lets a View environment verify all trusts that exist within a domain?
    a. Recursive Enumeration of Trusted Domains
    b. Verify Domains
    c. Verification of Trusted Domains
    d. Enumerate Verification of Trusted Domains

This chapter covers the following subjects:

- Optimizing the Operating System
- Configuring Virtual Hardware
- Installing the Agent
- Creating Customization Specifications

(This chapter covers Objective 3.5 of the Blueprint.)

CHAPTER 6

Optimizing the Operating System

Up to now, we have reviewed the steps necessary to install and configure View, and to provide an optimal delivery experience for users connecting to virtual desktops. However, for the best possible end-user experience, the virtual desktop itself must also be optimized. The first step in this optimization process is fine tuning the operating system (OS) to function well in a View environment. Windows operating systems were not initially designed for a virtual platform. Although they have been adapted in recent years to function in this type of environment, changes should still be made to ensure that they perform well. For example, in a virtualized environment, all components of a desktop exist as files. Therefore, optimizing storage resources when virtualizing a desktop is a critical step in ensuring proper performance. Some of these optimization steps are simple tricks that can result in an impressive performance improvement, not only for virtual environments but for physical environments as well. This chapter takes a look at these optimization methods.

"Do I Know This Already?" Quiz

The "Do I Know This Already?" quiz allows you to assess whether you should read this entire chapter or simply jump to the "Exam Preparation Tasks" section for review. If you are in doubt, read the entire chapter. Table 6-1 outlines the major headings in this chapter and the corresponding "Do I Know This Already?" quiz questions. You can find the answers in Appendix A, "Answers to the 'Do I Know This Already?' Quizzes and Review Questions."

Table 6-1 Headings and Questions

Foundation Topics Section	Questions Covered in This Section
Optimizing the Operating System	1–2
Configuring Virtual Hardware	3
Installing the Agent	5
Creating Customization Specifications	4, 6–10

1. What two guides can you use to optimize virtual desktops in a View environment?
   a. *VMware View XP Deployment Guide*
   b. *VMware View XP Optimization Guide*
   c. *VMware View Optimization Guide for Windows 7*
   d. *VMware View Optimization Guide for Windows XP*

2. Which setting immediately improves performance on a Windows virtual desktop?
   a. My Computer > Properties > Advanced Tab > Performance Options
   b. My Computer > Advanced Settings > Performance Options
   c. My Computer > Properties > Performance > Performance Options
   d. My Computer > Properties > Performance Options

3. What virtual hardware can you remove from a virtual desktop to optimize performance?
   a. vCPU
   b. vRAM
   c. Floppy drive
   d. Disk drive

4. What must be installed on the virtual desktop image to ensure the latest drivers and other performance improving features are present?
   a. View drivers
   b. VMware drivers
   c. VMware Tools
   d. View Agent

5. What feature must be installed on the master image to allow a desktop to be used for linked clones?
   a. View linked-clone agent
   b. View Composer Agent
   c. VMware linked-clone agent
   d. VMware Composer Agent

6. What should the BitLocker Drive Encryption Service be set to?
   a. Default
   b. Started
   c. Manual
   d. Disabled

7. Which service should be enabled on the master image but disabled for linked clones to help improve disk performance?
   a. Desktop Window Manager Session Manager
   b. VMware Composer Agent Service
   c. Disk Defragmenter Service
   d. Disk Defragmenter Session Manager

8. Which service should not be used to back up a virtual desktop?
   a. Centralized File Backup
   b. Backup with MS Software Copy Provider
   c. Windows Backup
   d. Centralized Profile Backup

9. A View implementation requires Superfetch and has been optimized to handle the increased I/O workload. When configuring Superfetch, what is the default setting?
   a. Cache boot files only
   b. Cache documents only
   c. Cache applications only
   d. Cache everything

10. What PowerShell script enables you to stop Windows services?
    a. `powershell set-service <service name> -startuptype "disabled"`
    b. `powershell setservice <service name> -startuptype "disabled"`
    c. `powershell setservice <service name> -servicetype "disabled"`
    d. `powershell set-service <service name> -servicetype "disabled"`

Foundation Topics

Virtual Hardware and Installation of the Operating System

Microsoft has been producing operating systems for a while now. I still remember my first DOS system and the first time I started using Windows with version 3.1. I've poked and prodded pretty much all of Microsoft's operating systems with the exception of Microsoft Me and Microsoft BOB. All of the Microsoft operating systems, with the exception of Windows 8, were pretty much designed for standalone hardware. This is particularly true for the desktop operating systems (XP, Vista, and 7). Windows 8, released as of the time of this writing, has been designed more for a tablet or touchscreen laptop. At this time, View does not support Windows 8. Although most environments deploy View during their next operating system refresh (usually from XP to Windows 7), quite a few are deployed with Windows XP, usually because of application dependency or end-user comfort.

VMware created two guides to help with optimization of both XP and Windows 7 operating systems in a View environment: the *VMware View Windows XP Deployment Guide* and the *VMware View Optimization Guide for Windows 7*. They are excellent references to keep handy. Remember to check the VMware website, because these guides are regularly updated as VMware finds new optimizations that can benefit organizations as they migrate Windows 7 to a virtual environment.

If I were to simplify the process of building and optimizing a virtual desktop, it would look something like the following:

1. Create a virtual machine as a template for your virtual desktops. Optimize the virtual hardware for the desktop during this step.
2. Install the latest version of VMware Tools.
3. Select a time-synchronization method where the virtual machine either synchronizes to the ESXi host or to the Active Directory time source.
4. Join the Active Directory domain.
5. If using VMware time synchronization in step 3, disable Windows time.
6. Install appropriate applications, and tune them for optimal performance.
7. Enable remote connections.
8. Install the View Agent.
9. Patch Windows desktops as needed. Note, this may require a reinstallation of VMware Tools and the View Agent.

Certain steps can be performed regardless of the OS used. By using local GPOs that prevent the use of themes, solid backgrounds, simple screensavers, and other similar settings like adjusting the Performance Options (right-click **My Computer >** click **Properties > Advanced** tab), you can realize a fair amount of performance improvement. Part of this process may require training your end users on how best to use their virtual desktops compared to what they might have been used to. Some organizations allow users a bit too much freedom with regard to the management of their desktops. The move to a virtual environment can be the perfect time to reassess end-user requirements and implement appropriate changes. As I often mention in class, one benefit of a virtual desktop infrastructure (VDI) deployment is that the organization regains ownership over the desktop as a tool provided to their end users and not something to use as their personal laptop.

Computers as personal devices have been around for decades, but it's only in the past 20 years or so that we've seen such an explosion of multipurpose need. Today, many organizations are leveraging bring-your-own-device (BYOD) or employee-owned IT (EOIT) policies. These policies enable employees to have a computer system that meets their specific needs and lets them personalize it without putting organizational data at risk. There would likely still need to be an organizational policy on what's allowed on the desktop versus what's not allowed, but this kind of configuration allows users flexibility while minimizing risk.

The main thing to keep in mind when it comes to virtual desktops is that services and processes that work well in a physical environment might not work well in a virtual environment. The emphasis placed on storage in a virtual environment may require changes to those services and processes. For example, in Windows 7, an indexing service runs continuously in the background. This adds roughly three to five input/output operations per second (IOPS) of read behavior on a disk. By itself, on a physical system, this is a negligible amount of IOPS. But when you have multiple systems all running regular indexing at the same time, utilizing storage from the same shared storage device, the collective amount of IOPS can result in a significant impact to storage performance. Disabling this service on the master image for a linked clone desktop pool reduces the possibility of unexpected resource contention for end users. The goal is to always ensure the same or better experience for end users than they had before virtualizing their desktops.

Configure Virtual Hardware

The first step in virtual desktop optimization is to optimize the hardware configuration. The best way to do this is when first creating the master image. Do not use a physical-to-virtual (P2V) conversion method to create the master image. Creating an image from a P2V results in a virtual desktop image that includes physical drivers and other components that might not behave well when virtualized. VMware recommends creating a new virtual machine and performing a fresh OS installation. Using the Microsoft Deployment Toolkit (MDT) is one way to ensure that the initial install meets the necessary requirements and allows for the creation of a unique ISO image that is specific to the environment. This ISO image can then be used as part of a zero-touch installation that requires no user interaction. By removing that interaction, you significantly reduce the chance of mistakes occurring. In addition, the MDT can install various applications as part of the base image install. These applications can include VMware Tools and the VMware View Agent. As mentioned earlier, the more interaction that is removed from the install process the better. In this case, by including VMware Tools and the VMware View Agent as part of the install, you ensure that they will automatically be part of the base image.

Many administrators simply accept the default virtual hardware when creating a new virtual machine. To ensure optimal performance, adjusting that hardware is worthwhile. This is often referred to as *right sizing* the environment and ensures that CPU, memory, disk, and network resources are sized exactly to what is needed by the environment. Removing any hardware that is not needed (such as a CD-ROM or floppy drive) can help keep the virtual machine optimized. Modifying the BIOS of the virtual machine can provide some benefit. For example, you can modify the BIOS to disable serial ports and parallel ports not in use on the virtual machine.

A part of this optimization process is sizing virtual CPU and virtual memory resources. As part of the initial planning of any VDI environment, an analysis of how the current environment is being used, including how the four "food groups" of CPU, memory, disk, and network are used, can help determine how many vCPUs are needed, how much memory is required, the proper sizing of the disks, and how much bandwidth is needed by the virtual desktops. For Windows 7, you can leverage the VMXNET3 virtual network adapter to help ensure better performance for virtual machine network activities.

After the virtual hardware is configured, a fresh install of the operating system should be performed, along with any required patches (as per organizational policy) and service packs. In addition to doing a fresh install, consideration should be given to minimizing the number of applications included with the master image. The fewer applications that exist on the image, the better it will perform and the better the end-user experience will be with it. This has the nice side effect of reducing application conflicts and reducing the number of support calls in relation to those conflicts. Ideally, applications should be virtualized using ThinApp and then streamed, either as a mapped drive to the desktop or through other methods. This will also result in a smaller image, which will allow for the faster deployment of images, whether fully provisioned or linked-clone provisioned.

After you have a basic clean image, you can clone this to create other "master" images for each of your use cases. Many organizations make the mistake of creating a single image with multiple levels of snapshots on it to represent different use cases. Having multiple images can result in a little more administration, but it allows for proper image management for each use case and not just from an operating system or application standpoint. An individual master image for each use case means that individual virtual hardware configuration can also be performed.

As mentioned in the steps listed previously, you must choose how to synchronize the guest operating system to a time source. This is a critical step, particularly with regard to Active Directory. As an experiment, I once tested what would happen when a virtual machine was not synchronized. Over an 18-hour period, the virtual machine drifted by 23 minutes! That is a significant time drift that can cause problems for things like Active Directory, and even some applications. As part of VMware Tools, the ESXi host can be selected as a time source. Alternatively, you can use a centralized time source, ideally the one that Active Directory uses. The rule I follow is that whatever you choose should be consistent across the board for all desktops, the Connection Servers, and Active Directory. For updates on how time changes with each ESXi version, check http://kb.vmware.com/kb/1318.

If you need to stop Windows time (W32Time), you can adjust it by modifying the following Registry entry type to **NoSync**:

```
HKEY_LOCAL_MACHINE\SYSTEM\CurrentControlSet\Services\W32Time\
Parameters
```

The last steps to perform are to install VMware Tools and the VMware View Agent. VMware Tools is needed to ensure that the latest drivers and other features specific to a virtual environment are in place. The VMware View Agent ensures that connectivity and management between the desktop and the Connection Server and between the desktop and the client are maintained. Keep in mind that as you install base applications and additional drivers you might need to reinstall VMware Tools again to ensure that the right drivers stay in place.

To install the View Agent, start by double-clicking the installer executable. This file is named VMware-viewagent-*xxxxxx*.exe, where the *xxxxxx* represents the build version. Remember to always read the release notes with each version to see whether a reinstallation of VMware Tools is required before or after upgrading the View Agent. Once the installer starts, complete the steps laid out in the following sections.

Installing the Agent

To install the Agent, follow these steps:

Step 1. On the first two screens (the Introduction and the End User Patent Agreement screens), click **Next**.

Step 2. Read the VMware end user license agreement. Then choose **I accept the terms in the license agreement** and click the **Next** button.

Step 3. Choose which options you want to use with the agent. See Table 6-2 for more details on the options shown in Figure 6-1.

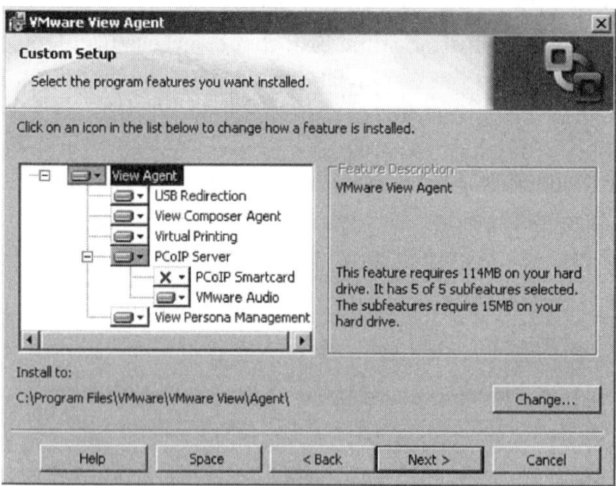

Figure 6-1 View Agent install options.

Step 4. Select the location where the View Agent will be installed if different from the default location of C:\Program Files\VMware\VMware View\Agent\, and then click **Next**.

Step 5. If Remote Desktop was not already made available, you will seen a screen asking if you want to enable Remote Desktop. Select the choice that is appropriate for the use case of the desktop and click **Next**.

Step 6. Read the summary page and ensure that all the choices are correct. Click **Next** and wait for the installer to finish.

If the installer includes USB Redirection, this forces the Windows OS to reboot to add a virtual USB device to the system.

Table 6-2 VMware View Agent Custom Installation Options

Option	What Does It Do?
USB Redirection	Allows for USB devices connected to the client to be passed through (if allowed by GPO and View Connection Server policy) to the virtual desktop to be used by the desktop.
View Composer Agent	Allows for the creation of special virtual machines as part of the composer process. This is required for master images that will be used to build linked-clone pools.
Virtual Printing	Allows users with the full Windows client to print to their local printer rather than to a network printer.
PCoIP Server	Allows users to connect to the desktop through the View Connection Server by using the PCoIP protocol. Note that by installing this piece on Windows Vista and Windows 7, guest operation will disable the sleep mode service. On Windows XP systems, this disables standby mode. This helps prevent desktops from going into a state that could make them unusable or appear otherwise hung.
PCoIP Smartcard	Allows users to authenticate with smart cards while using PCoIP. If the environment uses smart cards, this setting must be enabled to use them with the PCoIP protocol.
View Persona Management	Allows for profile synchronization from the virtual desktop to the repository to ensure that the user's profile is maintained.

Now that a master image has been created and virtual hardware has been configured, we can begin to optimize the OS.

Creating Customization Specifications

Before getting into the details of OS customization, it is worthwhile to review some of the options needed for Sysprep customized pools. In essence, the customization specification is key to the Sysprep process. Having it ready and tested before doing a pool deployment, whether template-provisioned virtual desktops or linked clones using Sysprep, can make the difference between a successful deployment and a frustrating one. The process to create a customization specification is straightforward:

1. Go to the Customization Specifications Manager found on the vSphere Client Home page.
2. Click the **New** button.
3. Choose the appropriate OS from the Target Virtual Machine OS. In this case, it is **Windows** because Linux is not a supported OS for View.

4. In the Customization Specification Information dialog box, enter a name. You can enter a description as well (helpful when multiple customization specifications exist). Click **Next**.
5. Enter the virtual machine owner's name and organization. This will likely be a generic owner name and the actual organization name. Click **Next**.
6. Specify that the computer name will be derived from the virtual machine name. This option *must* be selected for desktops that will be used with Sysprep. Select **Use the virtual machine's name** and click **Next**.
7. Specify a volume license and click **Next**.
8. Configure the local administrator and click **Next**.
9. Select the time zone and click **Next**.
10. (Optional) If there are scripts or commands that have to be run when the user first logs in, add them to the Run Once page. Click **Next**.
11. Network settings should always be set to **Typical settings** because Dynamic Host Configuration Protocol (DHCP) is currently the only supported addressing method for automated pools. Click **Next**.
12. Add appropriate domain information. The computer should be removed from the domain before you attempt to join the template to the same (or a different) domain. If the computer has not been removed, it is very likely that attempting to join the template to the domain will fail. Click **Next**.
13. Select **Generate new security ID (SID)** and click **Next**.
14. Click **Finish** to save all the settings.

This ensures that any new desktop created will have a consistent look and feel to it. Also, using a customization specification reduces the possibility of user errors interspersed in various desktops as part of their creation.

Most environments will deploy a VDI environment as part of an operating system refresh when moving from Windows XP to Windows 7. To that end, the focus in this chapter is on Windows 7 as the OS that will be optimized. Although the *Optimization Guide* does have two .bat scripts to turn services off, it is important to understand why it is necessary to turn off certain services and why some may be left on.

One of the big challenges with administering desktops is the reliance on the end user to keep the system up to date and to not perform activities that are harmful to the desktop and the network it is part of. In an attempt to reduce vectors of attacks and find ways to optimize performance, Microsoft moved a variety of tasks into service processes that could be automated. This ensures that activities like defragmentation of the disk occur on a regular schedule. As mentioned earlier, these processes were initially designed for physical systems and might not perform well for virtual machines with shared storage. Understanding what each service is, what it does, and whether to allow it to continue to run is a critical part of virtual desktop optimization.

Before looking at each service, note this one important thing: Even if a service is set to Manual, you might want to disable it to avoid the possibility that it might get restarted. You can adjust these services using a post installation script or by building the settings into the ISO image that is created.

The first service to look at is the *BitLocker Drive Encryption Service*. This service was introduced to encrypt whole volumes as an extra layer of protection against compromise, particularly if a laptop (or even just a disk) is stolen. The challenge with this service is that the constant encryption behavior performed by the service increases activity on the disk. This adds additional load for full-provisioned virtual machines that exist on a shared storage array. For linked clones, this method of encryption is unnecessary and would seriously impact performance for the shared C: drive of the replica. The setting for the service defaults to Manual, but you should definitely set it to Disable. Even if the image might be used with local mode, you should avoid the use of this feature. Local mode has its own encryption method, so using this feature would be unnecessary and would only impact performance. Put simply, this feature should not be used in a VDI environment.

The *Block Level Backup Engine Service* was created to allow workstations to perform a block-level backup rather than backing up individual files. This ensures that decentralized environments are backed up and data is protected. Because a VDI implementation relocates all data into the datacenter and allows for centralized backup to occur, this service is not needed. Again, this service defaults to Manual, but you should set it to Disable as a best practice.

Desktop Window Manager Session Manager, besides being a mouthful to say, is a service that may or may not be disabled for an environment. This service renders the desktop Aero environment if used. If the environment requires Aero, this service must be enabled. If Aero will not be used, set the value to Disable. By default, the service is enabled and set to start and run at boot.

One feature that has been part of Windows for a long time is disk defragmentation. Users often forget to do a disk defrag regularly, and as a result, disk performance slows down as fragmentation increases. Making this available as an automated scheduled service addressed this problem. However, having the defragmentation feature running on virtual disks causes unnecessary I/O, particularly for linked clones. The *Disk Defragmenter Service* should be run only on the master image. This will ensure that it is part of the replica, and then whenever a linked clone is refreshed, the disk will be optimized to begin with. By default, the service is set to Manual, but you should definitely set it to Disable for all virtual desktop types.

Sometimes, trying to determine what is causing problems on a desktop can prove challenging. The *Diagnostic Policy Service* was added to help identify problematic issues and to help end users troubleshoot them. For environments where end users need to perform troubleshooting, and for environments with various hardware and software footprints, this service can prove helpful. However, in a View environment, the master image remains unchanged and the hardware settings remain unchanged, so you have no need for this service.

Both the Home Group Listener service and Home Group Provider service were introduced to help make home networking and shared printer setup easier for the home environment. Within Active Directory environments, these services are unnecessary and should have their default setting of Manual changed to Disable for all systems, physical or virtual. Another networking service, the IP Helper service, should also be looked at. If your environment leverages IPv6, it is worthwhile to keep this service; otherwise, you should change its setting from the default of Automatic to Disable.

A number of services are not needed after a desktop is virtualized. These services may offer something for physical hardware, but they become unnecessary because we are leveraging virtual hardware. Leaving the following services running or potentially available could result in excess resource utilization or spikes in disk I/O by the guest OS:

- Microsoft iSCSI Service
- Tablet PC Input Service
- WLAN AutoConfig
- WWAN AutoConfig
- SSDP Discovery

If the desktop I was configuring were physical, I would have to consider whether these services might be needed. For example, the WLAN AutoConfig service is for wireless access, definitely an unnecessary service in a virtual environment because the virtual desktops reside in the datacenter. The Simple Service Discovery Protocol (SSDP) service was designed to help home and small business environments with network IP assignment without needing a full server to provide for things like DHCP and other similar services. Disabling SSDP also means that Universal Plug-and-Play (UPnP) service, the actual service that makes it easier to connect devices to PCs, will have to be disabled (because it is dependent on SSDP).

You still have to consider the use of some services, however, regardless of whether you want to use them because other services or functions might be dependent on the service in question. The Microsoft Software Shadow Copy Provider service, which is used by the Virtual Shadow Service (VSS) for backups, is one such example. If you back up the user data from a central location because of profile configuration, individual desktops do not necessarily need to be backed up and you might consider disabling this service. But if you are using View Persona Management, this service *must* be running because Persona Management utilizes the VSS to maintain the regular in-session backup of the profile between the user session and the repository. In fact, if you are using View Persona Management, even though this service is required, you should not use a VSS-based backup application. This can potentially cause corruption of files, which generally is not a good thing.

The Microsoft Software Shadow Copy Provider service, used as a mechanism for backup, should not be confused with Windows Backup. The Windows Backup service allows for the backup of individual workstations. But in a virtualized environment the desktops are located within the datacenter, and backups are performed either with the Microsoft Software Shadow Copy Provider service or with the backup mechanism that takes care of the centralized files, and personas are kept as per organizational policy.

Because the environment will be hosted within the datacenter and any remote sessions will come through either a View Security Server or a point-to-point VPN, the Secure Socket Tunneling Protocol Service is unnecessary. This service is meant for virtual private network (VPN) connections from the desktop to a VPN broker. Because the desktop has no need to do this, this is definitely a service that should be set to Disable.

The Security Center service might seem an odd service to turn off, but it is appropriate to set this service to Disable for virtual desktops because the features it provides are better provided outside of the guest OS in larger organizations. The Security Center service monitors whether security features like host-based firewall, antivirus, malware detection, and other security programs are running. Because these services often add additional I/O when using traditional versions of them (rather than versions optimized for virtual desktops), it is best not to use them. Products such as vShield Endpoint Protection and other similar vApps, where the protective service runs outside of the virtual machine, are better for overall disk I/O.

One thing that Microsoft attempted to do for Windows Vista (and tried to improve in Windows 7) was to be proactive about starting and loading applications to help speed up performance through the introduction of a service called Superfetch. It uses an algorithm based on commonly used applications to determine what applications would benefit from being cached in memory. Because memory for a virtual machine can be done at a disk level (vswp) as well as within the guest operating system (pagefile.sys), Superfetch use might cause problems for a virtual desktop.

This is one service that should be thoroughly tested to verify whether disabling it will adversely affect specific applications. For most virtual desktop environments, it is safe to disable this service. However, there are always unique cases where specific applications behave differently. One option is to "partially" leverage the Superfetch service by limiting it to just applications. You can also adjust the shadow storage size. The following steps describe how to adjust Superfetch settings. This should be done in the master image/template so that it is pre-optimized when clones are deployed:

Step 1. Click the **Start** button and type **regedit** in the Search box.

Step 2. Press **Enter**.

Step 3. Navigate to the following key location:

HKEY_LOCAL_MACHINE\SYSTEM\CurrentControlSet\Control\SessionManager\MemoryManagement\PrefetchParameters

Step 4. Double-click the **Enable Superfetch** key. By default the value will be 3. Change this value to one that is appropriate:

0 = Disable Superfetch

1 = Cache applications only

2 = Cache boot files only

3 = Cache everything (default)

Step 5. Choose the value and click **OK**.

Step 6. Select **File** from the top menu and click **Exit**.

Step 7. Click the **Start** button and type **C:\Windows\Prefetch** in the Search box.

A Windows Explorer window showing the contents of this location should open.

Step 8. Delete all the files in this location.

Step 9. Restart the Windows OS. The first reboot might take longer because Superfetch will need to repopulate the C:\Windows\Prefetch location with the appropriate files, depending on which option was chosen.

The decision as to whether to run Superfetch also depends on the kind of virtual machine being used and the disk density of the storage device. Those decisions are generally made during the design phase and are thus beyond the scope of this exam. As a best practice, an administrator should consult the appropriate personnel about the design before making these configuration changes.

Another service that can be disabled is the Themes service. Themes were first introduced with Windows 98 and the Plus! add-on. The idea was to enable end users to customize the desktop look and feel to whatever they wanted. Users could have dancing hamsters, leaves falling, or magical snowy backgrounds. All these animations increase the overall utilization of both CPU and memory resources, which can present a challenge for virtual desktops. VMware recommends disabling this service to reduce resource utilization and improve performance. However, it is a required service for Windows Aero and must be enabled if Windows Aero will be used. If a decision has been made to use Windows Aero, the environment should be tested to ensure that the functionality can be supported without undue performance impact. It might be that not every desktop will need Aero, or perhaps you can offer Aero as an optional desktop choice for some users. The default setting is for it to automatically start. If possible, though, you should set this to Disable.

During the Internet boom of the late 1990s and early 2000s, Windows was one of the more prolific operating systems and was the main target for worm, virus, and other malware creators. Most of these developers depended on users not being savvy with regard to the protection of their systems, and for the most part they were correct. Although Microsoft was not in the antivirus or antimalware business, it did recognize the need for these services. In 2004, it acquired GIANT AntiSpyware (originally developed by GIANT Company Software, Inc.). The idea was to include a combo antivirus/antimalware program as part of the OS so that users would not have to determine which third-party application they should trust. In 2006, Windows Defender was officially released as part of Windows Vista. The initial version of this application was limited to antimalware capabilities. Subsequent versions added an antivirus component, and today both Windows 7 and Windows 8 provide full coverage by default.

The inclusion of the antimalware portion was critical as users ventured more and more out to the Internet and spyware was becoming more and more prevalent. For home users and small offices, this is a nice piece of software to help secure desktops. However, in organizations, it is not sufficient because the user can turn off the protection. In addition, the program regularly scans the hard drive for any potential unwelcomed "visitors." For a virtual enterprise environment, using something like vShield Endpoint or a similar product, where the scan occurs in active processes through the hypervisor, results in less disk I/O impact compared to traditional system protection software. If Defender is going to be used in an enterprise environment, no change needs to be made. If an enterprise application will be employed, you should change this service from the default of Automatic to Disable.

Another service with similar conditions is the Windows Firewall service. This service began with Windows XP as the Internet Connection Firewall service (ICS), which was a basic firewall application. By default, the service was disabled, largely because of concerns about compatibility with existing programs. However, this mindset changed after the Blaster and Sasser worms began to ravage the Internet. With Windows XP Service Pack 2, the service was renamed and significantly improved. One of the main improvements was that the service was enabled by default. With each release, Microsoft has added significant improvements to this service. If this will be the only firewall for your virtual desktops, leave the service running. It is best to ensure that the settings for the service are controlled by Group Policy Objects (GPOs) and that appropriate settings for access are configured. If an organizational firewall will be in place, whether physical or software based, this service should be disabled.

It might seem odd to disable the Windows Error Reporting service, but the logic behind doing so is twofold. This service (originally known as Dr. Watson) was designed as a way for application developers to get error reports sent to them, over the Internet, when errors occurred. This would help lead to better programs and fewer issues. Although this is a good idea for the average home user, for organizations it is better for the IT team to be aware of any issues and address them as part of their support mandate. For an ideal virtual desktop environment, any support application would be virtualized and in a central location where logs would be collected. In addition, because of the nature of virtualization, the number of errors that occur due to conflict with other programs (the more common scenario) will lessen significantly. This brings us back to the clean image concept. Assuming a clean image was used, the need for this service is minimal, and the performance impact from using the service makes it disadvantageous. This service defaults to Manual, but you should set it to Disable.

The Windows Media Center was designed as a way for Windows to control various media devices and to provide access to various devices like TV tuners or FM access. The Windows Media Center Receiver service and the Windows Media Center Scheduler service are not needed for desktops because there is no access to a device like a tuner on the ESXi host. Both services default to Manual, but you should set them to Disable.

The states of the last three services that we look at here depend on use cases and fall into the "it depends" category. The utility of the Windows Search service, the Windows Update service, and the Offline Files service depend largely on how and if they are needed and used. The Windows Search service enables users to find files or folders on the desktop. If very little virtual desktop searching is necessary, you should disable this service. In environments where searching is necessary, it is wise to reduce the density of desktops found within the datastore to help reduce conflicting I/O behavior from the resulting searches against other desktops with similar activity.

The Windows Update service, another service introduced with Windows 98, was originally designed to give users access to additional themes, games, driver updates, and other features not found with the base operating system. Over time, however, this service came to be used for patch management, the most notable being the Y2K fixes. The ability to keep the system up to date in the face of challenges and threats from the Internet has been critical to keeping Windows systems running. However, for virtual environments (particularly linked clones), this service might not be needed. The base image and any patching should come from a central location after sufficient testing of the patch has been performed. (To this day, I still have nightmares over NT4 and Service Pack 6.) Linked clones should never have the Windows Update service running because a refresh would cause any updates to no longer exist. It is better to have the update applied to the base image and a recompose done to ensure that the whole pool has the updated features as part of the desktops. The default setting for the Windows Update service is Automatic, so this should be changed to Disable unless needed (say, for a local mode desktop or fully provisioned virtual machines).

The last service, the Offline Files service, was created to enable users to access files even when the network is down. Because the virtual environment is based on the network, this service is not really needed. Again, the exception would be for local mode desktops. The default for this service is Manual, but you should change it to Disable.

You can disable all of these services manually via the graphical user interface (GUI), or you can disable them through command-line options or even a PowerShell script. To do this via a script, use the following syntax:

```
Powershell Set-Service <Service Name> -startuptype "disabled"
```

The *VMware View Optimization Guide for Windows 7* comes with two batch-shell scripts, one for environments leveraging Persona Management and one for use without Persona Management. These scripts will disable all the services reviewed in this section. Because the scripts are text based, you can modify them as needed to ensure that master images are configured according to use case requirements.

A last thought with regard to these services is this: Disabling these services makes complete sense for virtual desktops that reside in the datacenter. If local mode will be used, any desktops that run locally can actually benefit from leaving these services running. While disabling the services can provide some performance optimizations, the use cases should be carefully considered before any changes are made.

Additionally, the services may still need to be used for any physical desktops that will exist in the environment. This highlights the importance of having a separate organizational unit (OU) for the virtual desktops apart from that of any physical desktops. Conversely, it might be important to block the effects of GPOs used for the physical desktops from being applied on the virtual desktops because those GPOs may have an adverse effect.

To help with the variety of GPOs that could be used within an environment, leverage loopback policy processing. This will tie the use of GPOs to the computer OU the user is in and ensure that the appropriate GPOs are applied, particularly when users move between different desktop OUs.

Although the majority of the optimization benefits come from disabling services, some benefits derive from GPOs being leveraged or through manual adjustments to the master computer image. The assumption may be that everything should be removed or disabled, but certain settings are required, such as enabling RDP access. If these settings are not configured as part of the base image and the user needs RDP to access the desktop, this would present an obvious challenge for accessing the environment. In this section, we take a look at adjustments that should be made using the GPO Editor. To get to the editor, follow these steps:

Step 1. Click the **Start** button.

Step 2. In the Search box, type **MMC**. This opens a blank Microsoft Management Console (MMC).

Step 3. Select **File** from the menu.

Step 4. Choose **Add or Remove Snap-ins**.

Step 5. From the Available Snap-ins list, find **Group Policy Object Editor**.

Step 6. Click the **Add** button.

Step 7. For the Group Policy Object, choose either **Local Computer** (beneficial for computer specific policies like Themes) or the appropriate domain.

Step 8. Click **Finish** and verify that the snap-in shows in the Selected Snap-ins window.

Step 9. Click **OK**.

Over the years, Microsoft has tried to get end users to realize the importance of addressing security issues and updates. Of equal importance was identifying when a Windows system did not have enough protection in place when the user was online. As Microsoft introduced more security features as part of the Windows OS, it became important to let users know when those security services (such as Windows Firewall or Windows Defender) or replacement services weren't running so that the user would be aware of the issue, and thus protect the OS. To that end, Microsoft added a mechanism to alert users when a vulnerability was present.

Originally known as the Windows Security Center, the Windows Action Center lets users know when those services are not enabled or available and it provides diagnostic advice on how to address maintenance issues (for example, patch updates). Given that the services might have been disabled as part of the optimization process, this could result in warnings that would be unnecessary in a virtual desktop environment and resources being used by the Action Center. By default, this service cannot be turned off completely. However, through a GPO setting, you can disable and remove the Action Center by changing the value of the Remove the Action Center Icon to Enabled in the Administrative Templates under User Configuration, as shown in Figure 6-2. This needs to be done for VDI environments because the security comes through mechanisms in the datacenter rather than through the Guest OS.

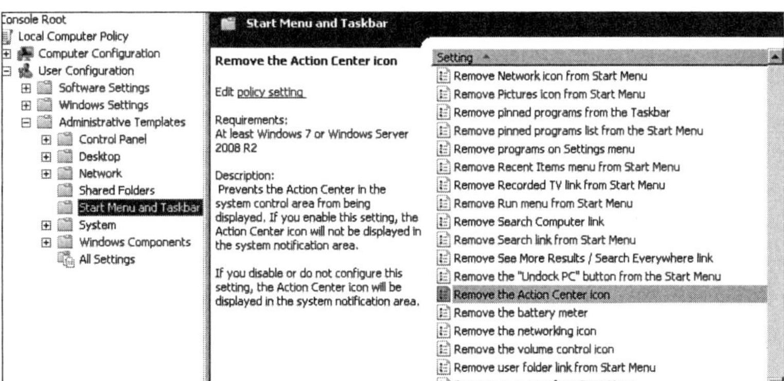

Figure 6-2 GPO of Action Center

Most applications leave a trail of their activities within the event log. This helps users troubleshoot when application issues arise. The default size of the logs is 1024KB (or 1MB). Depending on the number and complexities of applications on the desktop, the values for these logs might need to be adjusted. You can adjust the various log sizes, in chunks of 64KB, by going to the Event Log Service in the Administrative Templates under Computer Configuration. This particular setting would benefit from being specific to the image rather than applied from the domain.

The same is true for GPO configuration if the Windows Firewall is going to be used. If the Firewall service is disabled, there is no need for a GPO configuration. If the firewall is used, it will be necessary to adjust the settings for items such as Define Port Exceptions, Allow Logging, Allow Remote Desktop Exception, and other features would be necessary for a virtual desktop. The choices made will depend on the use case of the desktop. As part of the test of the master image, adjust each setting one at a time until you reach your required security level.

Internet Explorer is the browser that many users choose for their web experience. If this browser is used in your environment, you must be aware of two settings, one under Computer Configuration and one under User Configuration, that must be adjusted to ensure a better end-user experience. The first, Internet Explorer Settings (cache), is found under User Configuration. By default, Internet Explorer has a cache of 50MB. To improve performance and behavior, you can configure the setting for temporary Internet files to delete upon browser closure. This helps reduce the amount of space used by the browser on the desktops and ensures that data is not carried over from session to session, particularly for fully provisioned virtual machines that are in a floating pool. You can find this setting at **Administrative Templates > Windows Components > Internet Explorer > Internet Control Panel > Advanced Page**.

The second setting, Internet Explorer Settings (using the First Run Wizard), enables you to configure the default behavior of Internet Explorer when it is first launched. By default, Internet Explorer starts by going to the Welcome to IE page. However, this can be changed to a home page appropriate for your users. If you configure this setting in a GPO, you can prevent users from changing the default home page to another that could be detrimental to the performance of the virtual desktop. Because this setting is applied to the computer configuration, this can be done as part of the master image to ensure that it carries over to all users. You can find this setting in the Administrative Templates at **Windows Components > Internet Explorer**.

Each use case can have a different default home page if necessary because the home page option is configured under User Configuration and can be applied to different OUs. The default home page option is found in the Important URLs GPO under Internet Explorer Maintenance in the Windows Settings section. You can configure other URLs here, too, such as the Search bar URL and Online support page URL. You can configure each setting as appropriate for the organization.

When files are deleted on a Windows system they end up in the Recycle Bin. The files are not deleted until you choose Empty Recycle Bin, and even then the files are not actually deleted and can be recovered using the Restore option. Beginning with Windows Vista, the ability to recover recycled files became possible for each drive. The capability to allow or disallow the recovery can either be adjusted via GPO or configured in the Registry. In a virtual environment, enabling this setting using a GPO allows you to apply it based on each use case found within the environment rather than as a *carte blanche* setting. You can find this setting under **User Configuration > Administrative Templates > Windows Components > Windows Explorer**.

Although PCoIP is the default protocol for a View implementation, some end-user clients must use RDP. To ensure that those users can connect using RDP, and to enable the use of network-level authentication, you must enable the settings found in Administrative Templates under Computer Configuration. In the **Windows Components > Remote Desktop Services > Remote Desktop Session Host**, you can enable the Connections and the Security options.

In the information age, keeping up to date on information can be a challenge. One often used technique is to utilize Rich Site Summary (RSS) feeds. With RSS, websites can publish brief synapses of information to a browser link or other location so that interested individuals are made aware of changes or to aggregate website updates from a variety of sites. To help keep these feeds up to date on a Windows system, Windows 7 typically runs this service in the background. Not surprisingly, this can have an adverse performance effect. Some users (for example, power users or local mode users) might require this feature, so disabling it for them would not be beneficial. If a use case requires the feature to be disabled, you can do so in the Windows Components of the Administrative Templates under User Configuration.

Screensavers were first implemented as a way to save cathode ray tube (CRT) monitors from "ghost" burn-in of the desktop. Over the years, as newer technology was introduced, the need to use screensavers for that purpose lessened, and screensavers began to be used more commonly for security and/or entertainment purposes. The challenge with screensavers is that the more complex they are (for example, screensavers that show a lot of images or have many moving parts) the greater the possibility of a performance hit. In virtual environments, screensavers not only cause performance issues, but in some cases they have been known to cause the desktop to hang. So, the general rule is to not enable screensavers.

For environments that need screensavers (for example, in environments where users forget to lock their desktops), it is worthwhile to configure a GPO for users. As part of the configuration, you can configure specific features of the screensaver so that it works in a manner that benefits both the user and the organization. These features include configuring a requirement for a password to be used to unlock the screensaver, setting a timeout period of inactivity before launching the screensaver, and choosing a specific screensaver. Because these settings are tied to the user configuration under the Control Panel in the Administrative Templates, they will follow the user regardless of the desktop he uses (if that is the desired result).

As the Windows operating system became more and more mainstream, drivers, applications, updates, hardware changes, and more were added to the environment in so many different permutations that the resultant side effects could not be predicted. As a result, these variations could potentially leave a desktop unstable and unusable, frustrating users because of the time needed to perform a full reinstall or an in-place upgrade. These frustrations don't even account for the possibility of data loss. Because of this issue, Microsoft introduced System Restore, which allows the OS to be restored to a previous state that was functional (sometimes referred to as last known good state). This feature first appeared in Microsoft Me and has evolved over the years. For environments that have a wide variety of hardware/software combinations, this feature has saved more than a few users from having to do a full reinstallation due to the installation of faulty hardware or software.

Because virtual hardware never changes for virtual environments, and because the base Guest OS is configured based on the virtual hardware configuration, the need to return to a last known good state is lessened significantly. As a result, System Restore becomes an unnecessary feature, especially for desktops like those found in a linked-clone pool. So, it is beneficial to configure the Computer Configuration GPO to turn off System Restore. You can find this under the Administrative Templates in the System section.

The use of desktop wallpaper represents another challenge for desktops in a similar vein as screensavers do. The challenge with wallpapers is that they consist of complex images that can cause performance degradation. To alleviate performance concerns, you should configure the desktop to use either a solid-color background or no background. To configure the desktop not to use a background image (and use the default color associated with the desktop profile) using a GPO, go to the GPO Editor under User Configuration in the Desktop section of the Administrative Templates and set the value for Desktop Wallpaper equal to a blank space. The other option is to set the value to a nonexistent file. This will prevent user changes to the desktop background.

Although some might think that the Windows Sideshow service is related to a screensaver concept, it actually relates to how information is displayed on secondary display devices, including mobile phones, tablets, and so on. Because the desktop is located in the datacenter, this is not possible. So, disabling this feature via GPO is important because this will reduce the number of services active on the base image. You can find this particular GPO under Computer Configuration in the Administrative Templates within the subgroup of Windows Components. Just enable the **Turn Off Windows Sideshow** option.

Summary

This chapter covered a significant amount of information related to optimizing the virtual desktop by optimizing the underlying operating system. The operating system features enabled or disabled should not be chosen based only on the performance benefit but also based on the use case for the desktop. This will ensure that the configuration satisfies the use case while also providing the best possible performance. Without properly optimizing the virtual desktop, there is a good chance that the end user experience will suffer regardless of the chosen protocol.

In the next chapter, we look at a unique desktop configuration known as kiosk mode.

Exam Preparation Tasks

Review All Key Topics

Review the most important topics in the chapter, noted with the Key Topic icon in the outer margin of the page. Table 6-3 lists a reference of these key topics and the page numbers on which each is found.

Table 6-3 Key Topics

Key Topic Element	Description	Page
List	How to create a build and optimize a virtual desktop	136
Step list	How to install the View Agent	140
Table 6-2	VMware View Agent Custom Installation Options	141
Figure 6-2	Image showing the GPO for Action Center	151

Define Key Terms

Define the following key terms from this chapter and check your answers in the Glossary:

EOIT/BYOD, IOPS, P2V, MDT, ThinApp, master image

Review Questions

You can find the answers to these review questions in Appendix A.

1. An end user has difficulty logging in to his View desktop. Upon investigation, the administrator discovers that time synchronization is not configured. Which step should the administrator perform to correct the issue?
   - **a.** Let Active Directory reset the virtual machine time.
   - **b.** Set the virtual desktop to sync time with the ESXi host.
   - **c.** Set the virtual desktop to sync time with another virtual desktop.
   - **d.** Let Active Directory reset the virtual machine token time.

2. A CEO decides to let employees purchase their own laptops or tablets for use as a work device. Which of the following acronyms describes this policy?
   a. EOIT
   b. COIT
   c. BYOB
   d. PCOD

3. It is important to "right size" a virtual machine. What does this term refer to?
   a. Allocating maximum memory and CPU resources
   b. Using P2V to create the virtual desktop
   c. Sizing a virtual machine for all four "food group" types: CPU, memory, disk, and network
   d. Sizing a virtual machine for all four "food group" types: pizza, soda, ice cream, and chips

4. VMware recommends creating a master image from scratch. What method is strongly discouraged from being used to create a master image?
   a. Template-created image
   b. Clone-created image
   c. P2V-created image
   d. MDT-created image

5. What option is not a valid choice when installing the View Agent using custom installation options?
   a. View Composer Agent
   b. Virtual Printing
   c. RDP Smartcard
   d. View Persona Management

6. What service is needed if Aero is to be used in a Windows 7 virtual desktop?
   a. Desktop Window Manager Session Manager
   b. Aero Desktop Window Manager
   c. Desktop Windows Session Manager
   d. Aero Window Manager Session Manager

7. Which service should be disabled because the virtual hardware in a master image will not be altered?
   a. Diagnostic Policy Service
   b. Master Hardware Service
   c. Hardware Diagnostic Service
   d. Diagnostic Hardware Service

8. If you use a VSS backup service, what service should not be used?
   a. Roaming profiles
   b. Persona Management
   c. Profiles service
   d. Persona service

9. What is the main reason for disabling the Windows Defender service?
   a. Causes too much I/O during scans
   b. Not available in Windows 8
   c. Causes too much swapping
   d. Only works with Internet Explorer

10. What common Windows element should be disabled or locked via GPO to help improve a performance impact and to prevent the virtual desktop from locking up?
    a. Accessibility
    b. Screensaver
    c. Screen resolution
    d. RSS feeds

This chapter covers the following subjects:

- **Preparing for Kiosk Mode:** This section illustrates the steps required to prepare the environment for kiosk mode.
- **Enabling Kiosk Mode:** This section describes the use of the `vdmadmin` command.
- **Additional Configuration Options:** This section illustrates the different options available with the `vdmadmin -Q` command.

(This chapter covers part of Objective 2.11 of the Blueprint.)

CHAPTER 7

Kiosk Mode

You can use kiosk mode to automatically launch a VMware View Client from a locked-down PC or ThinClient after automatically logging in to the operating system. This would be useful for healthcare, hotel kiosks, airport kiosks, and so on. Kiosk mode is ideal anywhere an application could be used that you want to make available to your customers without having to worry about physically administering the machine or turning over access to a secure workstation. Getting kiosk mode up and running for a VMware View environment requires several steps, as you can probably imagine, and this chapter illustrates how to configure and enable/disable kiosk mode and discusses all the available options.

"Do I Know This Already?" Quiz

The "Do I Know This Already?" quiz allows you to assess whether you should read this entire chapter or simply jump to the "Exam Preparation Tasks" section for review. If you are in doubt, read the entire chapter. Table 7-1 outlines the major headings in this chapter and the corresponding "Do I Know This Already?" quiz questions. You can find the answers in Appendix A, "Answers to the 'Do I Know This Already?' Quizzes and Review Questions."

Table 7-1 "Do I Know This Already?" Foundation Topics Section-to-Question Mapping

Foundation Topics Section	Questions Covered in This Section
Preparing for Kiosk Mode	5
Enabling Kiosk Mode	1–3
Additional Configuration Options	4

1. Where do you enable kiosk mode for a View environment?
   a. View Manager
   b. vSphere Client
   c. VMware View Client
   d. VMware View Connection Server

2. What command do you use to enable kiosk mode on a Connection Server?
   a. vdmadmin -Q -clientauth -setdefaults -ou "OU=<Kiosk OU>,DC=<domain name>,DC=<top-level domain>" -noexpirepassword -group <group name>
   b. viewadmin -Q --clientauth -setdefaults -ou "OU=<Kiosk OU >,DC=<domain name>,DC<top-level domain>" -noexpirepassword -group <group name>
   c. kioskmode --enable
   d. vdmadmin -Q -enable --kiosk

3. What identifiers can be used to add a client account to Active Directory? (Select two correct answers.)
   a. MAC address
   b. IP address
   c. Account name
   d. SID

4. What does the command vdmadmin -Q -clientauth -removeall do?
   a. Resets all kiosk client passwords
   b. Removes all kiosk client accounts
   c. Removes all View users from Active Directory
   d. Removes the kiosk password requirement

5. Which of the following cannot be used as a kiosk machine?
   a. A physical PC running Microsoft Windows
   b. A physical PC running Linux
   c. A ThinClient
   d. A MAC Pro workstation

Foundation Topics

Preparing for Kiosk Mode

Kiosk mode allows client devices, or endpoints, to be used as kiosks for a wide range of applications. Common applications include hospital admission, hotel registration, and airline check-in. Kiosks could be used for these types of services. They also can be useful for providing web browsing stations in similar locations.

VMware View kiosk mode consists of a physical end device, or client device, with a minimal security footprint. This could be a device running a hardened Linux or Windows operating system, a ThinClient device, or a device with an embedded operating system. Older devices can also be repurposed as kiosk machines, especially if those devices no longer have the hardware to allow them to be useful as a standard View system. The physical client device will boot, and can log in to the operating system automatically if desired to reduce the amount of manual administration that is required. For this to be useful, the end device should be as locked down as possible to prevent someone from gaining control of the operating system and any potential data. On startup of the operating system, the device should automatically launch the VMware View Client in unattended mode via the command line. After the virtual desktop session has been established, the View Client automatically logs in to the desktop. The control bar usually visible at the top of the screen used to disconnect/attach USB devices and so forth will not be present. From this point on, the View desktop is indistinguishable from the local physical desktop.

Before you can utilize client devices as kiosks, you must complete some preliminary steps to ensure that the devices are secured and configured properly:

- Create an Active Directory organizational unit (OU) for use by the kiosk machines only.
- Configure the virtual machines to be used as kiosks.
- Build the desktop pool in View Manager for the kiosk systems.
- When creating a pool for the kiosk machines, it is best to create a manual pool with dedicated assignment. It is possible to configure the pool for automatic assignment, but because kiosk machines are going to have only one user, and you typically know exactly how many machines are needed, there's no need to create an automated pool.

NOTE Although there is no technical requirement for creating different OUs and groups in Active Directory for kiosk mode, it is highly recommended.

Enabling Kiosk Mode

Enabling kiosk mode requires many configuration steps and a fair amount of planning up front. It is not as simple as just deploying physical machines and creating VMware View pools (although that is involved). The following section outlines the general steps to configure kiosk mode at a high level. Throughout the rest of this chapter, we delve into these steps in a lot more detail.

Steps Required to Configure Kiosk Mode

To configure and enable kiosk mode at a high level, follow these steps:

Step 1. Configure Active Directory.

Step 2. Configure the Connection Servers to be used by the kiosks.

Step 3. Identify the MAC addresses of the physical client devices if you want accounts that are MAC address based.

Step 4. Add accounts for the VMware View Clients that will run in kiosk mode.

Step 5. Configure and enable authentication for the VMware View Clients that are running in kiosk mode.

Step 6. Check the configuration to verify kiosk mode has been set up properly.

Step 7. Test kiosk mode from the physical client devices.

Configuring Active Directory

You first need to configure Active Directory for the kiosks, so that they are separated from the rest of the environment. This way, settings applied to the kiosks will not affect other machines (the other View desktops, for example) or users who will not be using kiosk mode. This section assumes that we are not going to use existing OUs or groups or users.

In Active Directory, create a new OU and a new group. You should also create new user accounts for the kiosks to allow for the systems to automatically log in upon boot.

Configuring the Connection Server

On the Connection Server (and any Connection Server you intend to allow the kiosks to attach to), you have to use the `vdmadmin` command to configure the Connection Server to allow this connection. You can find the command in the following path: C:\Program Files\VMware\VMware View\Server\Tools\bin. You should either execute the command from this path or add the path to an environment variable. You should also run the command with a user who has been given the Administrators role. The command syntax is as follows:

```
vdmadmin -Q -clientauth -setdefaults -ou "OU=<Kiosk OU>,DC=<domain
 name>,DC=<top-level domain>" -noexpirepassword -group <group name>
```

The `vdmadmin -Q` command has additional options that we will explore in more detail. First, let's break down the `vdmadmin` command syntax:

- **`vdmadmin:`** The command to enable/disable kiosk mode.
- **`-Q:`** This option configures the account in Active Directory and in the View Manager configuration.
- **`-clientauth:`** This option enables authentication for the kiosk clients.
- **`-setdefaults:`** Uses the default values when the client accounts are added.
- **`-ou:`** This specifies the OU to use for the kiosks in addition to the domain name.
- **`-noexpirepassword:`** This option defines that an account password doesn't expire.
- **`-group:`** This option identifies the Active Directory group to associate with the kiosks and where the client accounts will be added. The group name must be the pre-Windows 2000 group name.

Here is an example of this command in an actual environment:

```
vdmadmin -Q -clientauth -setdefaults -ou "OU=kiosks,DC=vmware,DC=com"
-noexpirepassword -group KioskUsers
```

Table 7-2 outlines the settings available with the `vdmadmin` command.

Table 7-2 `vdmadmin` Command Options

Option	Notes
`-A`	**Agent logging:** Configure logging for the View Agent or to override the IP address that the View Agent provides. Suboptions for the `-A` option include the following: `-d - desktop`: Define the pool you want to manipulate. `-getDCT`: Create a Data Collection Tool (DCT) bundle and save it to a file. `-getlogfile` and `-logfile`: These two options can be used to define the name of the log file for saving a copy. `-getloglevel`: Retrieve the level of logging that is currently set for the View Agent. `-getstatus`: Retrieve the current status of the View Agent. `-getversion`: Get the current version of the View Agent. `-list`: List the log files for the View Agent. `-m`: Define the machine name of the virtual machine in the pool. `-outfile` and `-local_file`: These two switches enable you to define the name of the file to which you are saving the DCT bundle. `-setloglevel` *<level>*: Define the level of logging for the View Agent itself. The following are the valid logging levels: `debug`: Record error, warning, and debugging information. `normal`: Record error and warning events. `trace`: Record error, warning, informational, and debugging information. `-i -- ip_or_dns`: Define the IP address or DNS name. `-override`: Override an IP address. `-r - remove`: Remove an IP address that was overridden.
`-C`	**Connection Server group:** Define a name for the View Connection Server group so that it can be managed by Microsoft Systems Center Operations Manager (SCOM). There is one option to the `-C` command: `-c`: Define the name of the vCenter Connection Server group. If you do not define this option, the GUID is displayed. (`vdmadmin -C -c <View Connection Server Group>` or `vdmadmin -C`)

Option	Notes
`-F`	**Foreign security principals:** This option enables you to update the foreign security principals (FSPs) for allowing access through external domains. There is one option below the `-F` option: `-u`: Define an FSP for a user outside of the local domain. (`vdmadmin -F -u <External Domain Name>\<username>`)
`-H`	**Health status:** Display View Manager health status. This option has many different health monitors that the View Manager can use to view the health of the View environment. The following is a list of the health monitors: CBMonitor: View Connection Server health monitor. DBMonitor: Events database health monitor. DomainMonitor: Connection Server's local domain health monitor. SGMonitor: Security server and secure gateway service health monitor. TSMonitor: Transfer Server health monitor. VCMonitor: vCenter server health monitor The following `-H` additional options enable you to use one of these listed health monitors: `-instanceid`: View a specific health monitor instance. `-list`: View all of the health monitors. `-list -monitorid`: View all the monitors for the specific health monitor chosen. `-monitorid`: View a specific health monitor identifier.
`-I`	**Information:** Gather information on the View Manager. Additional options for the `-I` switch include the following: `-enddate <YYYY-MM-DD-HH:mm:ss>`: Define an end date for the information listed. `-list`: View all available reports. `-report`: Determine a specific report. `-startdate <YYYY-MM-DD-HH:MM:SS>`: Define a start date for the information listed. `-view`: Determine a specific view.

Option	Notes
-L	**Link or unlink a desktop to a user (assignment):** Can be used to assign or unassign a dedicated View desktop to a user. Additional options for the -L switch include the following: -d <pool name>: Define the name of the View desktop pool. -m <machine name>: Define the name of the virtual machine. -r: Remove assignment for an individual user (to be used with the -u switch) or for all assignments to the virtual desktop. -u <domain name\username>: Define the domain\username.
-M	**Machine information:** List virtual or physical machine configuration information. Additional command switches under the -M option include the following: -d <desktop pool>: View information about the specified pool. -m <machine name>: View information about the specified virtual machine. -u <domain\username>: View information for domain\user.
-N	**Domain filtering:** This option enables you to configure domain filters. In the case of large environments, it might be useful to limit the number of domains visible. This option requires additional settings: -add: Add a domain to the filtered list. -domain <domain name>: The domain to be filtered (NetBIOS name). -domains: Define the domain filtering setting. -exclude: Exclude the specified domain. -include: Include the specified domain. -list: View the excluded and included domains in the filter list. -remove: Remove a domain from the list. -removeall: Remove all the domains from the filter list. -s <Connection Server>: Define the Connection Server to which the filtering will be applied. If no Connection Server is defined, the filtering applies to all Connection Servers. -search: Specify the domain to search exclusion list.

Option	Notes
`-O`	**Assignments without entitlements:** Display desktop assignments for users who aren't entitled to those same desktops. Additional options for the `-O` switch include the following: `-ld`: Sort the output by desktop. `-lu`: Sort the output by user. `-noxslt`: Define the default stylesheet not be applied to the XML output. `-xsltpath <path>`: Define the path to the stylesheet to be used. There are XML stylesheets that can be applied to the output of the preceding commands to determine how the output is formatted for HTML. The stylesheets are located in the following directory: C:\Program Files\VMware\VMware View\server\etc
`-P`	**Policies (user):** Displays policies for users who aren't entitled to use the machine. When an administrator removes an entitlement for a user, the desktop assignment is not removed automatically.
`-Q`	This option can be used to enable/disable kiosk mode, add accounts, enable authentication, and verify the kiosk mode settings. This is the most common command option, and we use this option throughout this chapter.
`-R`	**Report user:** Lists the first user who accesses a desktop. There is one additional option for this command switch: `-i`: Define the IP address of the desktop. (`vdmadmin -R -i <IP address>`)
`-S`	If a Connection Server has been removed or decommissioned and is no longer being used, it will still show up in the View Manager. You can use the `-s` option to remove the entry.
`-T`	**Transfer Server split limit:** This option sets the split limit for packages of View Transfer Servers.
`-U`	**User information:** List information about users (desktops they are entitled to use, ThinApp application assignment, and VMware View roles). An additional `-u` option enables you to specify the domain and name of the user. (`vdmadmin -U -u <domain\username> -n -xml`)

Option	Notes
`-V`	**Virtual machine decryption:** This option can be used to lock or unlock virtual machines or to decrypt a virtual machine to recover data. This could be useful for a checked-out virtual machine (local mode desktop) whose physical device has been lost or stolen. Additional options include the following: `-d <desktop pool name>`: Define the name of the pool. `-infile <path to file>`: Define the .vmx or .vmdk file location for the virtual machine. `-u <domain\username>`: Domain\username for the desktop. `-e`: Unlock a virtual machine. `-m <machine name>`: Define the name of the virtual machine. `-p`: Lock a virtual machine. `-vcdn <vCenter distinguished name>`: Specify the distinguished name of the vCenter server. `-vmpath <path>`: Define the inventory location (path) of the virtual machine.
`-X`	**Fix duplicate LDAP entries:** Identify and repair any duplicate Lightweight Directory Access Protocol (LDAP) entries. Additional options include the following: `-collisions`: Enable detecting LDAP collisions for the Connection Server group. `-resolve`: Resolve all LDAP collisions.

The following are some examples of using the `vdmadmin` command:

- View the status of the View agent:

  ```
  vdmadmin -A -b <username>@<domain> * -getstatus -xml -d <desktop
  pool> -m
  <machine name>
  ```

  (Alternatively, the login could be domain\username, and the `*` option will prompt for a password. Otherwise, one could be defined here.)

  This redirects the output to an XML file for the specified pool and machine name of the virtual machine in that pool.

- Capture all the logs, including the most verbose, from the View Agent:

  ```
  vdmadmin -A -b <domain>\<username> <password> -setloglevel trace
  -d <desktop pool> -m
  <machine name>
  ```

(In addition, you could define the following log levels: `debug` for error, warning, and debugging; `normal` for error and warning messages; and `trace`, which records error, warning, informational, and debugging events.)

- Change the logging level for the View Agent to log everything for assistance in troubleshooting:

```
vdmadmin -A -d <desktop pool> -m <virtual machine name>
-setloglevel
trace
```

- Remove all assignments to a virtual desktop:

```
vdmadmin -L -d <pool name> -m <machine name> -r
```

- Add a domain name to the filtered list:

```
vdmadmin -N -add -domain <NetBIOS domain name> -include
```

NOTE If you are running this command as someone other than a user with the Administrator role, you can run the command specifying another user account. This is done by adding the following to the command:

```
-b <authentication>
```

Where `<authentication>` is domain\username, username@domain, or username domain; and `<password>` is that user account's password.

NOTE All `vdmadmin` commands can be used with several options to redirect the output to a file. The following are available:

`-csv` to output to a CSV file

`-n` to output to a plain text file

`-w` to output using UTF-16 characters

`-xml` to output to an XML file

Identifying MAC Addresses of the Physical Client Devices

This step is optional and is required only if you want to have accounts created based on the MAC address of the client. Creating accounts in this method makes sense because each physical device will have a unique MAC address. Perform this configuration using the following steps:

Step 1. Log in to the physical client device and open a command prompt (Windows-based device) or shell (Linux-based device).

Step 2. For Windows-based devices, enter the following:

```
C:\Program Files\VMware\VMware View\Client\bin\wswc
-printEnvironmentInfo
```

Step 3. For Linux-based devices, enter the following:

```
vmware-view -printEnvironmentInfo -s <Connection Server>
```

Where `<Connection Server>` is the name of your VMware View Connection Server

Both of these commands give you the same basic information, though the Linux command generates slightly more detail. The information provided includes the IP address, MAC address, and machine name.

Adding Accounts

Now that we've retrieved the MAC address for the physical client device, we can add the accounts to Active Directory. This command must be issued on the Connection Server (or one of the Connection Servers in the Connection Server group) to which the client device will attach. The following is the command syntax:

```
vdmadmin -Q -clientauth -add -domain <domain name> -clientid <MAC
address> -group <group name>
```

Where `<domain name>` is the domain name (for example, `VMWARE`), `<MAC address>` is the MAC address of the physical device you discovered in the previous step, and `<group name>` is the name of the group you want to add this account to.

If you do not want to use MAC addresses client identification, you can instead specify names for the accounts. If you choose this method, the accounts must start with the name *custom-*. If they do not, the prefix would have to be defined in the Active Directory Application Mode (ADAM) database (in the `pae-ClientAuthPrefix` multivalued attribute under cn=common, ou=global, ou=properties, dc=vdi, dc=vmware, dc=int on a View Connection Server). Using a naming convention other than *custom-* has some drawbacks: The prefix cannot exceed 20 characters, and each device should get its own specified name.

> **NOTE** Some ThinClients only allow account names that begin with custom- or cm-. When in doubt, check your vendor's documentation.

When adding this account, you can supply some additional information. For example, you can add a description to the account that will be listed in Active Directory to identify why the account was created. You could also specify passwords. Table 7-3 provides examples of additional options.

Table 7-3 Kiosk Mode Account Options

Key Topic

Option	Notes
-clientid	The name or MAC address of the VMware View Client or physical client device.
-description	This option can be used to describe the account and will be visible in Active Directory.
-domain	Defines the domain that the client is a member of.
-expirepassword	Sets the password expiration of the client account to the value defined for the View Connection Server or Connection Server group. If this option is not defined, the password doesn't expire.
-genpassword	Generates a password for the client account. The password that is generated with this option is a 16-digit, alphanumeric, mixed-case password. You can manually define a more complex password using the -password option.
-group	Defines the group to which the client account is added. This has to be the pre-Windows 2000 group name.
-noexpirepassword	Defines that the password never expires.
-nogroup	Does not add the client account to a group.
-ou	Defines the organization unit to add the account.
-password	Defines a password manually. After this option, you type the password. This option is used in place of the -genpassword option if a more complex password is required.

NOTE You can also add accounts by specifying a username rather than a MAC address. VMware recommends configuring kiosk account usernames with a *custom-* prefix to work with all physical devices. The following is the syntax for creating an account with a username:

```
vdmadmin -Q -clientauth -setdefaults -ou "OU=<kiosk OU>,DC=<domain
name>,DC=<top-level domain> -noexpirepassword -group <kiosk group>
```

Where <kiosk OU> is the organizational unit you created for the kiosks, <domain name> is the domain name, <top-level domain> is the top-level domain (.com, .net, and so on), and <kiosk group> is the group created for the kiosks in AD.

Configuring and Enabling Authentication

You configure authentication using the `vdmadmin` command on the Connection Server (any one of them in the group) that the client will connect to. The following is the command syntax to enable authentication of the client device:

```
vdmadmin -Q -enable -s <Connection Server FQDN>
```

Where `<Connection Server>` is the name of the VMware View Connection Server to which the client device will connect (NetBIOS name).

`-requirepassword` is the only additional option for this command. This option requires the View Client to enter a password.

> **NOTE** to disable authentication for a connection server, the syntax is as follows:
>
> ```
> vdmadmin -Q disable -s <Connection Server FQDN>
> ```

Checking Kiosk Mode Configuration

Verifying configuration of the kiosk mode client devices is also done using the `vdmadmin` command. Again, the command must be run from one of the Connection Servers. The following is the command syntax to verify the configuration:

```
vdmadmin -Q -clientauth -list
```

This command outputs information about the client devices, including client IDs, domain information, and authentication information. For example, the top of the list displays the authenticated users, while the bottom of the list shows the VMware View Connection Servers, whether the clients are authenticated and whether a password is required on the client device.

Testing Kiosk Mode

Now that the environment has been configured and verified, it should be tested from one of the client devices to ensure functionality. To automate the login process, you can launch the VMware View Client from the command line and create a script to be run on startup. A sample script has been provided for you in this location: C:\Program Files\VMware\VMware View\bin\kiosk_mode.cmd.

The command to launch the View Client varies by platform, and the syntax is as follows:

Windows Clients

```
C:\Program Files\VMware\VMware View\Client\bin\wswc -unattended
```

The `wswc -unattended` command assumes that the account was created using the MAC address and is connecting to the default VMware View Connection Server.

Table 7-4 describes some additional options for this client.

Table 7-4 VMware View Windows Client Command-Line Options

Key Topic

Option	Notes
`-serverURL`	Enables you to specify a Connection Server to connect to if you do not want to use the default Connection Server (or didn't define one when you installed the VMware View Client). This option requires the Connection Server IP address or fully qualified domain name (FQDN).
`-userName`	If you are not allowing the client to log in using its MAC address, you need to specify a user account here. Kiosk user accounts should all begin with *custom-* to be properly recognized.
`-password`	If you have set a password for the account that the client will use, a password must be defined in the command string.

An example using the additional options might look like this:

```
C:\Program Files\VMware\VMware View\Client\bin\wswc -unattended
-serverURL
<Connection Server FQDM> -userName <username> -password <password>
```

Linux Clients

```
vmware-view -unattended -s <Connection Server> --once
```

As with the Windows clients, this command assumes that accounts were configured using the client MAC address. Table 7-5 describes all the options available with this command.

Table 7-5 VMware View Linux Client Command-Line Options

Option	Notes
`--once`	Stops the View Client if an error message is generated. This is recommended because otherwise the client will continue trying to reconnect, and it might become necessary to terminate the process (vmware-view).
`-p`	Sets the password for the client account. If no password was defined, this option is not needed.

Option	Notes
`-s`	This option, followed by the Connection Server IP address or FQDN, tells the client where to connect.
`-u`	Sets the username for the client account if you didn't define the account by MAC address.

Additional Configuration Options

The commands and processes described in the preceding section are sufficient to configure kiosk mode for most environments. For custom configurations, other client configuration options are available. Table 7-6 explores all the options available with the `vdmadmin` command `-Q` option.

Table 7-6 Additional `vdmadmin -Q` Options

Option	Notes
`-add`	Adds a domain account for the client dedicated for kiosk mode.
`-clientauth`	Configures authentication of the kiosk mode client.
`-clientid`	Sets the name or MAC address of the client device.
`-description`	Provides a description for the account inside Active Directory.
`-disable`	Disables kiosk mode authentication on the VMware View Connection Server or group on which this command is executed.
`-domain`	Sets the domain name for the client account.
`-enable`	Enables kiosk mode authentication on the Connection Server or group on which this command is executed.
`-expirepassword`	Sets the password for the client devices to be the same as the Connection Server group.
`-force`	When removing an account for a kiosk mode client, this option suppresses the prompt asking for confirmation.
`-genpassword`	Generates a 16-digit, alphanumeric, mixed-case password.
`-getdefaults`	Obtains client account default settings.
`-group`	Defines the pre-Windows 2000 Active Directory group name to which the account will be added.
`-list`	Lists the configuration of kiosk mode, including client and Connection Server information.

Option	Notes
`-noexpirepassword`	Defines no password expiration.
`-nogroup`	Does not add an account to the default group.
`-ou`	Sets the organizational unit where the accounts are being added.
`-password`	Defines a password for an account. This option is needed if the generated password is either not complex enough or is too complex. After this option, you would then enter the password.
`-remove`	Removes the account from kiosk mode.
`-removeall`	Removes all accounts from kiosk mode.
`-requirepassword`	Requires clients to input a password when the View Client launches.
`-s`	Sets the Connection Server name.
`-setdefaults`	Sets up kiosk mode with the default settings.
`-update`	Updates a kiosk mode account.

Summary

This chapter discussed in detail how to set up kiosk mode, from the configuration of the physical endpoint devices all the way through configuring Active Directory and the View Connection Servers. The chapter also covered all of the various configuration options you have with the `vdmadmin` command.

At this point, you should be familiar with the process for enabling kiosk mode and with the general syntax of the `vdmadmin` command. You should be able to configure the Connection Servers to allow kiosks to attach and log in without requiring an end user to enter credentials. Kiosk mode does have some definite benefits, and you should now understand the steps that must be completed to properly configure the environment. You should be aware of the use cases that would benefit from kiosk mode (hospitality services, customer self-service portals, hotel check-in, airline check-in, and so forth). In fact, kiosk mode can be utilized anywhere it would be useful to have a dedicated desktop directly accessible to a customer without worrying about having any special security credentials.

Exam Preparation Tasks

Review All the Key Topics

Review the most important topics in the chapter, noted with the Key Topic icon in the outer margin of the page. Table 7-7 provides a detailed discussion of the key topics. Use this table as a quick reference to the settings you need to make or verify in any system. Examples of these and other settings are provided in the following sections.

Table 7-7 Key Topics for Chapter 7

Key Topic Element	Description	Page
Step list	How to configure kiosk mode	162
List	How to configure the Connection Server	163
Table 7-2	`vdmadmin` command usage	164
Step List	Identifying MAC addresses of physical clients	170
Table 7-3	Kiosk mode account options	171
Note	Kiosk mode account name	171
Table 7-4	VMware View Windows Client Command-Line Options	173
Table 7-5	VMware View Linux Client Command-Line Options	173
Table 7-6	Additional Configuration Options	174

Review `vdmadmin` Commands

Table 7-8 provides many of the commonly used `vdmadmin` commands. You can use this table to see how many of the commands you can remember.

Table 7-8 Command Reference

Objective	Commands	Notes
Configuring the Connection Server	vdmadmin -Q -clientauth -setdefaults -ou "OU=<Kiosk OU>,DC=<domain name>,DC=<top-level domain>" -noexpirepassword -group <group name>	Sets the Connection Server to which the client will attach. Must be enabled for kiosk mode authentication.

Objective	Commands	Notes
Identifying MAC addresses of physical client devices	Windows: `C:\Program Files\VMware\VMware View\Client\bin\wswc -printEnvironmentInfo` Linux: `vmware-view -printEnvironmentinfo -s <Connection Server>`	Provides information about the MAC address, IP address, and system name for use in account creation.
Adding accounts	`vdmadmin -Q -clientauth -add -domain <domain name> -clientid <MAC address> -group <group name>`	This account is executed on one of the Connection Servers to add the account to Active Directory.
Checking kiosk mode configuration	`vdmadmin -Q -clientauth -list`	Lists information about the kiosk clients and the Connection Servers and kiosk mode configuration options that are currently configured.

Define Key Terms

Define the following key terms from this chapter and check your answers in the Glossary:

kiosk mode, ADAM, FQDN, FSP

Review Questions

You can find the answers to these review questions in Appendix A.

1. Your organization wants to start using kiosk mode. On what physical devices can kiosk mode be used? (Select all that apply.)
   - a. Windows machines
   - b. Linux machines
   - c. ThinClients
   - d. Mac machines

2. How can accounts be created to ensure uniqueness when setting up kiosk mode? (Select two.)
   a. By MAC address
   b. By UUID
   c. By machine name
   d. With account names starting with custom-
   e. With account names starting with kiosk-

3. What guidelines should you follow when adding the kiosk machines to Active Directory?
   a. Place the kiosk machines in the same OU as the other View desktops.
   b. The kiosk machines do not need Active Directory accounts.
   c. Place the kiosk machines in a separate OU.
   d. Place the kiosk machines in the same OU as the Connection Server.

4. When creating Active Directory accounts for kiosk machines, which of the following commands would you use?
   a. vdmadmin -Q -clientauth -add -domain <reverse domain name> -clientid <MAC Address> -OU <AD OU name>
   b. vdmadmin -Q -clientauth -add -domain <domain name> -clientid <MAC Address> -group <group name>
   c. vdmadmin -L -clientauth -add -domain <domain name> -clientid <MAC Address> -group <group name>
   d. vdmadmin -Q -adauth -add -client <IP Address> -group <group name>

5. Which command switch is used with the vdmadmin command to enable and configure kiosk mode on the Connection Server?
   a. vdmadmin -A
   b. vdmadmin -L
   c. vdmadmin -Q
   d. vdmadmin -O

6. When configuring kiosks for automatic login, which of the following command-line account options allows for defining the password used for an account that will not expire?

   a. `-indefinitepwd`

   b. `-noexpirepassword`

   c. `-nopasswordexpire`

   d. `-password -noexpire`

7. What is the output of following command?

```
vdmadmin -A -b <username>@<domain> * -getstatus -xml -d
<desktop pool> -m <machine name>
```

   a. Lists the status of the Connection Server

   b. Lists the status of the kiosk machine

   c. Lists the status of the virtual machine

   d. Lists the status of the View Agent

8. What are the different logging levels for the View Agent to assist with troubleshooting? (Choose three.)

   a. Info

   b. Debug

   c. Normal

   d. Trivia

   e. Verbose

   f. Trace

9. How should you configure the View Administrator for kiosk machines?

   a. Use one connection server specifically for kiosk machines, and don't use it for anything else.

   b. Spread the kiosk virtual machines across desktop pools.

   c. Create a pool specifically for the kiosk machines.

   d. Use an existing desktop pool for the kiosk machines.

10. Where can you set up the accounts for use in kiosk mode? (Select two.)

   a. The Connection Server

   b. The Transfer Server

   c. The replica server

   d. The virtual desktop

This chapter covers the following subjects:

- **Local Mode Concepts:** This section explains the different options available for local mode desktops.
- **Local Mode Benefits:** This section describes the benefits (to administrators and end users) for running local mode desktops.
- **VMware View Transfer Server:** This section covers what a Transfer Server is, how to configure one, and additional settings.

(This chapter covers part of Objective 2.10 of the Blueprint.)

CHAPTER 8

Local Mode

Local mode allows a virtual desktop to be copied to a client device (referred to as *checked out*) to be used offline without the need for reliable network connectivity (or any network connectivity) to the View environment. There are some very useful reasons why an organization might want to allow a local mode desktop. For example, workers might need to take their work home or on the road, but they might not have network connectivity in some locations (for example, on a plane). In some cases, the work done in these situations could be extremely valuable, and there could be significant concern for the loss of data, either due to a hardware failure or if a laptop was lost or stolen.

Local mode virtual desktops can provide the ability to work offline from the View environment while minimizing the risks associated with lost data. If the physical device is compromised, the virtual desktop (and all data associated with it) still resides in the datacenter (less any work done while the desktop was checked out). In addition, any data that was on the compromised device is encrypted. If the device is stolen and someone breaks in to the operating system, even though they could access any files exposed to the OS, they still wouldn't be able to access the virtual machine containing the sensitive data.

Virtual desktops that are defined for local mode are still controlled by View Manager, allowing administrators to extend their control to these devices as well. In addition, because these virtual desktops are maintained in a vSphere environment, administrators can extend their business continuity and disaster recovery plans to protect these machines as well.

A special version of the View Client is required to use local mode desktops. This client is aptly named the VMware View Client with local mode. As opposed to all other View Clients, this client is available only for Windows operating systems.

"Do I Know This Already?" Quiz

The "Do I Know This Already?" quiz allows you to assess whether you should read this entire chapter or simply jump to the "Exam Preparation Tasks" section for review. If you are in doubt, read the entire chapter. Table 8-1 outlines the major headings in this chapter and the corresponding "Do I Know This Already?" quiz questions. You can find the answers in Appendix A, "Answers to the 'Do I Know This Already?' Quizzes and Review Questions."

Table 8-1 "Do I Know This Already?" Foundation Topics Section-to-Question Mapping

Foundation Topics Section	Questions Covered in This Section
Local Mode Concepts	1
Local Mode Benefits	2
VMware View Transfer Server	3–4

1. An end user is using a local mode desktop and wants to confirm that all changes made locally have been updated to the virtual desktop since checking it out. The end user also wants to continue using the virtual desktop. Which action should be taken to meet the user's need?
   a. Check in the desktop
   b. Initiate a replication
   c. Roll back the desktop
   d. Check out the virtual desktop again

2. What is the default encryption mode for a checked-out local mode desktop?
   a. 256-bit AES
   b. 192-bit AES
   c. 128-bit AES
   d. No encryption

3. Which method can be used to deploy a Transfer Server?
   a. Install the Transfer Server on a Windows 2008 R2 64-bit physical server
   b. Install the Transfer Server on a Windows 2008 R2 64-bit virtual machine
   c. Deploy the Transfer Server using a virtual appliance OVF file
   d. Install the Transfer Server on the vCenter Server virtual machine

4. What component do you need to configure to allow linked-clone desktops to be checked out with local mode?
   a. Replica Server Repository
   b. Transfer Server Repository
   c. Linked-Clone Transport
   d. Linked-Clone desktops cannot be used with local mode

Foundation Topics

Local Mode Concepts

Local mode allows for a great deal of flexibility to the end user while still enabling administrators to maintain suitable control. Many settings can be configured to control what end users can and cannot do. These settings are explored in this chapter. Before looking at those settings, let's start by reviewing some concepts that are unique to local mode:

- **Checkout:** The checkout operation copies the virtual desktop from the View environment to the end user's local device. The first time an end user initiates this operation can take quite some time because the entire image must be downloaded to the device. The page file and any unallocated blocks (unused space on the disk) are not copied to the client laptop during the checkout process. A copy of the virtual desktop remains in the datacenter, but it is locked so that no administrator can make changes to it while it is checked out. Checked-out desktops attempt to contact the View Connection Servers every 5 minutes by default to check for policy updates (for example, revoking permission to the desktop). A snapshot is taken of the copy housed in the datacenter so that the desktop can be reverted back to its original state if needed. This also allows for synchronization of changed data from the local device back to the datacenter copy.
- **Check-in:** The check-in operation replicates changes made to the virtual desktop since it was checked out. During a check-in, the virtual desktop is temporarily unavailable to the end user. When the operation completes, the desktop is relocated to the datacenter, the lock is removed, and the user can connect to the datacenter copy using the View Client. Check-in operations employ vSphere snapshots: A snapshot is taken on the end user's device, which gets consolidated with the snapshot for the virtual desktop in the datacenter when the desktop is checked in. While the check-in operation is taking place, deduplication is used so that only unique blocks get copied, reducing the time needed to complete the operation. The client machine performs the deduplication and sends a reference to any unchanged blocks instead of the blocks themselves. Data deduplication must be enabled in the Connection Server - General Settings and is disabled by default.
- **Replication:** Replication of a local mode desktop will copy all changes made to the desktop since it was checked out from the datacenter. While the operation is in progress, end users can still use their virtual desktop (no interruption

of service), and the desktop remains on the local device. As with check-in operations, data deduplication can be configured on the View Connection Server to reduce the time needed to complete the replication operation.

- **Rollback:** A rollback operation discards all changes to the virtual machine since the desktop was checked out, releases the lock on the virtual desktop in the datacenter, and redirects the user to this desktop via the View Client. During this operation, the virtual desktop is temporarily unavailable to the end user.

NOTE When a desktop is rolled back, the files that were copied to the client device are still present.

NOTE A license is needed to use the local mode feature. View Premier includes licensing for local mode desktops, whereas View Enterprise does not.

Local Mode Benefits

The benefits to local mode desktops extend beyond just providing security and business continuity to the desktop images. The following additional benefits apply:

- **Local resource utilization:** Because the local mode desktop, once checked out, is running on a client device, it is not bound by resource controls set within the datacenter either on the virtual desktop itself or on its parent resource pool.
- **Conservation of resources:** If users are using local mode desktops that are checked out a majority of the time, the locked datacenter versions of these virtual machines are not using any resources. This allows an organization to add local mode users without any performance impact (or increase in resource requirements) on the View environment. This would also allow for such initiatives as bring your own PC.
- **Backups:** As data changes on the local mode desktop, replication operations can be periodically performed to ensure that all data is backed up to the datacenter.
- **Rollbacks:** If something happens that corrupts data on a checked-out desktop, the rollback operation can be used to quickly restore the desktop to a known good state.

- **Security:** Local mode provides many features to ensure data is secure while checked out of the datacenter. These include
  - **Encryption:** Local mode desktops are encrypted to 128-bit AES encryption by default, configurable to 192-bit or even 256-bit encryption.
  - **Lockout:** View administrators can configure the local mode desktop to become inaccessible after a period of time. If a local mode desktop has been checked out and remains out of contact with the Connection Server for a given period of time, the desktop is locked and end users will no longer be able to access it. To reconnect to the desktop, the local device would have to connect to the corporate network, upon which access would be restored.
  - **Data Security:** The local mode desktop is not allowed to access the physical CD-ROM drive of the end-user device, limiting the ability to copy sensitive data. Furthermore, copy and paste is disabled between the local mode desktop and the client OS.

An initiative is taking place among several businesses today called bring your own PC or bring your own device (BYOD). This means an organization could allow an employee or contractor to utilize his or her own laptop to access the corporate environment. The laptop could remain outside the domain, with the View Client installed on it to access a corporate virtual desktop, even allowing for local mode operation. This allows the organization's data to remain secure while giving end users the freedom of using whatever computer equipment they want, including combining their personal and corporate computer systems into a single device. Local mode desktops are encrypted while checked out, and can be locked if they are out of contact with the Connection Server for a predetermined period of time. This minimizes the risk of loss of corporate information due to lost or stolen equipment.

When the VMware View Client with local mode is installed, a Type 2 (hosted) hypervisor is also installed on top of the local operating system. This allows end users to continue using their operating system for nonwork-related tasks and to then launch a View Client to connect to the local virtual desktop for business-related tasks.

NOTE ThinApp packages cannot be published to local mode desktops or managed through the View Administrator. They are also not supported on local mode desktops.

VMware View Transfer Server

The View Transfer Server is a required component for local mode desktops. The Transfer Server offloads processing from standard Connection Servers. It is responsible for transferring virtual desktop images from the View environment to the end user's device and for replication afterward to keep the datacenter desktop image synchronized with the image on the local device. It also handles authorization for local mode desktops, because it still acts as just another type of Connection Server. If linked clones are being used, the Transfer Server can also download the components of the linked clones into a repository (configured by the View administrator).

The Transfer Server must be installed to a virtual machine, because it must be able to access all the datastores used by the virtual desktops. It must be managed by the same vCenter Server that manages the virtual desktops. If you are using the pod and block design in a large environment, each block (or each section of the environment managed by its own vCenter Server) must have its own Transfer Servers. The Transfer Server must be installed on Windows 2008 R2 64-bit. It is a best practice to configure the Transfer Server virtual machine with two vCPUs, 4GB of RAM, and a static IP address, and to have at least two Transfer Servers deployed to provide for redundancy. The Transfer Servers do not necessarily have to be a member of the domain.

Installing the View Transfer Server is similar to installing a View Connection Server. During the install, you will be prompted to open the firewall ports needed for the Transfer Server automatically. After the install, the Transfer Server must be added to the View Manager. This is done by navigating to **View Configuration > Servers > Transfer Servers** and clicking **Add**.

Figure 8-1 illustrates where you would add the Transfer Server to the View Manager.

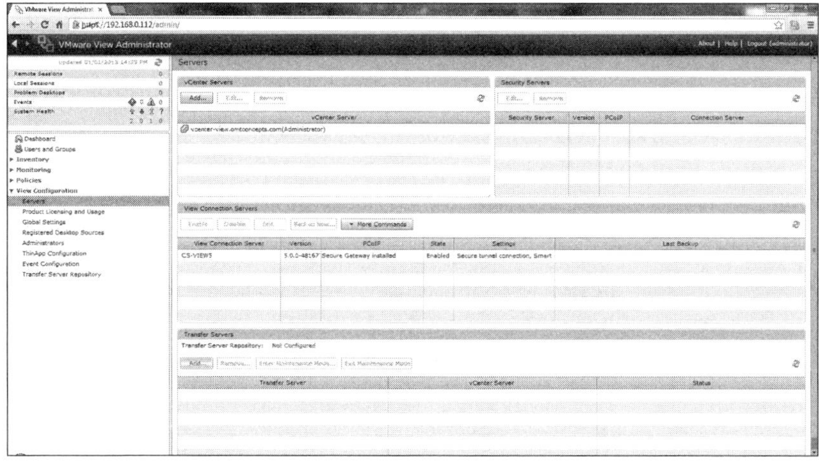

Figure 8-1 View Administrator, servers selected.

After the Transfer Server virtual machine is added to the View Manager, vCenter Server locks the virtual machine and performs the following actions:

- Three additional SCSI controllers are added to the virtual machine. This allows the Transfer Server to perform up to 60 transfers at a time. Note that this number is theoretical; the actual number of transfers depends on the network. VMware testing has shown that 20 concurrent operations will saturate a 1Gbps network connection.
- If the virtual machine is in a DRS (Distributed Resource Scheduler) cluster, the automation level for the virtual machine is set to manual.

View Transfer Server Repository

If local mode is to be used with linked-clone desktops, a Transfer Server repository must be configured. This allows the Transfer Server to copy the replica, OS disk (delta), and persistent disks for check-in/checkout operations. It is a best practice to add the repository after adding the Transfer Server to View Manager, but it is possible to add a repository while you are adding the Transfer Server to View Manager.

After a Transfer Server has been added to View Manager, the repository can then be added. The following are the steps required to add a Transfer Server repository:

Step 1. Under View Configuration on the left side of the View Manager, select **Servers**. At the bottom of the window is a list of Transfer Servers, and the one just added should be listed here. Select that Transfer Server, and then select **Enter Maintenance Mode**. This should be done for all Transfer Servers in the list when you are adding a repository.

Step 2. In the Transfer Server Repository panel, click the **General** tab and select **Edit**.

Step 3. In the Edit Transfer Server Repository window, specify whether the repository will be stored on the network or locally on the Transfer Server. This way, it's possible to use one specific network path for the repository of linked-clone images, and the Transfer Server doesn't necessarily need a lot of disk space.

- If the repository is going to be a network share, select the **Network Share** radio button, and enter the network path along with logon credentials and domain name. It is a best practice to use a network share with fast disks for the repository.
- If the repository is to be on the Transfer Server itself, select the **Local filesystem** radio button and enter the path for this directory.

Step 4. Click **OK**, select the Transfer Server, and then select **Exit Maintenance Mode**.

In the future, if you need to modify the network path for the repository, or change the directory you want to use for the repository, this is possible by modifying the repository you just created.

NOTE If you enter an incorrect path, you will receive an error message.

Publishing Linked-Clone Replicas

Now that a repository has been created for the Transfer Servers, the View environment can be configured to publish Composer base images or replica disks to this repository.

Step 1. Under View Configuration on the left pane of the View Manager, select **Transfer Server Repository**.

Step 2. Feel free to type something into the Description box to help illustrate what this base image is.

Step 3. Select the virtual machine that is the parent of the linked clones.

After you select the parent virtual machine, the image will begin publishing to the repository. After the image has been published, it is then compressed. The Status column will now show that the image is published; the Size column illustrates the size after compression.

Now that the linked clone's replica has been added to the repository, the desktop pools can be configured. To simplify administration, desktops intended for use by local mode can be placed in their own pool, but this isn't a requirement.

An HTTP cache can be configured if an environment such as a remote office needs to provision local mode desktops across a WAN link. The speed of the network link might cause View Composer to take an unacceptable amount of time to download local mode desktops for the first time, especially if you consider how large some of the desktop images can be. When you consider the operating system plus desktop applications, a desktop image could easily be several gigabytes in size. Using an HTTP cache, the base virtual desktop image is saved in the proxy server's cache after the first virtual desktop is downloaded. This way, subsequent checkouts will pull the base image from cache instead of from the WAN. Persistent and OS disks still have to be copied across the WAN, but these should be smaller than the base image itself. The procedure for configuring an HTTP cache is as follows. (Note that HTTP caching must be enabled on the Connection Server.)

Step 1. In the View Administrator, select **View Configuration** and then select **Servers**.

Step 2. Select one of the Connection Servers and then select **Edit**.

Step 3. Uncheck **Use SSL when provisioning desktops in local mode**. This is to allow the base image of the linked-clone desktops to be cached at the remote site.

Step 4. If the proxy server isn't going to be configured for HTTP CONNECT, click **Use SSL for local mode operations**.

Ensure that the Composer base image packages are broken down into files no larger than the proxy server's cache:

Step 1. On the Connection Server, open a command prompt.

Step 2. Enter the command `vdmadmin -T -packagelimit <size in bytes>`.

The `vdmadmin -T` command with no options will list the current package file sizes.

The client machines must be configured to transfer their virtual desktops through the proxy server. This must be configured by modifying the Registry of the client machines. You can do this through Group Policy if desired.

- On 64-bit clients, the following Registry key must be added: HKEY_LOCAL_MACHINE – SOFTWARE – Wow6432Node – VMware Inc. – VMware VDM.
- On 32-bit clients, the following Registry key must be added: HKEY_LOCAL_MACHINE – SOFTWARE – VMware Inc. – VMware VDM.

Step 1. After the appropriate key has been added, the following string value should be set for the key:

useProxyForTransfer

Step 2. Right-click the new entry, enter **true**, and then click **OK**.

Step 3. Configure the clients to use the proxy server.

Step 4. Open Internet Explorer.

Step 5. Go to **Tools > Internet Options**.

Step 6. Go to the **Connections** tab and select **LAN Settings**.

Step 7. Select **Use a proxy server for your LAN**, and then select **Advanced**.

Step 8. Enter the proxy server and port numbers, and then click **OK**.

Step 9. Set up the proxy server to then cache the Composer base images.

Step 10. Set the maximum size of the cache. This should match the package limit size defined on the Connection Server.

Step 11. Set the maximum file size that can be cached. (This should be greater than or equal to the maximum package file size that was earlier defined.)

Step 12. If Use SSL for Local Mode Operations was not selected, configure the access control list to open port 80 on the proxy and let the CONNECT method make the connection using this port. This allows for improved WAN performance because the CONNECT method establishes a tunnel between the proxy server and the Transfer Server.

Local Mode Policies

You can configure three types of policies for local mode: global policies, pool policies, and user policies. Although providing the most granularity, configuring policies at the user level can be difficult to manage. Conversely, configuring policies at a global level might not provide an effective level of control. As a result, most administrators configure policies at the pool level. By default, anyone who has been entitled to a pool can use local mode, but this might not be the desired configuration for all environments. Modifying these policies at each level works in a similar fashion to adjusting permissions in vCenter Server. Changes made at a more granular level take priority to changes made at a higher level. For example, an administrator can deny local mode as a global policy, but can then allow it on a pool level. This is actually a great example of what would be used in the real world, as it would allow only those desktops specifically desired to be used with local mode. It is a best practice to use pools to define which desktops can be used for local mode.

Table 8-2 illustrates the settings available for local mode.

Table 8-2 Local Mode Policies

Policy	Option	Default	Notes
Local mode	Allow/Deny	Allow	Allows the use of local mode. Recommended to set this policy at the pool level.
User-initiated rollback	Allow/Deny	Allow	Allows administrators to determine whether a user should be allowed to initiate a rollback operation on a linked clone.

Policy	Option	Default	Notes
Max time without server contact	__ days	7 days	Defines how long a local mode desktop can be checked out without Connection Server contact. If contact has not been made with the server before this time elapses, users will not be able to connect to their desktop until connectivity is reestablished.
Target replication frequency	No Replication/ At a specified interval	No replication	Configures a specified interval for replication to occur, set in days, hours, or minutes. By default, there is no automatic replication of checked-out local mode desktops. If the time configured is insufficient, replication can take longer than the specified frequency, forcing the next replication to wait until the pending replication finishes.
User deferred replication	Deny/Allow	Deny	Allows end users to put off replicating their checked-out virtual machines until later. Allowing this option provides some flexibility to the end user; however, the longer a checked-out virtual machine goes without replicating, the longer the resulting replication will take, and the more data would be lost if the local image is compromised. When a user defers a replication, the process will pause for 2 hours.
Disks Replicated	Persistent disks/ OS disks/OS and Persistent disks	Persistent disks	Specifies which disks on a linked-clone local mode desktop should be replicated. Because the data in the OS disk is discarded during a refresh or rebalance operation anyway, this setting can be configured to ignore this disk and focus on the persistent disk, which is where user data is saved.

Policy	Option	Default	Notes
User-initiated check in	Allow/Deny	Allow	Allows users to initiate check-in operations as needed. As long as replication is regularly occurring, it might not be necessary to check in the virtual desktops.
User-initiated replication	Allow/Deny	Allow	Allows end users to replicate their virtual desktops as needed. This is set to Allow by default. If automatic replication is configured, this setting can safely be set to Deny.

Client Devices

For an end user to be able to check out a desktop, the following conditions must be met:

- Local mode must be enabled (globally, at the pool, or for the user).
- For linked clones, the parent virtual machine must be published to the Transfer Server repository.
- The end user must have the correct version of the View Client.

The View Client with local mode is available only for Windows operating systems. The client is available in 32-bit or 64-bit. If an end user already has a VMware View Client, it must be uninstalled and the new client downloaded and installed. The easiest way to do this is to point a web browser to the connection server and download the local mode client (http://<connection server URL>). If a custom installation is employed, the component for local mode might need to be manually installed.

Because local mode essentially installs a hypervisor on the client system, the installation will not proceed if the end user already has a VMware hosted virtualization product installed, such as the following:

- View Client
- VMware Workstation
- VMware Player
- VMware Server
- VMware ACE

When an end user checks out a virtual desktop, the virtual desktop will utilize the physical resources on the client device. A checked-out virtual machine can potentially use more resources than what was defined for it by vCenter Server. The View Client with local mode automatically splits the memory on the physical desktop between the host operating system and the virtual machine. If the physical machine has less memory than what was defined for the virtual machine, the user cannot check out the desktop. The amount of memory split between the virtual machine and the host is based on a formula. What is not taken into account is the minimum amount of memory required for the host operating system and the virtual machine. The remaining memory is split between the virtual machine and the host OS. Table 8-3 outlines the amount of RAM for each OS.

Table 8-3 Local Mode Policies

Memory	Windows XP	Windows 7 and Vista
Minimum	512MB	1GB
Best Effort	512MB + (Available / 2)	1GB + (Available / 2)
Maximum	2GB	4GB

The locally checked-out View desktop can use 2 virtual CPUs as long as the host operating system is running Windows Vista or later. These are the default settings and can be modified as needed via Group Policy Objects (GPOs).

The virtual network adapter assigned to the checked-out virtual machine will use Network Address Translation (NAT) by default. The virtual desktop shares the host operating system's IP and MAC addresses.

When checking out a View desktop, remember that the physical client device must have sufficient disk space to store the image. End users can choose the installation directory when installing the View Client with local mode.

Summary

This chapter discussed local mode and the requirements for successfully using this feature. Although not all virtual desktops will need local mode access, this feature allows flexibility for use cases where a steady network connection is not available. The ability to safely and securely check out a virtual desktop provides benefit to the end user. Having that desktop automatically lock itself if it has been out of contact with the Connection Server for too long allows View administrators to sleep more easily. After all, dealing with a lost or broken laptop is hard enough before adding the fear of losing data.

Utilizing local mode does come along with some requirements and restrictions. Local mode only works with Windows-based end user devices, and a specific version of the client must be installed.

Finally, if you use local mode you must install a Transfer Server, though it is not actually employed unless you will be checking out linked-clone virtual desktops.

Exam Preparation Tasks

Review All the Key Topics

Review the most important topics in the chapter, noted with the Key Topic icon in the outer margin of the page. Table 8-4 provides a detailed discussion of the key topics. Use this table as a quick reference to the configuration of local mode desktops.

Table 8-4 Key Topics

Key Topic Element	Description	Page
List	Local mode concepts	186
List	Local mode benefits	187
Figure 8-1	View Administrator: Transfer Server	189
List	Changes made to the Transfer Server after being added to the View Administrator	190
List	Setting up the Transfer Server repository	190
List	Publishing linked-clone replicas	191
List	HTTP caching	192
List	Configuring a proxy server for the Transfer Server	192
Table 8-2	Local mode policies	193
List	Client device requirements	195
List	VMware products that cannot reside on a View Client with local mode	195
Table 8-3	Local mode policies	196

Definitions of Key Terms

Define the following key terms from this chapter and check your answers in the Glossary.

checkout, check-in, replication, rollback, Transfer Server, Transfer Server repository

Review Questions

You can find the answers to these review questions in Appendix A.

1. What is a Transfer Server repository used for?
   a. Transferring the disks for virtual desktops being checked out for local mode
   b. Storing published linked-clone images for local mode desktops to be checked out
   c. Transferring snapshots to/from vCenter Server
   d. Attaching to virtual desktops from outside a firewall

2. Which of the following cannot be used for a Transfer Server repository?
   a. Windows network share
   b. Local directory on the Transfer Server
   c. NFS
   d. Zip file

3. During which of the following operations would a virtual desktop remain available for use?
   a. Replication
   b. Check-in
   c. Checkout
   d. Revert

4. Which operation discards all of the changes made since the local mode desktop was checked out?
   a. Replication
   b. Rollback
   c. Revert
   d. Regress

5. Which of these types of disks is not copied to the Transfer Server repository for linked-clone virtual desktops?
   a. Persistent disk
   b. OS disk
   c. Replica disk
   d. Disposable disk

6. Which of the following operating systems support the View Client with local mode?
   a. Windows XP
   b. Ubuntu Linux
   c. Mac OS X
   d. SUSE Linux

7. Which of the following settings would prevent a user from logging in to a local mode virtual desktop after it has been checked out for a week?
   a. Lockout timer
   b. Target replication frequency
   c. User deferred replication
   d. Max time without server contact

8. Your organization wants to use local mode virtual desktops. Where can this feature be enabled? (Select all that apply.)
   a. On the desktop pool
   b. Globally
   c. For the user
   d. On the vCenter server

9. Which of these functions can a user perform with a checked-out local mode virtual desktop?
   a. Copy text to/from the virtual desktop
   b. Attach a CD/ROM drive and see the contents from the virtual desktop
   c. Attach to and use printers attached to the physical laptop from the virtual machine
   d. Log in to the local mode desktop as the current user

10. A user receives an error while attempting to install the View Client with local mode. Which of the following would prevent a user from installing the View Client with local mode? (Select two.)

a. The local machine has VMware Zimbra Desktop installed.

b. The local machine has a View Client already installed.

c. The local machine has a vSphere Client installed.

d. The local machine has VMware Workstation installed.

This chapter covers the following subjects:

- Troubleshooting the View Composer Install on vCenter
- Troubleshooting the View Events Database
- Troubleshooting Guest Operating System Customization
- Troubleshooting Accounts and Permissions
- Troubleshooting Connectivity Between VMware View Components
- Troubleshooting PCoIP Configuration
- Troubleshooting View Servers
- Troubleshooting View Persona Management

(This chapter covers part of the VCP-DT Objectives 4-1 through 4-8.)

CHAPTER 9

Troubleshooting

As View environments grow, there become multiple potential points of failure. As a result, when a problem does occur, an administrator might find it difficult to identify the root cause. This can be further complicated by server sprawl in the physical environment, virtual machine (VM) sprawl in the virtual environments, and potentially even virtual desktop sprawl. This chapter identifies many of the common problems customers have faced in View environments and provides tips and resources for determining the underlying cause of the problem. From identifying the correct log files (and their locations), to utilizing Group Policy Administrative (ADM) templates for Active Directory, we explore all the tools available to assist in troubleshooting a VMware View environment of any size.

"Do I Know This Already?" Quiz

The "Do I Know This Already?" quiz allows you to assess whether you should read this entire chapter or simply jump to the "Exam Preparation Tasks" section for review. If you are in doubt, read the entire chapter. Table 9-1 outlines the major headings in this chapter and the corresponding "Do I Know This Already?" quiz questions. You can find the answers in Appendix A, "Answers to the 'Do I Know This Already?' Quizzes and Review Questions."

Table 9-1 "Do I Know This Already?" Foundation Topics Section-to-Question Mapping

Foundation Topics Section	Questions Covered in This Section
Troubleshooting View Composer installation on the vCenter Server	1
Troubleshooting the events database	2
Troubleshooting guest OS customization	3
Troubleshooting accounts and permissions	4
Troubleshooting connectivity between view components	5

Foundation Topics Section	Questions Covered in This Section
Troubleshooting PCoIP configuration	6
Troubleshooting View Servers	7
Troubleshooting View Persona Management	8

1. Your organization wants to deploy linked clones. How do you deploy the Composer server?
   a. Simply deploy the virtual appliance provided by VMware.
   b. Install Composer on the same server as the View Connection Server.
   c. Install Composer on the same server as vCenter Server.
   d. Composer is installed automatically when the Connection Server is installed.

2. Which type of database can be used for the events database?
   a. MS Access
   b. MySQL
   c. IBM DB2
   d. MS SQL 2008 R2

3. How should guest operating systems be activated in a View environment?
   a. Volume activation.
   b. Each operating system must be activated by the user when they log in for the first time.
   c. Guest operating systems for virtual desktops don't need to be activated.
   d. None of the above.

4. An administrator deploys a desktop pool called Fin-Win7, but none of the desktop users can connect to the desktops through the Connection Server. What should you do? (Select all that apply.)
   a. Make sure that the users or groups are in the Remote Desktop Users group.
   b. Ensure that the users or groups are entitled to use the pool.
   c. Re-create the pool.
   d. Check for the use of tags on the pool and on the Connection Server.

5. A Security Server is paired with a Connection Server. A subsequent attempt to pair the Security Server with a replica server fails. Why?
   a. The Security Server was installed on a virtual machine.
   b. The Security Server has not been added to the domain.
   c. The pairing password timed out and must be re-created.
   d. A Security Server can only be paired with a single Connection Server.

6. Users outside the firewall are complaining that when they launch the View Client and attempt to connect to their virtual desktop they see a black screen. What could be the problem? (Select all that apply.)
   a. The organization is not using a WAN accelerator.
   b. The external URL defined for the Security Server differs from the one defined on its paired Connection Server.
   c. The display resolution inside the virtual machine is set too high for the physical monitors.
   d. The Connect Using SSL option has not been selected.

7. A View Replica Server is listed as having a problem in the View Administrator. What could cause a problem to be displayed?
   a. The Replica Server is in maintenance mode.
   b. The Windows Firewall service on the Replica Server has been stopped.
   c. The View Connection Server service has stopped.
   d. A snapshot of the Replica Server virtual machine was taken in vCenter Server.

8. An administrator wants to use Persona Management for physical and virtual desktops. The organization is currently using View 5.0. Persona Management is working successfully for the virtual desktops, and login times have been dramatically reduced. However, login/logoff operations are still taking several minutes on the physical desktops. What could be the problem?
   a. Persona Management does not work with physical desktops in View 5.0.
   b. Persona Management must be enabled for both virtual and physical desktops.
   c. The VIewPM.adm file has to be copied to Active Directory.
   d. The physical desktops need to update their View Client.

Foundation Topics

Troubleshooting the View Composer Installation on the vCenter Server

(This section covers Objective 4.1 of the Blueprint.)

To be able to use linked clones, the View Composer service must be installed on a vCenter Server (see Chapter 2, "Configuring the View Environment"). When installing the service, it is important to verify that the vCenter Server has enough available resources to handle both vCenter Server and Composer. In some cases, available disk space for Composer might not be sufficient after the vCenter Server installation. This section illustrates the problems you might run into during the Composer installation process.

As of View 5.1, the Composer service can be installed on a separate physical or virtual machine from vCenter Server, which allows for the use of linked clones with the vCenter Server virtual appliance. During the installation of Composer in 5.1, the Install Wizard asks for the vCenter Server through which to attach. You must specify a user account with appropriate privileges on the vCenter Server. For linked-clone operations to be successful, this account should have the following permissions (see Table 9-2).

Table 9-2 vCenter Permissions for the Composer Role

Privilege Category	Privilege Name
Datastore	Allocate space
	Browse datastore
	Low-level file operations
Virtual Machine	Inventory (all)
	Configuration (all)
	State (all)
	Provisioning
	Clone virtual machine
	Allow disk access
Resource	Assign virtual machine to resource pool

Privilege Category	Privilege Name
Global	Enable methods
	Disable methods
	System tag
Network	(all)

Many things can happen during the installation process that will result in a failed install. First, several database related issues can occur. The Composer service requires a SQL Server to connect to for storing linked clone data. The database can be on the vCenter Server, or a different database server can be selected. However, Composer supports NT authentication only if the database is on the same system as the vCenter Server. When setting up the database, the system account used for Composer to attach to the database must have sufficient privileges. If the database is not located on the vCenter Server, SQL authentication is required, and user accounts must be created inside SQL after the database has been created.

Because the default setting of this new account requires users to change their password on the next connection, the setting must be modified to allow for a static password for easier administration. If this step is not performed, when the Composer service attaches to the database for the first time, it would be prompted to change the account password. Because there is no way for Composer to do this, the service would not be able to attach to the database, so it would be unable to continue.

When supplying the database account for Composer, make sure the account has the DB Owner Fixed Database role on the database. If this is not configured, the Composer server will not have sufficient privileges to modify the database. Composer supports Oracle and SQL databases as shown in the following list. When the database has been successfully configured, an Open Database Connectivity (ODBC) connection (system type DSN [database source name]) must be created with the SQL Server Native Client.

- MS SQL Server 2005 Express
- MS SQL Server 2005 SP3 and newer
- MS SQL 2008 SP1 and newer
- MS SQL 2008 R2 Express
- Oracle 10g Release 2
- Oracle 11g Release 2 with Oracle 11.2.0.1 Patch 5

Composer uses RSA key pairs to encrypt data. If the Composer installation is replacing an existing Composer server and you are reusing the database, the RSA container that was created on the original Composer server must be copied to the new server.

The user account for the Composer server requires several Active Directory permissions. If one or more of these permissions is absent, somewhere in the process of deploying linked clones, errors are likely to occur.

The AD permissions that the Composer service account should have are as follows:

- Read All Properties
- Write All Properties
- Read Permissions
- Create Computer Objects
- Delete Computer Objects

In addition to the Active Directory permissions, the View Composer account for vCenter Server requires the following privileges in the following categories:

- Datastore
- Global
- Network
- Resource
- Virtual machine
- Provisioning

The View Connection Server administrator also has to be a member of the local Administrators group.

An easy issue to troubleshoot is if the installation fails due to insufficient disk space. Ensure that the vCenter Server (where you are going to install Composer) has enough disk space to allow for the Composer installation. VMware recommends 40–60GB of disk space for Composer.

If the install process is cancelled or interrupted, the Composer certificate can be corrupted. If this happens, any subsequent install attempts will fail with no error and the installer will roll back. To correct this issue, all Composer certificates must be manually removed.

The process for doing this is performed using the Microsoft Management Console (MMC):

1. Click **File** on the menu bar and select **Add/Remove Snap In**.
2. Click **Certificates** and select **Add**.
3. Select **Computer Account** and click **Next**.
4. Click **Finish**.
5. Click **OK**.
6. Expand **Certificates**.
7. Expand **Personal** and click **Certificates**.
8. You should be able to see VMware View Composer Certificates here. Select all of them and delete them. You should now be able to go back and successfully install Composer.

A final problem that you might encounter installing Composer (or any software component) is corrupted installation media. This could be a result of not using the checksum when downloading the install files. If the installer fails and all the configuration settings look right, double-check your install files. Any problems with the installation of Composer essentially come down to four things: a problem with permissions (either locally or for the database), an incorrectly set up database, a canceled previous installation, or a corrupt image.

Troubleshooting the Events Database

(This section covers Objective 4.2 of the Blueprint.)

It is strongly recommended that you configure an events database to assist with troubleshooting. However, what if a problem is encountered with the events database itself? This section explores the potential issues you may run into with this VMware View component.

One of the simplest problems to troubleshoot can occur when setting up the events database in the first place. If, during the database configuration, you are unable to establish communication, ensure that port 1433 is open and that you can communicate to the server that the events database is being hosted on. Also verify that the SQL Server Configuration Manager TCP Dynamic Ports field is empty. This can be done using the following steps:

Start > **All Programs** > **Microsoft SQL Server** > **Configuration Tools** > **SQL Server Configuration Manager**

Expand **SQL Server Network Configuration** and select **Protocols**.

Right-click **TCP/IP** and select **Properties**.

Select **IP Addresses**.

In the section titled IPAll, if there are any numbers in the TCP Dynamic Ports field, delete them. (This field should be blank.)

Ensure that port 1433 is entered for this SQL instance. If you need to enter this here, the service will have to be restarted.

When setting up the database, the following error can appear:

```
Database configuration error
An error occurred while attempting to configure the database.
Double check the database parameters and ensure that the database
is not down, restarting, or otherwise unavailable.
```

While it's nice that this error message attempts to give you some advice on resolving the issue, there could be several other reasons the error message was displayed, including another authentication issue, a problem with the database itself, a problem with the database server, or a communication issue. Begin by ensuring that the database server is up, that port 1433 is not being blocked, and that all services are running. Next, ensure that the account has appropriate permissions to the database. Check the ODBC connection for the database and ensure that SQL authentication was selected, or the Connection Server will not be able to make the connection. The Connection Server logs can be of some benefit in identifying the problem and are located at C:\ProgramData\VMware\VDM\logs.

NOTE The growth of the events database is not restricted. It is possible for the database itself to run out of space as historical tables grow.

Troubleshooting Guest OS Customization

(This section covers Objective 4.3 of the Blueprint.)

When virtual desktops are automatically deployed through the use of automated pools, guest OS customization issues can sometimes occur.

If a problem occurs with guest OS customization, the first place to look is, of course, the log files. The QuickPrep, Sysprep, and Composer Customization logs can be found in the following path on the linked-clone virtual desktop:

%system_drive%\Windows\Temp\vmware-viewcomposer-ga-new.log

The Composer log files are kept on the Composer server (vCenter) in the following locations:

- **Windows Server 2003**

  C:\Documents and Settings\All Users\Application Data\VMware\View Composer\Logs\

- **Windows Server 2008**

  C:\ProgramData\VMware\View Composer\Logs\

Virtual desktops can be configured with multiple virtual CPUs, but they should be configured as such only if needed to support HD video or multithreaded applications. These virtual desktops should be the exception and not the rule for all virtual desktops. Scheduling issues can arise from trying to schedule too many vCPUs on an ESXi host, resulting in resource contention and poor performance.

Along with CPU resources, memory resources should be carefully configured as well. Desktop pools should be defined based on use case and user/application requirements. The amount of memory configured will vary, but you can follow some guidelines to attempt to reduce memory contention. As with CPU, if you define too much RAM among all the virtual desktops, you can run into memory overcommitment. Too much overcommitment can force the use of disk-based memory, resulting in slow response and poor performance.

The following amounts of RAM are defined by VMware as guidelines for memory allocation based on OS selection:

- 1GB for 32-bit Windows Vista or Windows 7 virtual desktops
- 2GB for 64-bit Windows 7 virtual desktops
- 1GB for Windows XP virtual desktops

Another problem that can arise when using linked-clone virtual desktops occurs when an organization is not using Microsoft volume activation. Without volume activation, the same license key would be deployed over and over, causing activation errors.

Although not directly related to Guest OS customization, communication, as with any other component of View, is important for the virtual desktops as well. Be certain that name resolution is present and working for the View Agent on the desktops to be able to successfully connect to the Connection Server.

NOTE Make sure that desktop pool accessibility is entitled to all users requiring a desktop from any given pool.

Troubleshooting Accounts and Permissions

(This section covers Objective 4.4 of the Blueprint.)

Several issues can occur if a user, Connection Server, or desktop pool does not have the appropriate permissions to allow access. It's a best practice to create an organizational unit (OU) specifically for your View desktops and groups. You may also choose to have multiple View administrators, in which case it is a good idea to create a View Administrator Active Directory group. In the View Manager, desktop pools are entitled to groups (preferably), but they can also be entitled to individual users. For users to be able to successfully connect to their desktops, it is not enough to create a pool and entitle it. The virtual machine (or source VM, if it was part of an automated pool or linked clone) must have Remote Desktop enabled, and each user/group must be a member of the Remote Desktop Users group. A great way to verify that this is correctly configured is to see whether a user can establish a remote desktop connection directly to the virtual desktop in question.

By default, any user (or group) who is entitled to a pool can access that pool through any of the Connection Servers or Replica Servers. However, restricted entitlements can be used to restrict which desktop pools are accessible to which Connection Servers. This is determined by configuring tags and associating them with both the Connection Servers and the applicable pools. If a user or group is accessing a pool defined with a tag, the Connection Servers through which the user or group connects must have a matching tag. If a pool has a tag, but no tags have been defined on the Connection Server, access is denied. If a pool has a tag and the Connection Server has a tag, they must match, or access is denied. If the Connection Server has a tag defined, but the pool does not, access is permitted. Tag definitions can contain no spaces and have a limit of 64 characters maximum.

View 5 supports smart card authentication. This allows for greater security by not just requiring use of a hardware card but by also requiring the end user to have a PIN to be granted access. Smart card behavior is configurable. Users can be automatically logged out if they remove their card, for example, which would be advantageous for higher-security facilities. Smart cards are *not* supported with the View Client for Mac or for authenticating to the View Administrator. The readers specifically supported are those using PKCS#11 and Microsoft CryptoAPI.

View 5 also supports RSA SecurID. When this function is enabled, users must provide their RSA SecurID credentials before being prompted for Active Directory credentials. The credential is provided via a SecurID token that must first be registered with an RSA Authentication Manager. To use SecurID, the RSA software must be installed first, then SecurID must be enabled in the View Administrator, and finally the sdconf.rec file must be copied to the View Administrator from the RSA Authentication Manager.

If an organization requires the use of Secure Sockets Layer (SSL) connections for the View Client and View Administrator, the View Connection Server service itself must be restarted after this function has been enabled.

A Group Policy ADM template exists that can be used to define policies for all desktops/users. Policies are automatically applied at login. These files are present on the Connection Servers after installation and are located in a subdirectory off the directory where the application was installed:

\VMware\VMware View\Server\Extras\GroupPolicyFiles

The following ADM templates are located in this directory:

- Vdm_client.adm (View Client policies)
- Vdm_server.adm (View Connection Server policies)
- Vdm_common.adm (All view component policies)
- Pcoip.adm (PcoIP protocol policies)
- ViewPM.adm (View Persona policies)

Troubleshooting Connectivity Between View Components

(This section covers Objective 4.5 of the Blueprint.)

A common problem with all environments can be simple communication.

It is important to ensure the following ports are open to allow for successful communication between VMware View components:

- **443:** Remote Desktop Protocol (RDP)
- **4172:** PC-over-IP (PCoIP)
- **8009:** Security Server to Connection Server
- **4001:** Security Server to View Messaging Service
- **3389:** RDP from Security Server to the virtual desktop (View Agent)
- **4172:** PCoIP from Security Server to virtual desktop (View Agent)
- **4100:** Java Message Service Inter-Router (JMSIR)
- **389:** View Manager to AD and authentication
- **4001:** Java Messaging Service

On the public-facing interface of the View Security Server, port 4172 should be enabled if using PCoIP and port 443. Port 80 can also be opened, but should be redirected to 443. On Windows 2008 systems, the View installer automatically opens the required firewall ports. If there is a communication issue, first ensure that these ports are not blocked. Also verify that any external physical network equipment is not blocking any of these ports. Successful name resolution is also critical to proper communications, so ensure that all View servers can resolve each other's name. If there is a communication error, the problem will show up in the View Manager Dashboard.

The following is a VMware article detailing the complete list of ports required by View: http://pubs.vmware.com/view-51/index.jsp?topic=%2Fcom.vmware.ICbase%2FPDF%2Fic_pdf.html.

Finally, ensure that all View servers have static IP addresses.

Troubleshooting PCoIP Configuration

(This section covers Objective 4.6 of the Blueprint.)

Most View environments take advantage of the PCoIP protocol. Several best practices should be adhered to when configuring PCoIP for use with View, but issues can still arise. This section examines problems that can stem from misconfiguring the environment and looks at some potential problems with the protocol.

First, as with any troubleshooting exercise, it is important to isolate the problem. End users can be vague when reporting problems, and the most common complaint you are likely to hear is "it's slow." Although this is not very helpful as a problem statement, general slowness can be assumed to mean that the virtual desktop is performing slower than normally expected. The problem should first be narrowed down to one of three areas: network congestion, resource contention, or disk access issues.

To help narrow down the problem, first examine the available log files. The PCoIP log files are located here:

- **Windows XP:**

  C:\Documents and Settings\All Users\Application Data\VMware\VMD\logs

- **Windows Vista and Windows 7**:

  C:\ProgramData\VMware\VDM\logs

A common PCoIP connection problem occurs when users attempt to connect to a virtual desktop and instead receive a black screen. No desktop background is visible, and the connection eventually closes. This error can be caused by a number of issues that are well documented and include the following:

- The virtual machine is set to a display resolution higher than the physical monitor can support.
- The video RAM for the virtual machine is set to a level that is too low for the display resolution.
- The Group Policy Connect Using DNS Name has become corrupt.

If none of these issues are the source of the problem, the issue is likely communications based. Ensure that all required ports are open (TCP and UDP port 4172). If the problem exists when users try to connect to their desktop through the Security Server, first check to make sure that all the ports are open, then make sure that the public URL for both the Security Server and its associated Connection Server are the same (and are correct).

NOTE Remember, there is an ADM template file to assist with configuration and management of the PCoIP protocol on the Connection Server: C:\Program Files\VMware\VMware View\Servers\Extra\GroupPolicyFiles\pcoip.adm

Troubleshooting View Servers

(This section covers Objective 4.7 of the Blueprint.)

If you wind up troubleshooting issues related to one or more View server components, one of the great things about the View Manager is that you can get a quick status of the entire environment. When you select Servers on the left side of the View Manager, the main pane of the window displays the status of the Connection Servers and Replica Servers as well as the vCenter Server, Transfer Server, and Security Server. If a problem exists with any one of these servers, it should be indicated by the status. This screen should be reviewed if a problem is indicated on the dashboard in the upper-left corner of the View Manager.

Be aware that a View configuration consisting of one Connection Server is not a scalable or highly available solution. For this reason, multiple Connection Servers (or replica servers) should be deployed. These servers automatically replicate to each other, so administrators must log in to only one server and changes will populate to all of them. To provide proper scalability, it would then be beneficial to deploy a third-party load balancer in front of the Connection Servers and Replica Servers.

Problems with any of the View servers (Connection, Replica, Transfer, and Security Servers) can usually be isolated to one of four areas: communications (networking), applications (service failures or stops), operating systems (blue screens, virtual machine stopped), or misconfigurations. The first question that should be asked when a problem is reported with any View component should be, "Has it ever worked?" If so, when did it stop working, and what happened? Sometimes this information can be easy to track down (someone walked into the datacenter and tripped over a cable), or the nature of the problem could take a little more work to isolate.

For example, suppose the Connection Server service is stopped on one server in the environment. If there is a load balancer in front of the Connection/Replica Servers an attempt to log in could very well be unsuccessful due to being routed to the downed server. Subsequent login attempts might or might not be successful depending on which server the load balancer routed the connection attempt to. This could make it difficult to pinpoint the location of the problem. In all cases, the View Administrator should be the first place to look.

In the upper-left corner of the View Administrator, you can quickly identify the state of View components and the overall environment. Green up arrows indicate that everything is working fine. Red down arrows indicate a View server or component is unavailable or has malfunctioned. Yellow arrows show that a component is in a warning (potentially prefailure) state, and question marks indicate that the View Administrator cannot ascertain the functionality of the component. You should be able to click these indicators to find out more information and perhaps identify the root cause. For example, if a View component or vCenter Server is showing a red down arrow, this usually indicates that communication cannot be established. Verify that the servers can resolve each other's names and that all services are running. If the arrow indicates a desktop issue, try to establish what the problem is. (For example, are you able to RDP into the desktop?)

If a Connection Server's health status is red, first verify whether the previous settings are correct. If so, another problem that can cause a communications issue is if the various clocks of the VMware View components are not in sync with each other.

For Transfer Servers, there are some unique issues. Common Transfer Server issues include the following:

- A checkout operation fails at 10% with the error message "No Available Transfer Server." This is most likely because the virtual desktop cannot see the Transfer Server or the Transfer Server cannot see the virtual desktop's files (for example, if the virtual desktop is using a local datastore, and the Transfer Server is on a different ESXi host).

- The first checkout succeeds, but subsequent checkouts fail. This can happen as a result of the Connection Server losing the encryption key for the virtual desktop.
- The login window takes several minutes or times out. This can happen if the Connection Server is not reachable.
- The Transfer Server is listed as Pending in the State field on the Servers section of the View Administrator.
- The Transfer Server cannot enter maintenance mode. If there are checkouts, check-ins, or replications taking place or an administrator is publishing a linked-clone desktop to the Transfer Server, it will not be able to enter maintenance mode until any outstanding operations complete.
- The Transfer Server repository is not present, is invalid, or cannot be connected to. By default, a repository for linked-clone desktops is not defined. The repository can be a local directory on the Transfer Server, or it can be a network path. If a path was defined and is now showing invalid, verify that the Transfer Server can still reach the network path.
- The Transfer Server fails its health check. This can occur if one or more of the services on the Transfer Server are not running. Verify whether all transfer services are running and whether the Transfer Server can reach the Connection Server (and vice versa).
- Recover a local desktop. If a virtual machine was powered off while it was being updated, a recovery may be needed. You would need to launch the View Client from the command line to fix the problem:

```
Wswc -desktopName <VM Name> -username <username> -domainName
<domain name> -repairLocalDesktops
```

Troubleshooting View Persona Management

(This section covers Objective 4.8 of the Blueprint.)

If a Persona Management issue arises, you might need to review the applicable log file. The default location of the Persona Management log is as follows:

- **Windows XP:**

  C:\All Users\Application Data\VMware\VDM\logs\VMWVvp.txt

- **Windows 7:**

  C:\Program Data\VMware\VDM\logs\VMWVvp.txt

If the log file is not present, logging might be disabled. The Logging flags group policy setting must be enabled to turn on Persona Management logging (this is typically enabled by default).

If folder redirection does not appear to be working, or the profile is not loading when the user logs in, a simple problem could be that Persona Management was never enabled. It is important when installing the VMware View Agent inside the virtual desktop (or parent desktop image) that the View Agent with the View Persona Management setup option is selected. If the agent is not installed with this option, Persona Management will not function. It is also worthwhile to note that once Persona Management is enabled you do not want to use roaming profiles for your virtual desktops. You can still use roaming profiles to manage physical machines. It is best practice to use one profile for the virtual environment and a separate profile for the physical machines.

If a user's ThinApp'd applications are not functioning properly, it is important to verify that the user's sandbox is included in the profile. Otherwise, every time the user launches the application, it will be in a freshly installed state.

If users have large files that must be downloaded, be aware that this takes time. Even though Persona Management does a "just in time" retrieval of user data, large files or applications still may take some time to copy across the network to the desktop.

> **NOTE** When using Persona Management to manage user profiles, you must copy the ViewPM.adm Active Directory Template file to the Active Directory server or the parent virtual machine.

Other important things to confirm when it comes to configuring Persona Management include the following:

- The path to the users' profile has to be in the same Active Directory forest as the user.
- The folder has to be large enough to contain all the users' folders.
- The full profile path must be created where the profile's folders were created. If this is not done, Windows could create a user's folder under \\server\<Persona Repository> and append the %username% for the first user who logs in, preventing everyone else from accessing anything underneath it.

- If a user has to switch between Windows XP and Windows Vista or Windows 7 virtual desktops, the user needs two separate profiles. The reason for this is that XP virtual machines use version 1 user profiles, and Windows Vista/7 use version 2, and the two are not interchangeable.
- There is an issue with Windows XP where the Registry is not cleaned out when a user logs out. For Windows XP virtual desktops only, UPHClean (User Profile Hive Cleanup Service) must be installed.
- View Persona Management cannot be used with local mode desktops.
- If you are using antivirus scans inside the virtual machine, configure Persona Management to load all the files in the profile up-front instead of as needed.
- If users need to save a large number of files (or large files), use persistent virtual disks and do not remove the local Persona at log off.

NOTE The previously mentioned ADM template for Persona Management can also be used for troubleshooting. On the Connection Server, the file is located here: C:\Program Files\VMware\VMware View\Server\Extras\GroupPolicy\Fles\ViewPM.adm.

Summary

This chapter examined some common problems that sometimes arise during the installation, configuration, and administration of a VMware View environment. The larger the environment, the more complexity in that environment, and the more likely issues are to crop up. To assist with troubleshooting, administrators must know where to find information that can help identify and resolve issues. Reviewing the log files and working with the events database should help with this task.

As you learned in this chapter, some problems are not easily resolved. However, many of these problems stem from simple misconfigurations such as blocked ports, making it important to know the paths of communication.

Upon completion of this chapter, you should now understand how to resolve many common issues that may impact your environment.

Exam Preparation Tasks

Review All the Key Topics

Review the most important topics in the chapter, noted with the Key Topic icon in the outer margin of the page. Table 9-3 lists a reference of these key topics and the page numbers on which each is found.

Table 9-3 Key Topics

Key Topic Element	Description	Page
Table 9-2	vCenter Permissions for the Composer Role	206
List	Supported databases	207
List	Composer service account permissions	208
List	Composer vCenter role permissions	208
File location	Connection Server log file	210
File location	Composer log file locations	211
List	Memory allocations	211
List	ADM template files	213
List	Port numbers	213
File locations	PCoIP log file locations	214
List	Black screen causes	215
List	Transfer Server common issues	216
File locations	Persona log file locations	217

Troubleshooting Scenario

Your organization tells you that users connecting from home are seeing a black screen upon launching their virtual desktops. They are able to connect to the Security Server and select their virtual desktop pool, but when the connection launches, all they see is a black screen. How would you resolve this issue?

Ensure that the virtual machine resolution is not set too high.

Ensure that the virtual machine has enough video RAM defined.

Ensure that Group Policy has not become corrupt.

Ensure that the required ports are open.

Ensure that the external address is the same for the Connection Server and Security Server.

Refer to Appendix A for the answers.

Define Key Terms

Define the following key terms from this chapter and check your answers in the Glossary:

> Composer, linked clones, Connection Server, QuickPrep, Sysprep, View Agent, replica server, tag, PCoIP, ODBC, DSN, OU, RSA SecurID, ADM template, RDP

Review Questions

You can find the answers to these review questions in Appendix A.

1. In View 5.1, how can the Composer Server be deployed?
   - **a.** Simply deploy the virtual appliance provided by VMware.
   - **b.** Install Composer on the same server as the View Connection Server.
   - **c.** Install Composer on the same server as vCenter Server.
   - **d.** Install Composer on a separate virtual machine from vCenter Server.

2. Which type of database cannot be used for the events database?
   - **a.** IBM DB2
   - **b.** Oracle 10g
   - **c.** Oracle 11g
   - **d.** MS SQL 2008 R2

3. Which of the following would cause a checkout operation to fail at 10% with the error message "No Available Transfer Server"?
   - **a.** The virtual desktop is on the wrong domain.
   - **b.** The Transfer Server has not been installed yet.
   - **c.** The virtual desktop is a linked clone with more than one persistent disk.
   - **d.** The Transfer Server cannot see the virtual desktop's virtual disk

4. Which TCP port is required for the connection to the events database?
   a. 443
   b. 9443
   c. 1433
   d. 903

5. Which port is required for PCoIP communication?
   a. 1433
   b. 4100
   c. 4173
   d. 4172

6. A user is entitled access to a virtual desktop pool that has a tag of Development. Under which circumstances will that user be allowed access to the View environment?
   a. The pool is tagged for Sales, and the Connection Server is tagged for Development.
   b. The pool is tagged for Development, and the Connection Server is tagged for Sales.
   c. The pool is tagged for Development, and the Connection Server is not tagged.
   d. The pool is not tagged, but the Connection Server has a tag of Development.

7. Which of the following would be a valid tag to use with Connection Servers and pools?
   a. Internal_Contract-Workers Corporate_Office
   b. Internal_Contract_Workers_East
   c. Internal_Contract_Workers_East_Atrium_West_Sixth_Floor_Data_Center_Side
   d. View Internal Contract Workers

8. The PCoIP logs are found in which directory on a Windows XP machine?
   a. Windows XP does not store PCoIP log files.
   b. C:\Documents and Settings\All Users\Application Data\VMware\VMware View\PCoIP\logs
   c. C:\Program Files\VMware\VMD\logs
   d. C:\Documents and Settings\All Users\Application Data\VMware\VMD\logs

9. Which of the following is *not* a valid ADM template file?
   a. 1433vdm_client.adm
   b. 4100vdm_common.adm
   c. 4173vdm_persona.adm
   d. 4172viewPM.adm

10. Which of the following could cause the Transfer Server repository to be listed as "invalid" in the View Administrator?
    a. The Transfer Server repository was never configured.
    b. The Transfer Server repository is on an unreachable network share.
    c. The Transfer Server repository is on a separate virtual disk.
    d. The Transfer Server does not have VMware Tools installed.

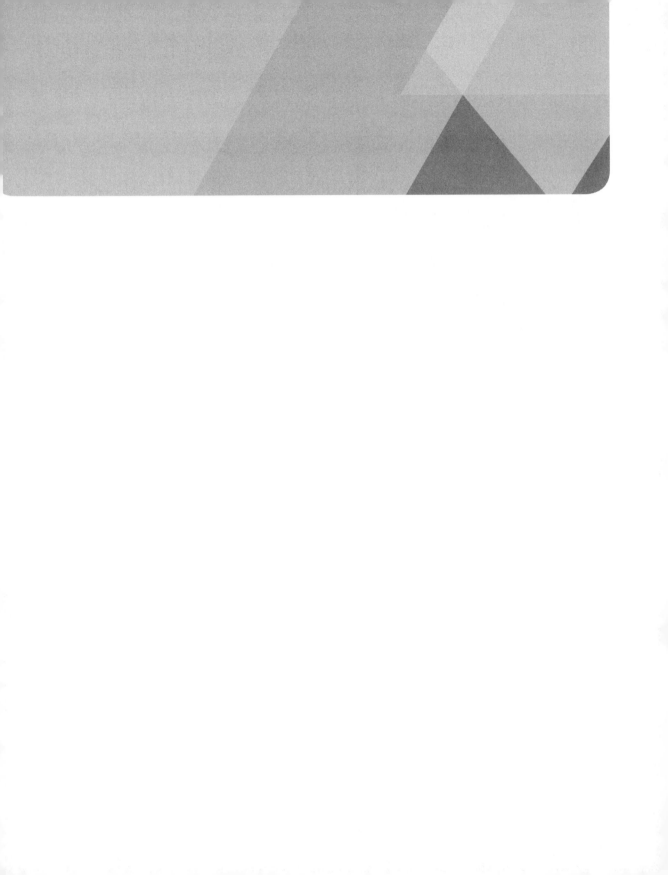

APPENDIX A

Answers to the "Do I Know This Already?" Quizzes and Review Questions

Chapter 1

Do I Know This Already?

1. D
2. B
3. D
4. A
5. A and C
6. A and C
7. D
8. A
9. A
10. C

Review Questions

1. C
2. C
3. B
4. C
5. A
6. B
7. A
8. D
9. D
10. D

Chapter 2

Do I Know This Already?

1. D
2. B
3. A
4. D
5. C
6. B
7. C
8. B
9. A
10. B and D

Review Questions

1. C
2. A
3. C
4. B
5. B
6. D
7. B and D
8. C
9. B
10. B

Chapter 3

Do I Know This Already?

1. B
2. D
3. B
4. A
5. C
6. C
7. C

Review Questions

1. A
2. B
3. B
4. A and C
5. B
6. A
7. C

Chapter 4

Do I Know This Already?

1. B
2. D
3. A
4. B
5. C
6. C
7. A
8. C
9. D
10. C

Review Questions

1. B
2. B
3. C
4. A
5. B
6. D
7. D
8. B
9. C
10. D

Chapter 5

Do I Know This Already?

1. A
2. C
3. C
4. A
5. D
6. B
7. B
8. A and B
9. A
10. A

Review Questions

1. C
2. A
3. C
4. A
5. B
6. C
7. A
8. C and D
9. A
10. A

Chapter 6

Do I Know This Already?

1. A and C
2. A
3. C
4. C
5. B
6. D
7. C
8. C
9. D
10. A

Review Questions

1. B
2. A
3. C
4. C
5. C
6. A
7. A
8. B
9. A
10. B

Chapter 7

Do I Know This Already?

1. D
2. A
3. A and C
4. B
5. D

Review Questions

1. A, B, and C
2. A and D
3. C
4. B
5. C
6. B
7. D
8. B, C, and F
9. C
10. A and C

Chapter 8

Do I Know This Already?

1. B
2. C
3. B
4. B

Review Questions

1. B
2. D
3. A
4. B
5. D
6. A
7. D
8. A and B
9. C
10. B and D

Chapter 9

Do I Know This Already?

1. C
2. D
3. A
4. A, B, and D
5. D
6. B
7. C
8. A

Review Questions

1. C and D
2. A
3. D
4. C
5. D
6. B and C
7. B
8. D
9. C
10. B

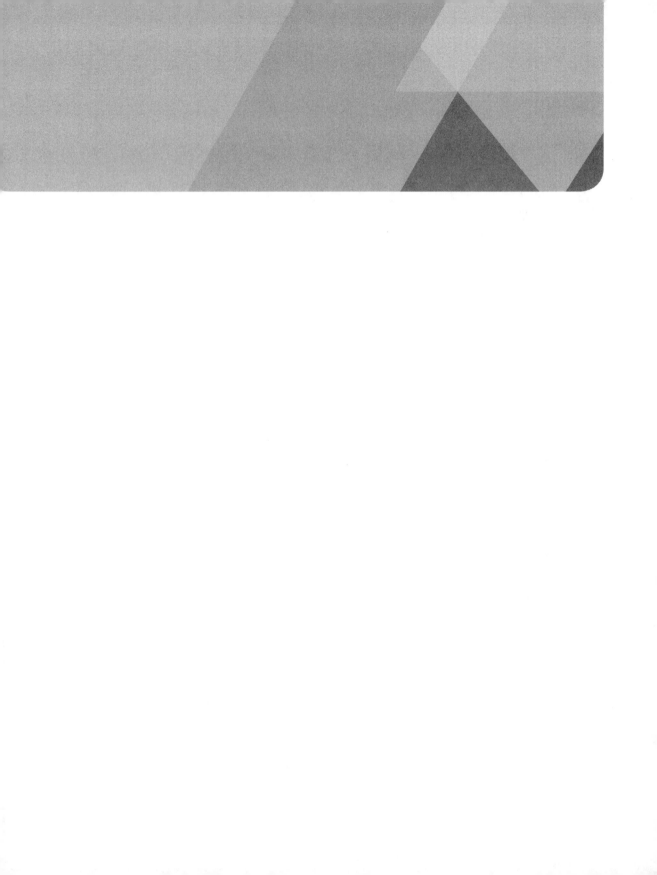

GPOs

Windows 2003 only: HKEY_LOCAL_MACHINE\SYSTEM\CurrentControlSet\Services\Tcpip\Parameters

HKEY_LOCAL_MACHINE\SOFTWARE\VMware, Inc.\VMware VDM\Plugins\wsnm\tunnelService\Params

ADM Templates

Table B-1 VMware View GPO Templates

Template	Description
vdm_agent.adm	This template applies to configuring policy settings related to the View Agent. These will apply to the desktop that the end user will connect to.
vdm_client.adm	This template applies to configuring policy settings related to clients that connect from within the domain. Any clients outside of the domain that the View Connection Server is a member of will not be affected by these policies.
vdm_server.adm	This template applies policies that affect the View Connection Server. This includes any View replica servers that are associated to the initial View Connection Server.
vdm_common.adm	This template allows policies to be applied on all View components (specifically, the View Agent, the View Client, and the View Connection Servers).
pcoip.adm	This template policy applies to the PC-over-IP (PCoIP) display protocol. If the remote connection uses Remote Desktop Protocol (RDP), these Group Policy Objects (GPOs) will not be applicable.
ViewPM.adm	This template applies policies related to View Persona Management.

Table B-2 View PCoIP General Session Variables

GPO	Description
Configure Clipboard Redirection	Defines whether to allow clipboard copy from the client to the View desktop only, View desktop to client only, both directions, or disabled. The default value is Enable client to server only (from View client system to View desktop).
Configure PCoIP Client Image Cache Size Policy	Sets the size of the PCoIP client image cache. This cache ensures that not all images have to be re-sent over and over again (for example, desktop icons). The default value is 250MB and can be adjusted to a size ranging from 50MB to 300MB. This GPO affects only the Windows and Linux clients. At the time of this writing, Mac and other VMWare View Clients do not support a PCoIP client image cache.
Configure PCoIP Image Quality Levels	Defines how PCoIP will display images when the network is congested. There are three values. The first is Minimum Image Quality, which defines how the image and frame rate will initially appear. This defaults to a value of 50 and can be changed to anything from 30 to 100. The lower the value, the faster an image/frame is displayed; however, this is done at a cost of quality. Images will appear fuzzier at lower values. In addition, this value cannot be higher than Maximum Initial Image Quality. Maximum Initial Image Quality helps to reduce the peaks that could be created by additional pixels (for changed areas) being sent during the initial stage. This value cannot be less than Minimum Image Quality. It defaults to 90 and can be set to any value from 30 to 100. It's important to consider what kind of images you are viewing. It's possible to make this value (and other graphic values) lower, but if image quality is required to be high (for example, medical imaging or CAD/CAM images) lowering these values could be detrimental. Maximum Frame Rate helps to control how much average bandwidth a user may utilize by limiting how often the screen is updated per second. The default value is 30 frames per second (FPS). (Films use 24FPS, and U.S. television often uses 30FPS.) The value can be anything from 1 to 120. Setting this value too low may result in stuttering of motion video. This GPO applies to the soft host only. If the GPO is disabled or not configured, it will use the default values (Minimum Image Quality will be 50 while Maximum Initial Image Quality will be 90).

GPO	Description
Configure PCoIP Session Encryption Algorithms	Determines which algorithm will be used for the session negotiation. At least one algorithm must be selected. By default, both AES-128-GCM and Salsa20-256round12 are enabled. If FIPS140-2 approved mode is selected, the Disable AES-128-GCM encryption option will not be available, because AES-128-GCM is required for FIPS140-2.
Configure PCoIP USB Allowed and Unallowed Device Rules	Determines which USB devices are allowed or not allowed to be used with zero clients; these are clients that use the Teradici firmware to connect to a View desktop. The default setting is to allow all devices to connect. For both the authorization and unauthorization tables, a maximum of 10 rules. The rules can be either a combination of a vendor ID (VID) and a product ID (PID) or it can define a class of USB devices. For a class rule, it can allow or disallow a whole device class, a subclass, or a protocol within a class. The rule format for VID/PID usage is `Rule#VIDPID` and is formatted as `1aaaazzzz`, where 1 is the rule number; *aaaa* is the VID hexadecimal, and *zzzz* is the PID hexadecimal. For example, if I want to block all 8GB Apple Nano devices (fourth generation), I just create a rule for the VID of 0x05ac and a PID of 0x1263, so it would be `105ac1263`. If I specifically want to allow webcams, I can use the rule of `22030eXXXX`. This means regardless of the vendor, webcams will be allowed. If a device is listed in the USB unauthorization table, it will not be allowed to be used, and if the device is listed in the USB authorization table, it will be allowed to be used.
Configure PCoIP Virtual Channels	Defines the virtual channels that are allowed or disallowed to be used during PCoIP sessions.
Configure the Client PCoIP UDP Port	Defines the UDP to be used by the software PCoIP clients. It identifies the base port to use and possible port range. (This allows for other ports to be used if the base port is unavailable.) The default values are a base port of 50002 with a port range of 64. (This means the range starts at 50002 and could possibly be 50066 as its highest value.)
Configure the TCP Port to Which the PCoIP Host Binds and Listens	Defines what TCP port the View Agent, on software PCoIP desktops, will attempt to bind to and what port range might be used (a value between 0 and 10). The base port depends on which version of the View Agent it is. The default value for View Agents that are version 4.0.x or earlier is 50002, and the default value for View Agents that are version 4.5 and later is 4172.

GPO	Description
Configure the UDP Port to Which the PCoIP Host Binds and Listens	Defines what UDP port the View Agent, on software PCoIP desktops, will attempt to bind to and what port range might be used (a value between 0 and 10). The base port depends on which version of the View Agent it is. The default value for View Agents that are version 4.0.x or earlier is 50002, and the default value for View Agents that are version 4.5 and later is 4172.
Enable Access to a PCoIP Session from a vSphere Console	By default when a PCoIP session is active, the vSphere Client console screen is blacked out to ensure privacy of the desktop (often a requirement of policies such as the Health Insurance Portability and Accountability Act [HIPAA] and the Sarbanes-Oxley Act [SOX]). In environments where this is not a requirement, you can enable access (both to see and interact with it) through the vSphere Client console. To enable seeing the desktop through the vSphere Client console on Windows 7 desktops, the virtual hardware must be version 8 or later. (Hardware version 8 is only found on ESXi 5.x and later.) To allow for vSphere Client input on Windows 7, any hardware version is allowed. For Windows XP or Vista systems, the hardware version can be any version.
Enable the FIPS 140-2 Approved Mode of Operation	Ensures that only FIPS 140-2 approved cryptographic algorithms and protocols are used for PCoIP sessions. When this is enabled, it prevents AES128-GCM from being disabled, because this is a required cryptographic algorithm for FIPS 140-2. Note that this GPO is only available for View 4.5 and later. If View 4.0 and earlier is being used, this GPO is ignored. This setting can be applied to the agent, the client, or both. Ideally, it would be used for both to ensure that all algorithms can be used since single-endpoint enablement reduces the effectiveness of the algorithms used.
Enable/Disable Audio in the PCoIP Session	Audio tends to be a large bandwidth waster and this particular GPO can be an easy way to alleviate excess bandwidth usage by disabling the use of audio. Most employees will not need it. This setting determines whether audio will be allowed when using the PCoIP. The default setting is enabled.
Enable/Disable Microphone Noise and DC Offset Filter in PCoIP	Either allows or prevents the use of microphone noise and DC offset filters for microphone input while in a PCoIP session. This can be applied against the View Agent and Teradici audio driver only. (At the time of this writing, this can be found only in the Windows View Client.) By default, the use of microphone noise and DC offset filters is enabled.

GPO	Description
Turn on PCoIP User Default Input Language Synchronization	This allows the View Agent to determine what language the client is inputting via the keyboard (for example, French, English, Korean). By default, the View Agent does not do any synchronization. Note that this setting can be applied only against the View Agent.

Table B-3 View PCoIP Session Bandwidth Variables

GPO	Description
Configure the Maximum PCoIP Session Bandwidth	Defined in kilobits per second, the maximum bandwidth sets the absolute maximum a specific session may use. This setting includes all graphics, audio, USB, control traffic, and the virtual channels. The PCoIP server (View Agent) will adhere to the value set, which could prevent poor performance or packet loss. You should set this value to the maximum capacity you want the session to have. It should be equal to or less than the value of what the endpoint can handle. For example, if the endpoint has a 10MB network interface card (NIC) and connects to the Internet through a 4Mb connection, the value should be equal to or less than the 4Mb. (If you need a quick conversion of kilobits to megabytes to megabits, you can visit http://www.easycalculation.com/bandwidth-calculator.php.) If the client and the View Agent have different values, the lowest of the two values is used when transmitting data. This value can be applied to both the View Client and the View Agent. The default value is 90000Kbps.
Configure the PCoIP Session Bandwidth Floor	Defined in kilobits per second, this sets what the lower limit of a session can be set to. This can prove helpful for networks that are particularly congested, by reserving bandwidth for sessions and thus ensuring that the end user does not have to wait for the congestion to clear. It is important, however, to plan appropriately and ensure that the sum total of all the "floors" does not exceed the bandwidth itself. By default, no minimum bandwidth is configured. (The value of 0 is used.) Although this setting can apply to both the View Agent and the View Client, it will affect only the endpoint that is configured for it.

GPO	Description
Configure the PCoIP Session MTU	Defines the maximum transmission unit (MTU) size for only the UDP packets of a PCoIP session. The default size of the packets is 1300 bytes, but the value could be set to anything between 500 and 1500 bytes. It would be rare to change this value. However, in cases where the network has a unique configuration, adjust the MTU to avoid fragmentation of the packets. Both the View Agent and View Client can have this attribute applied to them, but if the values differ, the lowest size of the two is used.
Configure the PCoIP Session Audio Bandwidth Limit	Defines the maximum amount of bandwidth that can be used for audio (sound replay) for PCoIP sessions. The default value is 500Kbps (which allows for high-quality stereo audio but compressed). The minimum value can be set to 50Kbps (which could mean no audio or audio being disabled). A value greater than 1600Kbps means uncompressed high-quality stereo audio. Values between 50Kbps and 450Kbps can result in qualities similar to that of FM radio or phone calls. This value applies only to View 4.6 and later. If the View environment is 4.0 and earlier, it will ignore this GPO.
Turn Off Build-to-Lossless Feature	Defines whether to build images to a lossless state. By default, Build-to-Lossless is enabled, and to disable this feature you have to agree to this (check the **I accept to turn off the Build-to-Lossless feature**) and enable this GPO setting. For environments that do not require pristine "every pixel" images, enabling this GPO can result in performance improvements.

Table B-4 View PCoIP Session Variables for the Keyboard

GPO	Description
Disable sending CAD when Users Press Ctrl+Alt+Del	By default, when users press Ctrl+Alt+Del, it might try to lock the local Windows client and the remote desktop. To help avoid confusion for end users, this setting can be enabled, which results in users pressing Ctrl+Alt+Ins to lock/unlock the remote desktop session when using PCoIP. By default, this GPO is not enabled.

GPO	Description
Enable Right Shift Behavior When a PCoIP Client Is Connected	If you use View Agent 4.5 or earlier and access an RDP session from within the PCoIP session, the right Shift key does not work as intended. Enabling this GPO allows to substitute the right Shift key with the left Shift key. This applies *only* to the View Agent. For View Agents 4.6 and later, this GPO has no impact.
Use Alternate Key for Sending Secure Attention Sequence (SAS)	This GPO allows you to define an alternate key other than the Insert key for sending the Secure Attention Sequence (SAS) to lock/unlock a remote desktop session using PCoIP. This particular GPO is particularly helpful for environments where the vSphere Client is used to access the console of a virtual machine on ESXi or vCenter on the remote desktop through PCoIP. By setting this, you avoid confusion between the SAS for the remote desktop and the one to use for the vSphere Client console. If this value is enabled, you *must* select a value for the third key in the SAS sequence from the drop-down.
Use Enhanced Keyboard on Windows Client If Available	Before you enable this GPO, the Windows client *must* have the keyboard filter driver (vmkbd.sys) installed and configured. If VMware Workstation, Player, or the View Client with Local Mode is installed, this driver is already installed and configured. This GPO allows for the use of special keys found on extended or enhanced keyboards (for example, Win+L) to be recognized by the PCoIP remote desktop. This can also be used for international keyboards.

Table B-5 View Agent Configuration ADM Template

GPO	Computer	User	Description
AllowDirectRDP	X		Enabled by default, this setting allows non-View clients to connect directly to View desktops using Remote Desktop Protocol (RDP). By disabling this, you can force clients to connect through the Connection Server only to get to the desktop. Note that because of the way that the Mac client works this GPO should not be disabled, because it will prevent them from connecting to the environment.

GPO	Computer	User	Description
AllowSingleSignon	X		Enabled by default, this setting allows for the use of single sign-on (SSO). For an end-user experience, this can be helpful. However, for environments that require extra security, it may be beneficial to disable this GPO.
CommandsToRunOnConnect	X		List any commands or lists of commands that are needed to run when the user connects, for the first time, to the desktop.
CommandsToRunOnReconnect	X		If any of the commands or lists of commands need to run again after first connect, ensure that they are listed here.
Connect Using DNS Name	X		Disabled by default, this setting can be helpful for environments that have a Network Address Translation (NAT) in place when the View Client or View Connection Server cannot connect directly via IP address.
ConnectionTicketTimeout	X		By default, the connection ticket timeout is set to 900 seconds (30 minutes). You can change this, as needed, depending on security requirements. This setting determines how long the View Clients use the connection ticket for verification and SSO requirements. If authentication does not occur within that time, the session times out.
CredentialFilterExceptions	X		In some cases, the credentials passed through the agent are not needed or wanted for specific files. You can specify which files you do not want to load the agent CredentialFilter. No path or suffix should be used. And when there is more than one filename, use a semicolon (;) to delineate between various filenames.

GPO	Computer	User	Description
Disable Time Zone Synchronization	X	X	Disabled by default, in some situations it will be necessary to let the desktop keep the time zone that it was created in rather than the time zone that the client is in. Note that if this setting is enabled, the Disable Time Zone Forwarding GPO setting for the client is not enabled.
Enable Multi-Media Acceleration	X		Enabled by default, this setting ensures that multimedia redirection (MMR) sends multimedia content to the client to decode instead of having the virtual desktop do it. This can result in a better end-user experience, but only if the client has sufficient resources to do so. In addition, the View Client has to have overlay support. This setting will not apply to local mode desktops.
Force MMR to Use Software Overlay	X		MMR uses hardware overlay where possible. However, if the client has multiple monitors, MMR often only applies to the primary monitors, and moving any multimedia content to any secondary monitors will result in it not being displayed. Enabling this ensures that MMR will utilize a software overlay to allow for this behavior. This particular setting is disabled by default.
ShowDiskActivityIcon	X		This setting is no longer supported.
Toggle Display Settings Control	X		Enabled by default, this setting ensures that when using the PC-to-IP (PCoIP) display protocol the Settings tab is available in the Control Panel. Kiosk-type desktops may benefit from having this setting disabled.

Table B-6 View Client Configuration ADM Template: Scripting Definitions

GPO	Description
Connect All USB Devices to the Desktop on Launch	Defines scripting option to ensure all devices are connected at launch. (Devices such as smart cards, USB printers, barcode scanners, and other dependent devices would benefit, as would kiosk systems.)
Connect All USB Devices to the Desktop When They Are Plugged In	Similar to the preceding GPO, this autoconnects devices when attached. Kiosk systems, barcode scanners, and other optional devices can be autoconnected when the client detects them after login to the desktop.
DesktopLayout	Specifies the layout options that users can have upon login, including the following: ■ Full Screen ■ Multimonitor ■ Window - Large ■ Window - Small The GPO DesktopName to Select setting must be set as well.
DesktopName to Select	Identifies which desktop to use.
Disable 3rd-Party Terminal Services Plugins	This setting, when enabled, disables the ability for the View Client to check for third-party Terminal Services plug-ins. (These are often installed as normal RDP plug-ins.) Keep in mind that this will not affect any View-specific plugs like USB redirection and so forth.
Logon DomainName	Specifies the NetBIOS domain name (derivative of the AD domain name) to be used by the View Client.
Logon UserName	Allows the script to insert the username that the View Client will use for authentication.
Logon Password	Specifies the password to be used. Keep in mind that this will be stored in clear text in the AD.

GPO	Description
Server URL	Identifies the URL for the Connection Server to be used by the View Client. For example, it could be http://view.company.com, which could either be the address directly to the Connection Server or the load balancer that will lead to the Connection Server.
Suppress Error Messages (When Fully Scripted Only)	When enabled, it hides error messages when the View Client logs in. However, this only works when the login is fully scripted.

Table B-7 View Client Configuration ADM Template: Security Setting

GPO	Computer	User	Description
Allow Command Line Credentials	X		Enabled by default, this GPO allows for user credentials to be passed through the command line. However, this means that SmartCardPIN and password options are not available for use.
Servers Trusted for Delegation	X		For environments where you may have some end users coming in from a non-domain location and some from within the domain (for example, internal employees and external partners), you can specify which Connection Servers will recognize Log In as Current User and which ones will not use this. By default, all Connection Servers accept this information. When setting a specific server to use these settings (and thus, enabling others to not use this), you can specify the server by entering the server information in one of three formats: ■ domain\system$ ■ system$@domain.com ■ The SPN (service principal name)

GPO	Computer	User	Description
Certificate Verification Mode	X		This setting configures the default value for the View Client and prevents users from changing this option, although they can see what the setting is set to. The option can be configured to one of the following three options: ■ **No Security:** This means that the View Client doesn't check nor verify the certificate. ■ **Warn but Allow:** The View Client checks the certificate, and if it is not signed, is expired, or is not valid, it gives a warning. ■ **Full Security:** This forces the View Client to use a signed and valid certificate. If the certificate is not valid, is expired, or is unsigned, the user will not be able to connect. If this GPO is not enabled, the default behavior of the View Client is to Warn but Allow. In addition, end users can change this setting on the client itself. Alternatively, CertCheckMode can be enabled on the client system. For 32-bit Windows systems: HKLM\Software\VMware, Inc.\VMware VDM\Client\Security For 64-bit Windows systems: HKLM\Software\Wow6432Node\VMware, Inc.\VMware VDM\Client\Security For this Registry key, changing the value sets the client system to use one of the earlier described options: 0 = No Security 1 = Warn but Allow 2 = Full Security If both the GPO and Registry key are used, the GPO overrides the Registry key.

GPO	Computer	User	Description
Default Value of the 'Log in as Current User' check box	X	X	By default, this GPO is not enabled. However, if all end users are going to be from within the domain, this can help ensure SSO (single sign-on) behavior for an environment and reduce the number of times users have to enter their log in information. If a user logs in to the View Client via the command line with the command `logInAsCurrentUser`, those values override this setting.
Display Option to Log in as Current User	X	X	By default, this GPO is enabled. If you disable this option, end users will have the option to select or deselect the option Log in as Current User. This can be helpful for users who access the View environment from both within the domain and outside the domain.
Enable Jump List Integration	X		By default, the View Client keeps a list of recently accessed View Connection Servers. For a client system that is shared by multiple users, disabling this feature ensures that others will not see the Connection Servers for other users.
Enable Single Sign-On for Smart Card Authentication	X		This setting allows the View Client to temporarily cache the smart card PIN in memory when logging in to the end user's desktop. If this option is disabled, the View Client will not display the smart card PIN dialog for login.
Ignore Bad SSL Certificate Date Received from the Server	X		This setting suppresses any errors that relate to the date on the certificate, usually after the date has passed for the certificate. Only applies to View 4.6 and earlier releases.
Ignore Certificate Revocation Problems	X		This setting suppresses any errors that relate to a certificate being revoked. Only applies to View 4.6 and earlier releases.
Ignore Incorrect SSL Certificate Common Name (Host Name Field)	X		This setting suppresses any errors that relate to a certificate hostname that does not match the hostname of the server that sent the certificate. Only applies to View 4.6 and earlier releases.

GPO	Computer	User	Description
Ignore Incorrect Usage Problems	X		This setting suppresses any errors that relate to a certificate being used that was intended to be used for something other than verifying the sender and ensuring that the connection is encrypted. Only applies to View 4.6 and earlier releases.
Ignore Unknown Certificate Authority Problems			This setting suppresses any errors where the server certificate is associated to an unknown certificate authority (CA), usually the result of a certificate signed by an untrusted third-party CA. Only applies to View 4.6 and earlier releases.

Table B-8 View Client Configuration ADM Template: RDP Settings

GPO	Description
Audio Redirection	The default setting is to redirect the audio to the client. However, you can explicitly set the audio behavior to one of the following: ■ **Disable Audio:** This setting does as it says: disables audio from being played. This can help reduce bandwidth. ■ **Play VM (this is needed for VoIP USB support):** Audio will be played on the View desktop and requires a USB audio device on the client system. ■ **Redirect to client:** Audio will be redirected to the client system. Remember that this setting is for RDP only. If audio is redirected as part of MMR, it will be played on the client system and not the View desktop.
Audio Capture Redirection	By default, this setting is disabled. If enabled, this will redirect audio input from an audio input device connected to the client to the remote View desktop.

GPO	Description
Bitmap Cache File Size in XX for YY bpp Bitmaps	This setting sets the size of the bitmap cache (in kilobytes or megabytes) for the bitmap color settings, or color depth, (specifically in a bits per pixel or bpp sizing). The options for this setting are as follows: KB/8bpp MB/8bpp MB/16bpp MB/24bpp MB/32bpp
Bitmap Caching/Cache Persistence Active	To help improve performance, you can enable the persistent bitmap. However, this increases disk space usage by the client.
Color Depth	This setting can specify the color depth of the View desktop as 8bit, 15bit, 16bit, 24bit, or 32bit. For Windows XP systems, you need to enable the Limit Maximum Color Depth policy in **Computer Configuration > Administrative Templates > Windows Components > Terminal Services** and ensure that it is set to 24 bits, the maximum for that operating system.
Cursor Shadow	This setting will either enable or disable the cursor shadow. By disabling this, you can improve performance.
Desktop Background	This setting will either enable or disable the desktop background when a View client connects to a View desktop. By disabling the background, you can improve performance.
Desktop Composition	This setting can be used only with Windows Vista or later. If you enable this setting, Windows Aero can be enabled and leveraged through video memory, which then renders it to the display. Depending on the bandwidth available, this can either degrade performance or improve the end-user experience.
Enable Compression	This setting is enabled by default. Disabling this may adversely affect bandwidth usage.
Enable Credential Security Service Provider	This setting is disabled by default. If you are using Windows Vista or Windows 7 desktops that have Network Layer Authentication (NLA) enabled, this setting must be enabled. In addition, both the client and the View desktop must support the use of NLA. This setting also can only be used in a direct connect mode and is not supported in tunneled connection.

GPO	Description
Enable RDP Auto-Reconnect	This setting is disabled by default and, when enabled, only works with View Agent 4.5 and later on the remote desktop. This setting ensures that the RDP client tries to connect again when the RDP connection fails.
Font Smoothing	This setting applies only to Windows Vista or later Windows operating systems. This setting will enable font anti-aliasing where needed when enabled.
Menu and Window Animation	Enables animation for menu and windows. Enabling this could adversely affect performance.
Redirect Clipboard	When enabled, allows for local clipboard information to be copied to the View desktop.
Redirect Drives	By default, this setting is enabled. This setting allows for local drives on the client system to be redirected to the View desktop. If data security is of concern, disabling this would be a better option. Alternatively, disabling folder redirection for remote sessions by setting the GPO Do not allow drive redirection is another way to ensure a secure desktop.
Redirect Printers	This setting allows for local printers to be redirected to the View desktop.
Redirect Serial Ports	This setting allows for local COM ports to be redirected to the View desktop.
Redirect Smart Cards	This setting allows for local smart cards to be redirected to the View desktop. This particular setting applies to both RDP and PCoIP sessions.
Redirect Support Plug-And-Play Devices	This is not the same as the USB redirection piece of the View Agent. This will allow, when enabled, local plug-and-play devices and point-of-sale (POS) devices to connect to the View desktop.
Shadow Bitmaps	Enables bitmap shadows except in full screen mode. Enabling this could adversely affect performance.
Show Contents of Window While Dragging	When enabled, it displays the contents of a folder when dragging that folder to a new location. Enabling this could adversely affect performance.
Themes	When enabled, allows themes to be used by end users on their remote desktop. Enabling this could adversely affect performance.
Windows Key Combination Redirection	When set, this allows you to redirect key combinations (for example, Shift+F2) to the remote View desktop. When this is not set, all key combinations apply locally only.

Table B-9 View Client Configuration ADM Template: General Settings

GPO	Computer	User	Description
Always on Top		X	Enabled by default, this setting ensures that the View Client will be the topmost window on the client system. However, this prevents the Windows taskbar from covering the View desktop.
Default Exit Behavior for Local Mode Desktops		X	By default, when a user connects to a local mode desktop, it shuts down. This behavior can be changed to a simple logoff (the virtual machine will remained powered on) if needed.
Delay the Start of Replications When Starting the View Client with Local Mode	X		Delaying the start of replication after starting the View Client with Local Mode helps to ensure that the local client system has been given enough time to ensure that it has network connectivity. This would be the first replication done. Remaining replication would be done as per the interval setting value in the View Administrator local mode policies. The value is done in seconds and has a default value of 900 seconds (15 minutes). Setting this value too low may not give enough time to ensure that the network is active.
Determines If the VMware View Client Should Use proxy.pac File	X		A PAC file (Proxy Auto Configured) is a JavaScript file that identifies a specific proxy for a specific URL. This setting, when enabled, allows the View Client to use a PAC file (proxy.pac). Note that if this setting is enabled on a multicore system, the WinINet application (part of the View Client that looks for the proxy.pac) may crash. This setting affects only direct connections and does not work with tunneled connections. Only applies to View 4.6 and earlier releases.
Disable Time Zone Forwarding	X		This setting, when enabled, ensures that the View Client will not synchronize its time with the local client system.

GPO	Computer	User	Description
Disable Toast Notification			Toast notifications are those little pop-up messages that you get when you receive an email or when a new instant message comes in. These messages normally appear at the corner of the screen; actual location varies depending on the application. Note that if this setting is enabled, this prevents the 5-minute warning for session timeout from appearing.
Don't Check Monitor Alignment on Spanning		X	By default, this setting is disabled. This means that the View Client will not span multiple monitors if multiple monitors are connected to the View Client.
Enable Multi-Media Acceleration		X	When this setting is enabled, multimedia redirection (MMR) is allowed on the client if the client operating system allows it and if the client hardware supports it. This means that the underlying hardware must have overlay support.
Enable the Shade		X	By default enabled, this setting allows the shade bar at the top of the remote desktop session if available. By default, this setting is disabled in kiosk mode desktops.
Redirect Smart Card Readers in Local Mode	X		By default enabled, the View Client redirects card readers to the local mode virtual machine. In some environments, this may need to be disabled if the smart card is not used with the local mode desktop.
Tunnel Proxy Bypass Address List	X		This setting would be populated with specific addresses that the proxy would not be used with. The separator for each address is a semicolon (;).
URL for View Client Online Help	X		If the end user cannot access the remote help (for example, local mode desktops that are not connected to a network), an alternative URL can be used.
Pin the Shade		X	By default enabled, this setting shows the pin option for the shade. If the shade is disabled (kiosk mode connections), this setting has no impact on the shade.

Table B-10 View Agent Configuration ADM Template: Device-Splitting Settings

GPO	Description
Allow Auto Device Splitting	By default, this value is undefined. This can allow for automatic splitting of composite USB devices.
Exclude Vid/Pid Device from Split	By default, this value is undefined. When set, a device can be excluded from being split. The syntax for this comes in the form of {m|o:vid-AAA1_pid-BBB2[;vid-AAA2_pid-BBB2]. The value must be specified in hexadecimal, and an asterisk (*) can be used as a wildcard to replace specific digits within the ID.
Split Vid/Pid Device	By default, this value is undefined. When set, you can have the various parts of the composite USB each be treated individually. The syntax format for this comes in the form of `{m|o}: vid-xxxx_pid-yyyy(exinfo:zz[;exintf:ww]).` The `exintf` value allows you to exclude components by their interface number. This value must be specified in hexadecimal, and an asterisk (*) can be used as a wildcard to replace specific digits within the ID. Note that View will not automatically include any component that is not excluded. A filter policy such as Include Vid/Pid Device will be required to include those components.

Table B-11 View Agent Configuration ADM Template: Agent-Enforced Settings

GPO	Description
Exclude All Devices	The default value is undefined and equates to false. If the value is set to true, the Include settings to allow specific devices or family of devices to be passed through can be used to forward devices. If this value is set to true, it overrides the settings that the View Client may have set.

Exclude Device Family	The default value is undefined. This allows the exclusion of devices by family (for example, smartphones and flash drives). The syntax for this is as follows:
	
	`{m|o}: family_name1;family_name2...`
	
	For example, to exclude Bluetooth, you use the following syntax:
	
	`o:Bluetooth`
	
	When automatic device splitting is enabled, View looks at the device family of the whole composite device.

GPO	Description
Exclude Vid/Pid Device	The default value is undefined. This setting allows for a specific device or devices and the syntax is as follows: `{m|o}: family_name1;family_name2...` The device ID numbers must be done in hexadecimal, and you can use an asterisk (*) to replace individual digits for the device.
Include Device Family	The default value is undefined. This allows the option to identify which device family or families would be included in the forwarding of USB devices. The syntax is as follows: `{m|o}: family_name1;family_name2...` The device ID numbers must be done in hexadecimal, and you can use the asterisk (*) to replace individual digits for the device.
Include Vid/Pid Device	The default value is undefined. This allows the option to identify which specific devices would be included in the forwarding of USB devices. The syntax is as follows: `{m|o}: family_name1;family_name2...` The device ID numbers must be done in hexadecimal, and you can use the asterisk (*) to replace individual digits for the device.

Table B-12 View Agent Configuration ADM Template: Client-Interpreted Settings

GPO	Description
Allow Audio Input Devices	The default value is undefined. This allows for audio input (USB specific) to be used.
Allow Audio Output Devices	The default value is undefined. This allows for audio output (USB specific) to be used.
Allow HIDBootable	The default value is undefined. This allows for human interface devices (USB specific), or HIDs, that are neither keyboards nor mice to be used if they are discovered at boot.
Allow Other Input Devices	The default value is undefined. This allows for non-HID boot devices or keyboards with integrated pointing devices (USB specific) to be used.

GPO	Description
Allow Keyboard and Mouse devices	The default value is undefined. This allows for keyboards with integrated pointers (USB specific) to be used. Integrated pointers include device types like mouse, trackball, or touch pad.
Allow Smart Cards	The default value is undefined. This allows for smart-card devices (USB specific) to be used.
Allow Video Devices	The default value is undefined. This allows for video devices (USB specific) to be used. Video devices could include webcams and other similar devices.

Table B-13 Results of Combined Disable Splitting Policies of View Agent and View Client

Policy for View Agent: Allow Auto Device Splitting	Policy for View Client: Allow Auto Device Splitting	Effected Result of Combined Policies
Set to default of Allow	False (disable autosplit feature)	Splitting will be disabled.
Set to default of Allow	True (enable autosplit feature)	Splitting will be enabled.
Set to default of Allow	Not defined	Splitting will be enabled.
Override Client-Side Allow	Any or not defined	Splitting will be enabled.
Not defined	Not defined	Splitting will be disabled.

Table B-14 View Client Configuration ADM Template: USB Splitting Modifiers for View Agent

Modifier	Result
merge (m)	This modifier ensures that the View Client will apply the device-splitting policy set by the View Agent in addition to the View Client.
override (o)	In this case, the View Client will use the View Agent's device-splitting policy in place of what the View Client may have had.

Table B-15 View Common Configuration ADM Template: Log Configuration

Setting	Description
Number of Days to Keep Production Logs	By default, View keeps 7 days of logs. In some environments, either because of organizational policy or legal requirements, this may not be a sufficient time.

Setting	Description
Maximum Number of Debug Logs	By default, this value is 10. Again, in some environments this might not be sufficient due to organizational policy or legal requirements. The policy will automatically delete the oldest log to maintain the number.
Maximum Debug Log Size in Megabytes	This value is 50MB by default. This refers to the maximum log file size before it closes the file and creates a new one. Exercise caution when increasing this and the number of debug logs. If a particular log starts "spewing" (writing nonstop), space on a particular View component could be completely used up and render that particular component unavailable.
Log Directory	When not specified, the View component writes logs to its regular location. However, setting this value can change this to a directory that would fit better with organizational policy. It is important to ensure that the new location has write permissions. For client logs, there will be an additional folder created with the client name to identify it compared to other clients (which proves helpful when multiple client share the directory).

Table B-16 View Common Configuration ADM Template: Performance Alarm Settings

Setting	Description
CPU and Memory Sampling Interval in Seconds	How often, in seconds, CPU and memory is polled for information.
Overall CPU Usage Percentage to Issue Log Info	Sets the threshold at which CPU information, in the form of a percentage, is recorded to the log. In components that have multiple CPUs, this value represents the total percentage of all CPUs.
Overall Memory Usage Percentage to Issue Log Info	Sets the threshold at which committed system memory, in the form of a percentage, is recorded to the log—basically, the percentage of memory that is utilized by a process, whether actual physical memory (whether that is truly physical or virtual machine memory) or whether using the guest operating system's page file.
Process CPU Usage Percentage to Issue Log Info	Sets the threshold at which CPU information for individual processes, in the form of a percentage, is logged. This can prove helpful in determining whether a particular process is causing disruption on a particular component.

Setting	Description
Process Memory Usage to Issue Log Info	Sets the threshold at which memory usage for individual processes, in the form of a percentage, is logged. This can prove helpful in determining whether a particular process is causing disruption on a particular component.
Process to Check, Comma Separated Name List Allowing Wild Cards and Exclusion	Individual processes can be identified and listed, delineated by comma, for the purpose of being logged for CPU and memory sampling. In addition, specific characters translate into wildcards or exclusion options: Asterisk (*) means a match of 0 or more characters in the process (for example, `vdm*`). Question mark (?) refers to a single character difference in a process (for example, `wsnm????.exe`). Exclamation mark (!), sometimes referred to as bang, would mean excluding this process (for example, `!vmware-svi-ga.exe`).

Table B-17 View Common Configuration ADM Template: General Settings

Setting	Description
Disk Threshold for Log and Events in Megabytes	This has a default value of 200MB. When no value is set, it uses the default value of 200MB. This value refers to the minimum remaining space on a disk for logs and events.
Enable Extended Logging	This value should really be set only at the suggestion of either VMware support or Teradici support. And even then, it should be done for a limited time, because it will increase logging behavior significantly. This setting, when enabled, adds both trace and debug events to logs.

Glossary

ADAM/AD LDS Active Directory Application Mode/Active Directory Lightweight Directory Services is a lighter version of Active Directory and is meant to allow applications to leverage AD Lightweight Services without the need to modify the native Active Directory domain(s).

ADM template This is an Active Directory file that adds functionality to Active Directory for use in management. The Active Directory templates for use by View, for example, allow greater levels of control for establishing what users are able to do in a virtual desktop environment. This is needed because Active Directory was not built with things such as virtual desktops and PCoIP in mind. A variation of this, ADMX, was introduced by Microsoft as part of the Windows Vista/Windows 2008 release. Although essentially the same, there is one main difference: The ADMX file is written in the standard adhering to XML format.

automatic pools Automatic pools are desktop pools that are created on-the-fly by vCenter/Composer.

build-to-lossless PCoIP uses this technique as a way to build images quickly for end users. The process can be broken down into three parts: The first presentation of images appears fuzzy but discernable to the viewer; as more packets are received, the picture gets clearer to a perceptually lossless state until it gets to the final stage of lossless.

check-in Updating the vCenter version of the virtual machine with the changes that have taken place (files written on the local desktop) since the checkout. The desktop is unavailable while the check-in operation takes place, and when complete, the end user's View Client is redirected to the vCenter virtual machine.

checkout Saving a local copy of the virtual desktop for use when the network is unavailable.

Composer View Composer is the server that is installed either on the same physical or virtual server as vCenter, or in View 5.1, installed on a separate physical or virtual machine. Composer is required for using linked clones in a View virtual desktop environment.

Connection Server The VMware View Connection Server is the connection broker that handles the connections of the View Clients and passes them off to their respective virtual desktops. The Connection Server is the first VMware View administrative server that is installed.

Connection Server restriction tags Restriction tags are identifiers that are used to limit pools to specific Connection Servers for either security reasons or to force manual balancing of connections.

DMZ Demilitarized zone; it comes from the neutral area between two combative sides. Originally coined during the 1950s to refer to part of the area between North and South Korea, it is also now used to refer to the network perimeter of an environment between the internal organization and the wilds of the Internet.

DSN (data source name) When establishing an ODBC connection, a data source name must be provided of System type to allow the communication. The data source name is where the information about the connection (such as database to connect to, authentication, and so on) is stored.

EMF This is the Enhanced MetaFile, which is used by Windows as the printer spool format.

EOIT/BYOD Employee-owned IT or bring your own device refers to when organizations allow employees to provide their own laptop/tablet device to connect to the organizational environment. The employee is responsible for supporting and troubleshooting the physical hardware, and the organization provides a virtual desktop.

FQDN Fully qualified domain name (for example, vmware.com).

FSPs Foreign security principals are domains that are trusted by the present or current domain.

GDI The graphics device interface is the mechanism that takes a print job from an application and turns it into an EMF to be passed to the print driver.

GPO Group Policy Objects are settings that are applied against specific operating system features or application-specific features. Instead of manually going through each application or system specific setting, you can apply GPOs against whole groups or computers found within the domain.

IOPS Refers to input/output per second. For virtual desktops, this often refers to disk activities in the form of reads/writes per second. A single virtual desktop, on average, may have 10 to 25 IOPS, but when a number of desktops exist on the same datastore, this can prove detrimental for overall VDI performance.

Kiosk mode Kiosk mode is a way to configure a VMware View Client to automatically log in to a virtual desktop for the purposes of allowing dedicated access to a specific application or desktop.

linked clones Linked clones are special clones of virtual machines that are not like typical full clones created in vCenter. Linked clones are deployed using a special API from VMware snapshots. With linked clones, the master virtual machine, called the parent, is a powered-off virtual machine that we take a snapshot of in this powered-off state. Composer is used to select this snapshot, and is used as the basis for a replica disk. The replica becomes the direct parent of all the cloned virtual machines that will be linked to it. The replica disk is a read-only copy of the operating system's System drive. When new linked clones are deployed, they each get a delta, or change file (as in the delta file from a snapshot), so that all changes written to the system drive write to the delta, instead of to the replica disk. This allows for faster provisioning time and for advanced options like easier and faster patching.

location-based printing Refers to printing that depends on where the client is. Sometimes referred to as "follow me" printing. The determination as to which printer to use can be based on factors such as IP address or address range, MAC address, user, group, and so on.

manual pools Manual pools are desktop pools that are created out of preexisting virtual machines/physical desktops.

master image Interchangeably used with golden image, template image, and similar terms, master image refers to the image created for end-user desktop pools. Most commonly, this term is used in reference to the image used for linked-clone pools.

MDT The Microsoft Deployment Toolkit allows administrators to create customized ISO images of Windows operating systems. This can include disabling/enabling services in addition to installing additional applications and options for the ISOs.

NLA Network Layer Authentication was added to RDP to improve security by verifying the computer connecting to another via RDP.

ODBC (Open Database Connectivity) This is a connection that allows connectivity to a database or data source.

OU Organizational units are object groupings found within Active Directory. These are used as points to apply GPOs against instead of doing the changes on individual object basis.

P2V Physical-to-virtual creation of virtual machines has been around for a while. This process can be done with VMware Converter, but often comes with a variety of caveats and challenges with leftover physical hardware drivers interfering in a virtual environment. This is *not* a recommended method of creating a virtual desktop.

PCoIP PC-over-Internet Protocol was created by Teradici as a remote connection protocol. The protocol was designed with encryption and speed without compromising security.

persistent disk A persistent disk is a special disk that can be assigned to a linked clone desktop when using dedicated pool assignment option.

.print Refers to the specific driver that is used by ThinPrint.

QuickPrep QuickPrep is a customization tool that can be used to give operating systems new identities. This is for provisioning new virtual desktops. QuickPrep is lighter weight than Sysprep and does not do all the functions that Sysprep does. QuickPrep will join a machine to the domain and change the computer name of the operating system, but that is the extent that QuickPrep customizes the OS, and it does not require a reboot.

RDP Microsoft's Remote Desktop Protocol is a mechanism, like PCoIP, to allow machines to attach to other machines while providing a user-friendly interface. RDP presents a desktop session through a window or full-screen session that enables users or administrators to use the regular Windows interface on a remote machine.

replica A full copy of the master image created by Composer. The replica is a read-only version.

replica server The VMware View replica server is a second or more instance of a Connection Server. Only the first server that is installed is a Connection Server. All other Connection Servers are replica servers, and replica servers are all siblings. This means that instead of only attaching to the web management portal of the Connection Server, administrators could log in to any one of the replica servers as well. Any change made on one is replicated to all the other Connection Servers and replica servers.

replication Updating the vCenter version of the virtual machine while still allowing the end user to access the local copy of the virtual desktop.

rollback Discarding the changes inside the local copy of the virtual desktop and reverting to the pre-checked-out state. The virtual desktop is unavailable while this takes place, and when complete, the user is redirected to the vCenter copy of the virtual machine.

RSA SecurID This two-factor authentication system allows for greater levels of security than a simple username and password. It consists of a card that the user inserts into a card reader to allow access to a system, but also requires users to insert a PIN code before they are allowed access.

Security Server This server is a proxy server to allow end users to connect safely to their desktop without risking the connection server.

Sysprep Sysprep is much more involved than QuickPrep, but as the name implies is not as fast as QuickPrep because a lot more changes are being made and a reboot is required. Sysprep generates a new SID, removes local accounts, removes the parent from a domain, can be used for language, regional settings, date, and time customization. Sysprep does require the configuration files to be loaded into the file structure of the vCenter Server or vCenter Virtual Appliance for Windows XP machines.

tag When using multiple Connection Servers, administrators can use tags to define which users have access to which Connection Servers. Once tags are used, they can be defined on the desktop pool as well as a Connection Server, so that if users wants to log in to the View environment where tags are being used they have to have a matching tag on the Connection Server for their pool. This would allow some users to be able to access their virtual desktops from outside the corporate environment, but not everyone.

ThinApp VMware's ThinApp product allows for virtual applications to be virtualized into their own runtime environment. Note that this is not a virtual machine. The runtime environment has its own virtual Registry and virtual file structure that maps to the native Registry and file structure on the Windows system that the ThinApp'd application runs on top of.

ThinPrint Refers to the client piece that allows for printing to the client printers. This was added as part of a partnership with Cortado.

Transfer Server This server helps with the downloading of system images, change replication between local and remote desktops, and data transfer during the check-in and checkout of local desktops.

Transfer Server repository If you want to check out linked-clone virtual desktops, a repository must be created to store the files in the linked-clone desktop to then be transferred to the desktop for checkout.

View Agent The VMware View Agent is the service installed on the virtual machine that allows the Connection Server to manage it and from which View Clients can connect.

View Composer Composer is used to create linked clones for VMware View environments. Using technology similar to virtual machine snapshots, this allows for the creation of desktops that can be deployed quickly and that utilize up to 90% less storage space.

View Connection Server Sometimes referred to as the Connection Server, the broker, the standard server, the replica server; this is the web server that provides access to desktops for end users as well as the administrative interface for the View environment.

View events View events are records of events as they happen in the View environment, both successful and not successful. These are recorded in simple English and include items such as "User A logged in successfully to Desktop01" and similar.

View global policies Global policies are settings that are used to configure what users are allowed to do or not do. Examples include the ability to use USB or MMR. These policies can be modified at either the pool level or on a per-user override policy.

View global settings Global settings are used to configure the View environment with regard to settings that would be used by all the Connection Servers. Examples of what is covered include items such as a login message and administrator timeout.

Index

A

B

C

D

E

J-K

L

M

N

O

Q-R

S

W-X-Y-Z